In Search of Susanna

SINGULAR LIVES: THE IOWA SERIES
IN NORTH AMERICAN AUTOBIOGRAPHY
ALBERT E. STONE, SERIES EDITOR

In Search of Susanna

By Suzanne L. Bunkers

FOREWORD BY ALBERT E. STONE

University of Iowa Press ⍦ Iowa City

4 February 1997

Dear Janet and Kelly,
In recognition of our shared interest in women's stories and lives.
Best wishes,
Suzanne Bunkers

University of Iowa Press, Iowa City 52242
Printed in the United States of America

Design by Karen Copp

Printed on acid-free paper

Library of Congress Cataloging-in-Publication Data
Bunkers, Suzanne L.
  In search of Susanna / by Suzanne L. Bunkers.
      p.   cm. — (Singular lives)
   ISBN 0-87745-538-4 (paper)
     1. Bunkers, Suzanne L.—Family.   2. Women college teachers—
United States—Biography.   3. English teachers—United
States—Biography.   4. Mothers and daughters—Middle West—
Biography.   5. Women pioneers—Middle West—Biography.
6. Luxembourgers—Middle West—Biography.   7. Genealogy—
Middle West—Methodology.   8. Family—Middle West.
9. Simmerl, Susanna.   I. Title.   II. Series.
PE64.B86A3   1996
929'.2'0893—dc20   96-3396
                                                               CIP

01   00   99   98   97   96   P   5   4   3   2   1

The memory is a living thing—it too is in transit.
But during its moment, all that is remembered joins,
and lives—the old and the young, the past and the present,
the living and the dead.
—Eudora Welty, *One Writer's Beginnings*, 1984

FOR RACHEL SUSANNA

Contents

Foreword

By Albert E. Stone

Calling *In Search of Susanna* an auto/biography is at once accurate and ambiguous. "Susanna" is three different persons brought together from a European past and an American present. Susanna Simmerl Youngblut is the ancestor who, having birthed an "illegitimate" daughter in her native Luxembourg village, emigrated in 1857 to Iowa. This book is in part her biography. Her great-great-granddaughter is Suzanne, the autobiographer and mother of Rachel Susanna, now a preteenager. One strand knitting the trio together is the fact that Suzanne Bunkers is a single—that is, unmarried or "natural"—Minnesota mother. Along with other members of an extended family, all three Susannas have shared Iowa and Minnesota homeplaces; the Roman Catholic faith, with its devotion to the Virgin Mary; and a staunch self-sufficiency, the full extent of which the youngest Susanna has yet to claim as her birthright. Yet their common story is truly autobiography. For Suzanne Bunkers, a teacher of English and women's studies at Mankato State University, has made it. She presides at its center. Around her is built a family history within social and cultural circumstances uniting two rural worlds 4,500 miles and a century or more apart. Throughout, Bunkers' emphasis is upon women's identities, capacities, histories, destinies. Where men figure in this bold narrative—as in chapter 3, "In the Name of the Father"—they are seen through the eyes of mothers, wives, lovers, relatives—women who are themselves breadwinners and homemakers, teachers and students, travelers and communicants. "Home" in its widest sense has women at its heart.

In Search of Susanna, then, is unique, yet allied to other women's stories about roots and uprooting, relationships, ruptures, and the search for a stable self amid the often-fragmented circumstances of family, emigration, church, love, career. Though the differences are dramatic, so too are the parallels between Bunkers' book and two others that describe the lives of Midwestern women. One, from nineteenth-century Iowa, is *"A Secret to Be Burried": The Diary and Life of Emily Hawley Gillespie* (Iowa, 1989). This voluminous diary covers thirty years, spent mostly on Iowa farms and in a small town near where Susanna Youngblut lived. Gillespie's detailed but guarded entries illuminate some of the darknesses (if not secrets) still surrounding the immigrant woman from Luxembourg. Mystery persists despite Bunkers' best efforts to make European archives and American oral histories, diaries, newspapers, and photographs disclose her ancestor's actions and motivations. Nevertheless, Bunkers' autobiographical intentions make for profound differences. Such congruences and contrasts are heightened when we note that Suzanne Bunkers has edited the diary of Emily's daughter, Sarah Gillespie Huftalen (Iowa, 1993).

In very different terms, a daughter's and granddaughter's account of seeking her roots across the Atlantic also links *In Search of Susanna* with Patricia Hampl's autobiography, *A Romantic Education* (1981). "Where do I come from? Who am I?" are common and urgent questions. But Hampl's Prague and Bunkers' Feulen are vastly dissimilar European destinations, just as Bunkers' consciousness as an American traveler is a less sensitive register of nuances than Hampl's. This writer, after all, is a teacher and scholar, not a poet. Yet surprisingly, Bunkers' autobiography is the more confessional. Nothing in *A Romantic Education* can quite match the candor of Suzanne Bunkers' anguished and triumphant account of the circumstances surrounding the birth of her daughter "out of wedlock." "This has not been an easy book to write" is a statement made about many women's autobiographies. *In Search of Susanna*, however, is more ambitious than many, incorporating as it does "strands of history, genealogy, psychology, and personal experience" into a narrative that openly resembles a "word quilt."

History is a major strand that Bunkers here weaves with scholarly care. Extensive references and apt quotations from archival documents and newspapers characterize many sections of this story. The Luxembourg theme in this immigration study makes it unusual, for the villages in that tiny country are seldom mentioned in standard histories. So, too, to a different degree, are the American lives of Midwestern women caught in the coils of emigration, marriage, working-class daily life, and childbearing. Most misunderstood of all is childbearing outside of wedlock, whether in Catholic Luxembourg in the 1850s or the American Midwest of the 1980s. Thus as this historian delves more deeply, her focus grows tighter, more personal, more dangerous. Breaking silence has its price, here as elsewhere in women's writings. Indeed, this is a lesson that most autobiographers ultimately learn: curiosity and joy often prove inseparable from shock, disillusionment, and depression.

If portions of *In Search of Susanna* read like an immigration history and memoir, this autobiography also shows its deep roots in the author's loving use of literature. Storytelling is a traditional art as well as a family tradition for Suzanne Bunkers. While arresting photographs dot this text, demonstrating her desire to recover the past as convincingly as possible, dialogue, scene-setting, image, and metaphor show the touch of an imaginative writer who knows that in any autobiography the authorial self is usually more available than the past actor. Bunkers' language authenticates her search, constantly anchoring her history in personal style and vision. Furthermore, the litany of literary guides is a long one: Sarah Orne Jewett, Patricia Hampl, Adrienne Rich, Meridel Le Sueur, W. S. Merwin, Anne Morrow Lindbergh, T. S. Eliot, W. H. Auden, Willa Cather, Wallace Stevens, Hannah Foster, Nathaniel Hawthorne, Katherine Anne Porter, bell hooks. These share space with less-literary inspirations, like the unknown poets of Luxembourg sentimental postcards and the biblical author of "Susannah and the Elders." It is not difficult to detect the common thread in a number of these admired models: a single, sometimes unmarried, woman's troubles and triumphs.

Towering above Hester Prynne, Ántonia, Eliza Wharton, even Joan of Arc and Susannah of the Book of Daniel, is the figure of Mary, the Virgin Mother. She presides over this autobiography as the archetypal "out of wedlock" mother. Catholic from girlhood, Suzanne Bunkers has private moments and churchly memories on which her mature reflections are based. These help to support her in the face of prejudice and condemnation, usually delivered by men. All seek to punish her for bearing a "filia naturalis," as her ancestor's child was once termed back in Feulen. Both her beautiful child and this abuse are realities to confront and survive. This has been possible with help from the

"Higher Power," the Virgin Mary. From her example and others in fiction and prose, Suzanne labors to become "the good mother" that the first Susanna may or may not have been, since she—Susanna Simmerl—left her daughter behind in Luxembourg. The mystery and model of "the good mother" is, then, the central metaphor of self that this reader takes away from *In Search of Susanna*. The ideal (and sometimes the reality) of this feminine identity is daily confirmed by the youngest Susanna in her love for her mother. But the mother-daughter tie is made even stronger by family example: the mother, grandmother, and others in the extended family who refuse to condemn or excommunicate. If such quarrels and condemnations *have* occurred in life, they find no place in this re-created life. Similarly, bitter recognition of paternalism, sexism, and bigotry about bastards among some, including the clergy of the Catholic Church, is a minor note in this narrative. What stands out is a stronger sense of the feminine power to love, to create, to forgive—embodied since Suzanne's girlhood in the Virgin Mary.

Autobiography, we have learned from the critics, is a capacious, many-faceted mode of storytelling. A work like *In Search of Susanna* may (and I believe does) successfully recapture historical experiences, making them as convincing a picture of reality as possible through diaries, documents, photographs, interviews. Personal histories like this one may also reconfirm the self of the story through its own artful, overdetermined language—the terms and tropes through which ideals like "the good mother" are given the illusion of flesh and blood. Thus modern autobiography can and does express an inner, ineffable self whose re-created dreams and deeds do not need to be confessed as sins or errors in order to seem emotionally coherent and convincing. Suzanne Bunkers, practicing Catholic though she remains, never confesses as sin what she knows and shows as earthly, imperfect emanations of divine love. She dares to point to Mary as model for a life in these last decades of the twentieth century, though without exploring in theological or psychological detail the fuller implications of this act of faith. As personal history, *In Search of Susanna* is a testimonial to a courageous rather than a saintly life, one written in media res. Suzanne Bunkers' story is an apology only in the autobiographical sense that many women's life histories are—a defense of difference and devotion.

Acknowledgments

This book, a work of creative nonfiction, is based on the interaction of history, memory, and imagination. To protect the privacy of individuals whose stories are told on these pages, some names have been changed.

I would like to thank the individuals and organizations listed below, who have helped make this book possible.

The Council for International Exchange of Scholars (Fulbright Commission), the National Endowment for the Humanities, the Iowa Humanities Board, and Mankato State University for helping to fund my research.

The State Historical Society of Iowa, the Wisconsin State Historical Society, the Minnesota Historical Society, the Bach-Dunn Luxembourgiana Collection at the University of St. Thomas in St. Paul, Minnesota, the National Library of Luxembourg, the National Archives of Luxembourg, the Royal Albert I Library of Brussels, the National Archives of Belgium, and county, district, commune, and parish records offices, in the United States, Luxembourg, and Belgium, for providing information essential to my research.

Editors in whose journals earlier versions of some portions of this book have appeared: Ginalie Swaim of the *Palimpsest* and Valerie Staats and Carolyn Hardesty of *Iowa Woman*.

Opportunities to present my research and read from my work at these professional conferences: Modern Language Association, Midwest Modern Language Association, Iowa Congress of Historical Organizations, the Society of Europeanists Meeting, and the 23rd International Congress of Genealogy and Heraldry.

Colleagues and friends who have provided valuable feedback on the book-in-progress: Aimée Alençon, Ilene Alexander, Victoria Amador, Elizabeth Baer, Zoé Barta, Jeanne Braham, Donna Casella, Kathryn Cullen, Diane D'Amico, Kate Hallet Dayton, Pamela Esty, Diana Gabriel, Gwen Griffin, Becky Hogan, Joe Hogan, Doris Ikier, Lynda Jacobson, Sandra Loerts, Jan McInroy, Neala Schleuning, Judy Stallmann, Al Stone, Trudee Svaldi, Judy Nolte Temple, Joaquin Vilá, Sandra Woods, and Jerome Zuckerman; two colleagues who have helped me translate documents, John Janc and James Booker; other colleagues and friends, past and present, who have supported my work; and the many students who have participated in my autobiography workshops.

Cousins, colleagues, and friends in Luxembourg and Belgium who have helped me with my research: Erny, Nico, and the late Nick Linden; the Bonert, Krieps, and Steiwer families; and Jul Christophory, Chris Cooleman, François Decker, Fernand Emmel, Jean Ensch, Jean-Claude Muller, Rogér and Colette Pierret and family, Liliane and Piet Stemper, Milly Thill, and Lois Triffin.

Cousins in the United States who have shared genealogical information and family photographs: Raymond Bunkers, Marie Hellman, Jeff and Michelle (Youngblut) Lindquist, Sister Callista O'Connor, the late Virginia O'Connor, Elaine Thoma, Charlotte Witry, Mary Beth Youngblut, Paul Fried, Florence Miller, James and the late Barbara Jacobs.

Above all, I want to thank my family: my parents, Verna Klein Bunkers and the late Jerome (Tony) Bunkers, whose love of their children and appreciation of family stories are a meaningful legacy.

My sister, Linda Bunkers Kennedy; my brothers, Dennis, Dale, and Dan Bunkers; my sisters-in-law, Barbara Ahrens Bunkers and Julie Castillo Bunkers; my brother-in-law, Dan Kennedy; and my nieces and nephews, Kim and Kelly Bunkers; Matt, Megan, and Ryan Kennedy; Margery, Lisa, Lori, and Jennifer Castillo; and Daniel Bunkers, Jr., whose stories have become part of this book.

My cousin, Father Frank Klein, whose generosity, insights, and love of family history helped make this book a reality.

And, finally, my dear daughter, Rachel Susanna, who has been the impetus for this book. Without her, it would not have come to exist.

In Search of Susanna

1. In Search of Susanna

The problem is, I think, that the lines of narrative
never jell. When it gets too bad, you do what I have
done: chuck it aside and go on a pilgrimage, hoping to
bring back the initial sense of joy and curiosity, and
find the tale whose telling will bind the scattered
lives of a family line.
—Kem Luther, *Cottonwood Roots*, 1993

On a muggy August day in 1980, I sat at an old oaken table in my room at the Maison des Vacances in Niederfeulen, Luxembourg, poring over black leather–covered books containing the Feulen parish records. I was midway through a two-week trip to Luxembourg with my cousin Father Frank Klein. We had come to see what we could learn about our Klein ancestors, who had left their native villages of Oberfeulen and Niederfeulen and immigrated to the United States in the mid-1800s.

As I studied the lists of baptisms, marriages, and deaths, jotting down names of Klein ancestors, my eyes paused at one name: Simmerl. I reached for my diary, where I had copied vital statistics on ancestors taken from the records of St. Joseph Parish in Granville, Iowa. There it was—Simmerl—the same name. Coincidence. Pure chance. Still, Simmerl was not a common name, either in Luxembourg or in the United States. Could it be that not only my maternal ancestors, the Kleins, but also my paternal ancestors, the Simmerls, had once lived in Oberfeulen and Niederfeulen?

On that summer day, as I skimmed the pages of yellowed church records, I encountered "Simmerl" again and again. I jotted down each reference, thankful that my knowledge of Latin and French was making it somewhat easier for me to decipher the tiny inscriptions in that intricate scrolled handwriting. Eventually I came upon this baptismal record:

Die Trigesima Decembris 1856, hora septa matutina nata eademque die baptista fuit Barbara, filia naturalis Angela Simmerl ex Oberfeulen, levantes erant Petrus et Barbara Simmerl.

[On December 30, 1856, at seven in the morning, was born and baptized that same day Barbara, the natural daughter of Angela Simmerl of Oberfeulen. Godparents were Peter and Barbara Simmerl.]

The summer before, I had seen the names of Angela and Barbara Simmerl in the St. Joseph Parish death register. Barbara Simmerl Bunkers was my great-grandmother. Her tombstone in St. Joseph's cemetery mistakenly listed her birth date as January 1, 1856, and listed her date of death as February 4, 1943, seven years before I was born. My first clue that Barbara Bunkers' maiden name was Simmerl had come from a penciled-in notation in the death register: "Grand-daughter of Angela Simmerl."

Armed with that name, Simmerl, I had leafed back through the death records until I found this entry: "Simmerl, Angela. Died July 15, 1897. Old age. Age 90. Funeral July 17, 1897. Granville, Iowa." Penciled in between "Simmerl" and "Angela" were the words "Grandmother of Barbara (Simmerl) Bunkers." So Angela Simmerl had been the grandmother of Barbara Simmerl Bunkers. That made Angela my great-great-great-grandmother. But who had been the link between Angela and Barbara? Had Angela's son been Barbara's father? Who had been her mother? The St. Joseph Parish death register held no clue to that mystery, and I had no idea how to find out.

Now, looking over the Feulen, Luxembourg, parish records, I did. I glanced again at Barbara Simmerl's baptismal record. Something did not make sense. How could Barbara have been the daughter of Angela, who had been a forty-eight-year-old widow in 1856? What did "*filia naturalis*" mean? Why was no father's name listed on Barbara Simmerl's baptismal record?

These questions swirling around in my mind, I closed the parish books and took a walk with my cousin Frank to the home of Monsieur François Decker, the local historian, whose study, *Feulen, 963–1963,* had been so helpful to us at the start of our research.

Sitting in Monsieur Decker's study, conversing haltingly in French, I confessed my preoccupation with the mystery of Barbara Simmerl's birth. Monsieur Decker smiled and gestured up to the top shelves of his bookcase, where tattered shoeboxes lined the wall. "Here," he said, "are my copies of the civil records for every person who has ever lived in the Feulen area. We will study the Simmerls. Perhaps I can help you answer your questions."

Down came the shoebox marked "S," and Monsieur Decker's eyebrows knitted together as he glanced at index card after index card. "Yes," he explained, "the Simmerl family in Oberfeulen can be traced back to the mid- to late 1700s. Joseph Simmerl, born in Bissen, Luxembourg, about 1758, married Maria Joanna Gilson, also from Bissen. By 1800, the couple was living in Oberfeulen, where Joseph was the Deputy Burgermeister. Theodore Simmerl, the second of their children, was born in Oberfeulen in 1797. He eventually became a teacher in Oberfeulen."

Monsieur Decker continued: "The Hottua family's roots in Niederfeulen can also be traced back to the mid-1700s. The Hottuas lived in the "Schmidden" house and were Hufschmieds (blacksmiths or horseshoers). Peter Hottois married Catherine Glesener in 1779. Their daughter, Angela Hottua, was born in 1808. In 1827, Angela married Theodore Simmerl of Oberfeulen."

Finally, he pulled one more index card from the box. "'Barbara Simmerl. Born in Oberfeulen, December 30, 1856.' You are right. Barbara was the granddaughter of Angela Hottua Simmerl and her late husband, Theodore Simmerl. And the mother of Barbara was Susanna Simmerl, the daughter of Angela and Theodore."

Monsieur Decker paused. "You see, Susanna Simmerl was not married when she gave birth to Barbara. *'Filia naturalis'* means 'illegitimate daughter.' Barbara was listed in the parish records as the daughter of her grandmother, Angela Hottua Simmerl, not her mother, Susanna Simmerl. But the civil records tell another story. They say that Susanna Simmerl was Barbara's mother."

So Susanna was the missing link, the piece to the puzzle I had been trying to complete. Susanna Simmerl. My great-great-grandmother. She had borne the same name as I, although my parents could not have known that when I was born in 1950 and named Suzanne because, as my mother liked to joke, she loved the song "Oh, Susannah."

I knew I needed to think more about that phrase *filia naturalis.* Surely, in nineteenth-century Luxembourg, an illegitimate daughter would not have been viewed in the same light as a legitimate daughter. Why had Barbara Simmerl's baptismal record listed her grandmother Angela as her mother? Why had Barbara's biological mother, Susanna, been wiped out of existence? How could I find Susanna again?

There may come to be places in our lives that are second spiritual
homes — closer to us in some ways, perhaps, than our original
homes. But the home tie is the blood tie. And had it meant nothing
to us, any other place thereafter would have meant less, and we
would carry no compass inside ourselves to find home ever, not
anywhere at all. We would not even guess what we had missed.
—Eudora Welty, "Place in Fiction," *The Eye of the Story and Other*
Essays, 1956

For many years Eudora Welty's words have inspired me to ask, "What is the 'home tie,' the 'blood tie,' in my life? What defines 'home' for me?" My sense of the home tie, the blood tie, derives not only from places but also from people. My sense of "home" is linked to my roots in Iowa and Luxembourg, and it is linked to my search for Susanna.

Susanna Simmerl was born on April 2, 1831, in Oberfeulen, Luxembourg, the third child of Theodore and Angela (Hottua) Simmerl. On December 30, 1856, at the age of twenty-five, she gave birth to her first child, a daughter named Barbara. Then, in the spring of 1857, along with her older brother Peter Simmerl, Susanna immigrated to the United States. Her infant daughter, Barbara, remained in Luxembourg with Susanna's mother, Angela Simmerl. Six months later, in December 1857, Susanna married Frank Youngblut, another Luxembourger, who had immigrated to the United States in 1852. The couple began farming near Gilbertville, Iowa, a small community just outside Waterloo. Susanna and Frank had nine children, and they farmed for many years, then retired and moved into town. Frank Youngblut died on May 11, 1892. When Susanna died fourteen years later, on May 20, 1906, she was buried next to her husband in the Youngblut family plot in the Immaculate Conception Parish cemetery in Gilbertville.

I was born on April 20, 1950, at Sacred Heart Hospital in Le Mars, Iowa, the first child of Tony and Verna (Klein) Bunkers, who lived twenty-five miles away in Granville, Iowa. I was baptized Suzanne Lillian Bunkers at St. Joseph Catholic Church. The oldest of five children, I grew up in Granville, and I left home at the age of eighteen to attend Iowa State University in Ames. Six years later, I moved to Madison, Wisconsin, to attend graduate school at the University of Wisconsin. After completing my doctoral degree in August 1980, I came to Mankato, Minnesota, to teach English at Mankato State University.

On October 17, 1985, I became the mother of a baby daughter, Rachel Susanna. Our family continues to live in Mankato.

These facts briefly outline the particulars of two women's lives. But, as I have learned during the past fifteen years, facts are only the tip of the genealogical iceberg; they do not tell the whole story. To create the story told on the pages of this book, I have needed to search in unconventional places, and I have needed to come to terms with a complicated web of ideas and feelings about the meanings of "motherhood," "family," and "home."

When I think of "home," I think of the first home I remember: the tiny white-shuttered house my parents rented on Elm Street across from St. Joseph Church in Granville. Then I think of the green three-bedroom rambler at 620 Long Street that my parents built in the mid-1950s. I spent the first eighteen years of my life in these two houses, one at the east end, the other at the west end of our town of 350 people. Even though it has been more than twenty-five years since I have lived there, when someone asks me, "Where's your home?" I still say, "Granville."

When I think of "home," I also think of Luxembourg, the tiny European country that my maternal and paternal forebears left in the mid-1800s. My ancestors were farmers, and when they began arriving in the United States, they settled near Dubuque, Iowa, in the small farming communities of Guttenberg, Dyersville, New Vienna, and Luxemburg. From eastern Iowa, some family members went south to Gilbertville, Iowa, others west to Granville and Remsen, Iowa, others to the Dakotas and Minnesota. Today, their descendants number in the thousands.

In Search of Susanna is about my family and my ongoing fascination with its history. Over the years, as I have worked on this book, I have wondered if I was writing history or literature, nonfiction or fiction. Now I no longer think in these either/or terms about this book or about the lives chronicled and imagined in it. This book is based on historical records about the individuals whose lives are reconstructed on its pages. At the same time, this book is based on the ways my imagination has interacted with historical records to re-create a sense of time, place, and character.

How and when did *In Search of Susanna* begin? In early 1980, my cousin Father Frank Klein and I began researching and writing *Good Earth, Black Soil*. This book, a study of several generations of Frank's paternal and my maternal Klein ancestry, was based on our research in Luxembourg and the United States. Because Frank and I decided early in our work that we wanted our book to be more than a compilation of genealogical charts, we decided to shape each chapter of the book as a narrative told by one of our ancestors. In the book's preface, we explained, "Rather than recite a chronology of names and dates, we wanted to create a sense of real people and authentic situations in our family's history. Doing so has involved combining historical fact with imaginative detail to shape what might be called a work of historical fiction."

When I wrote the chapter titled "The Tadler Home," I told the story of my great-great-grandmother Mary Müller Klein Flammang. As a young woman, she married Michel Klein, and the young couple lived in Tadler, Luxembourg, where their sons Nicholas and Jacob were born. Then Michel Klein died unexpectedly, leaving Mary pregnant with their third son, Theodore, born six months after his father's death. Mary Klein raised her three sons from her first marriage; she eventually remarried, had a fourth son, Franz Flammang, and was widowed again.

One by one, Nicholas, Jacob, and Theodore Klein immigrated to the United States. Years later, they bought their mother, Mary, and their half brother, Franz, tickets to join them in northwest Iowa. As I began writing "The Tadler Home," I was haunted by the image of Mary Klein standing before the grave of her first husband, Michel, just before she sailed for America, knowing she would never return to Luxembourg. That image became the cornerstone of my chapter and the heart of Mary's story.

It was while working on the story of Mary Müller Klein Flammang that I first learned of the existence of Susanna Simmerl Youngblut, another of my great-great-grandmothers. The more I found out about Susanna, the more determined I became to piece together the story of her life. To do this, I have studied the history of Luxembourg, the many reasons why Luxembourgers left their homeland for America, and the varied lives of those immigrants and their descendants once they arrived in this country.

Dailiness is central to this book. As Bettina Aptheker explains, "The search for dailiness is a method of work that allows us to take the patterns women create and the meanings women invent and learn from them. If we map what we learn, connecting one meaning or invention to another, we begin to lay out a different way of seeing reality." By using diaries, letters, newspaper clippings, church and census records, autograph books, photographs, holy cards, oral history inter views, and family stories to lay out patterns of dailiness, I hope to make more visible the lives of individual women within the context of families, generations, and cultures.

I call this book an auto/biography because it interweaves details of my ancestor Susanna's life with some of my own observations and experiences. To make this book, I have gathered and selected "fabric," cut "squares," laid them out to create the book's "pattern," and stitched them into the finished "word quilt."

As I have studied my ancestor Susanna's life, I have been stitching my own diary entries, my research on nineteenth-century women's lives, and my understanding of my family's history into the book that you are now holding. Stories from my life as a daughter and mother as well as from my work as a teacher and writer make up some of the pieces stitched into this word quilt. So do excerpts from the diaries I have kept since I was ten. I know that what I write in my diaries represents my own point of view and my own version of events, not anyone else's.

I have spent many years working on this word quilt. Since 1978, I have combed census, church, and county records in the United States and in Luxembourg. Two brief visits to Luxembourg in 1980 and 1984 initiated my research there. In 1988 a Fulbright senior research fellowship made it possible for my daughter and me to live in Brussels, Belgium, for six months, where I continued my study of nineteenth-century women's lives in the farming villages of Luxembourg and Belgium. At the Bibliotheque Nationale in Luxembourg City and at the Royal Albert I Library in Brussels, I had access to historical materials, civil and church records, letters, photographs, and village demographics. For a good deal of our time there, Rachel and I stayed with cousins who still live in Niederfeulen. Since 1988, I have returned to Belgium and Luxembourg three more times to conduct further research and to synthesize my findings.

My research has helped me place my ancestor Susanna into the context of nineteenth-century working-class life in Luxembourg, a country with a tempestuous history. I now have a better understanding of the economic and political matrix surrounding Luxembourgers' immigration to the "New World." I have gained a wider perspective on the experiences of working-class immigrant women in nineteenth-century America. And I am able to appreciate Susanna's relationship with her daughter, Barbara, through the filter of my relationship with my daughter, Rachel.

This has not been an easy book to write, for my work on *In Search of Susanna* has presented its own special challenges. My research process has had many twists, turns, and surprises. It began, and it has continued, based on hypothesis formation and testing. At the same time, it has included a healthy dose of coincidence and chance. This book is not the result of an objective, scientific study. It is intensely personal. It reflects my thoughts and feelings about myself and others, and not everything I have written here will please all those who read it. At the same time, the stories in this book are as true as I can make them, given that my interpretations of people and events bear the marks of my own experience and personality.

I am a teacher, a writer, a daughter, and a mother. This last fact, more than any other, has drawn me to the story of my ancestor Susanna. During the past seventeen years, as my life has changed, I have formulated and discarded many theories about who Susanna might have been. At every turn, my study of my ancestor's life has been fueled by encounters with others who, like me, are trying to relate their lives to the lives of those who came before them. Like these searchers, I want to explore the generations of my family, reconstruct their lives, and tell their stories, so that someday these stories will give my descendants a "family map" that will help them discover where they have come from.

In *Cottonwood Roots*, Kem Luther tells the compelling story of his search for his genealogical roots. Early in his book, he explains what makes his work difficult: "The presence of the story is what makes genealogy hard to write. The rest, the construction of the sequence from the network, can be learned by rote. The real problem is how to follow and develop the narrative. It is so difficult that it is a wonder that it gets done at all."

I had to laugh when I first read those words; they summed up just how I felt about my search for Susanna. For years, my attic study has been overflowing with genealogical charts, letters from relatives, childhood memorabilia, old family photographs, thirty years' worth of diaries, and hundreds of books. How would I ever manage to pull everything together into a meaningful whole? Only by seeing the problem that Kem Luther describes, then doing what he suggests: "The problem is, I think, that the lines of narrative never jell. When it gets too bad, you do what I have done: chuck it aside and go on a pilgrimage, hoping to bring back the initial sense of joy and curiosity, and find the tale whose telling will bind the scattered lives of a family line."

In the end, it is the interaction of the writer's imagination with the cultural records that makes the story meaningful and the search worthwhile. Like Kem Luther, I have gone on a pilgrimage to find the tale whose telling will bind the scattered lives of my own family line. My search for Susanna embodies that tale.

2. My Luxembourg across the Sea

But the dearest of all visions and the one I love
  the best,
'Tis of mother dear, her whom I long to see,
God bless you, darling mother, my true heart will
  never rest,
Till we meet again at home across the sea.
—"My Luxembourg across the Sea"

Luxembourg is at the crossroads of invading armies. Conquerors
have marched through this land while its people have tried elabo-
rately to pretend that they have not been there. Rulers may make
Luxembourgers a subject people, but all the while they have never
forgotten their right to be free. Their birthright of freedom is a pas-
sion that centuries of occupation cannot dim.—Eugene Fodor, Belgium and Luxembourg, 1975

Luxembourg: 999 square miles. 55 miles long, 34 miles wide.
Through the northern half of the country run the lush forests of the
Ardennes. To the south lie rolling farmlands, iron mines, and the
Moselle valley, renowned for its fine wines. Neatly sandwiched be-
tween Belgium on the north and west, Germany on the east, and
France on the south, the Grand Duchy of Luxembourg is home to more
than 395,200 inhabitants.

How did Luxembourg begin? Its official history dates back to the
tenth century, when Count Siegfried acquired from the Abbey of
St. Maximin of Trier a small, rocky promontory called the Bock, where
there stood a small castle called Lucilinburhuc (Little Burg). In return,
the count relinquished land near the area called Viulna. Lucilinburhuc
eventually became part of the powerful fortress of Luxembourg, and
the area known by its Latin name, Viulna, became known as Feulen.

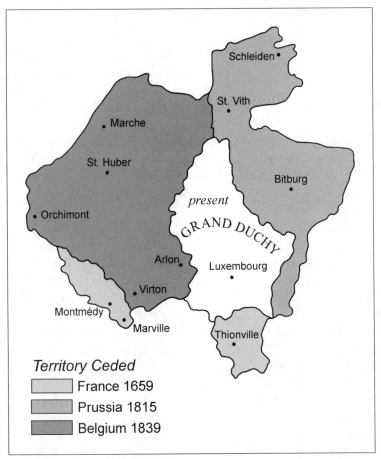

Map of Luxembourg, indicating the three partitions. From James Newcomer,
The Grand Duchy of Luxembourg, *redrawn by Pat Conrad.*

Thus, the founding of my ancestral home, Feulen, dates back to
963 A.D. In 1963 Feulen celebrated its 1,000th anniversary.

In his time, Count Siegfried became a powerful feudal lord of
the region, which, over the preceding centuries, had been conquered
by many armies (Julius Caesar's Roman army, Attila the Hun's pil-
lagers, and Charlemagne's Frankish forces, to name a few). Numerous
counts of the Ardennes succeeded Siegfried until Countess Ermesinde,
the daughter of Henry IV of Namur, took power in 1196. As James

Newcomer explains in *The Grand-Duchy of Luxembourg*, Countess Ermesinde led Luxembourg into the "intellectual, artistic, and religious renaissance that characterized western Europe."

But Countess Ermesinde's reign did not last. For centuries, Luxembourg was ruled by the House of Burgundy (1443–1506), Spain (1506–1684), France (1684–97), Austria (1714–95), and France (1795–1814). Finally, in 1815, after Napoleon's defeat, the Congress of Vienna established Luxembourg as a grand duchy that would serve as part of a vast defensive system. In *The Making of a Nation, 1815 to the Present*, Christian Calmes explains that Luxembourg would be "strong enough to constitute an English and a European corridor, capable of defending itself at least in an initial phase until allied reinforcements could arrive." Thus, according to Calmes, the State of Luxembourg "was born out of the interplay of geo-political and military factors" that resulted in "the decision to create a State in the interests of security and peace in Europe."

The area to the east of present-day Luxembourg was ceded to Prussia in 1815. In 1839, when the Treaty of London was signed, the western portion, including Bastogne, Arlon, and Bouillon, became part of Belgium. The eastern portion, under the rule of the grand duke, became an independent European state and a member of the German Confederation. This partitioning meant that those living in the western part of Luxembourg became Belgians by law, even though many of them continued to think of themselves as Luxembourgers.

The partition of 1839, according to Calmes, resulted in "the loss of 4,730 square kilometres and half the population of the Grand Duchy (175,000 inhabitants). After this diminution, the land area of the country was only 2,586 square kilometres." Even today, more than 150 years later, many inhabitants of the Luxembourg Province of Belgium consider themselves Luxembourgers.

During the past century and a half, Luxembourg has again been overtaken, most recently by German occupation forces during World War I and again during World War II. In the Place d'Armes at the center of Luxembourg City, a large stone tablet on the front wall of the Cercle Municipale proclaims Luxembourgers' gratitude to the American soldiers who helped restore their freedom more than fifty years ago:

On this square on 10th September 1944
The people of Luxembourg warmly welcomed its liberators,
The valiant soldiers of the U.S. 5th armored division
And their Royal Highnesses Prince Felix of Luxembourg
And Prince John, Hereditary Grand Duke of Luxembourg.

Today the Grand Duchy of Luxembourg is once again free. It has a constitutional monarchy, with hereditary sovereignty residing in the family of the House of Nassau.

Throughout the centuries, the inhabitants of Luxembourg have maintained their independent state of mind, embodied in the national motto: Mir wolle bleiwe wat mir sin. [We want to remain what we are.] But what does this motto mean? Historian James Newcomer notes that the motto "is not an idea as old as time in Luxembourg" and that it "has not been a motto in the mouths of Luxembourgians for much more than a century." Nonetheless, the motto has gained symbolic importance each time the people of Luxembourg have withstood an attempt by invaders to overpower them and subsume them under another culture.

An equally important aspect of Luxembourg's cultural and historical identity has been the survival and evolution of Lëtzebuergesch, the spoken daily language of Luxembourgers. Today more than 350,000 people, including neighbors across the Belgian and German borders, speak Lëtzebuergesch. Drawing upon the work of Luxembourgish linguist Robert Bruch, Jul Christophory has recently traced the origins of Lëtzebuergesch to texts of the ninth and tenth centuries, and he has outlined the rules governing its grammar and usage in Mir Schwatze Lëtzebuergesch [We Speak Luxembourgish].

Along with this analysis, Christophory has provided what he calls a "rough character-sketch of the Luxembourger." Christophory explains that, among other things, the Luxembourger "values roots, similarity and permanence" and that the Luxembourger is "slow, cautious, and serious-minded . . . a hard worker." Christophory notes that the Luxembourger is "conservative and conformist at heart in spite of a cavilling, sneering and grumbling facade." Christophory asserts that, because of centuries of subjugation, the Luxembourger has "an instinctive hate for hierarchic organization and for military or pedantic reglementation" and that the Luxembourger is "a natural democrat, proudly independent and reasonably European."

Regardless of whether Christophory's character sketch is generalizable to all Luxembourgers, it is useful in providing a sense of the mythos of the national character of Luxembourg as it has developed over the centuries. Determination, endurance, and independence—these have been and continue to be the watchwords of Luxembourgers on both sides of the Atlantic Ocean.

Perhaps, if you go to the old country seeking, as third or fourth generation Americans often do, a strictly personal history based on

bloodlines, then the less intimate history of the nation cannot im-
pose itself upon you very strongly. History is reduced to genealogy,
which is supposed to satisfy a hunger that is clearly much larger. . . .
      But if you go on a journey like this not to find somebody, but
just to look around . . . the country's history is infused with the ur-
gency of the classic search for personal identity. The country itself
becomes the lost ancestry and, one finds, the country is eloquent.
Its long story, its history, satisfy the instinct for kinship in a way
that the discovery of a distant cousin could not. For it is really
the longing for a lost culture that sends Americans on these
pilgrimages.—Patricia Hampl, *A Romantic Education,* 1981

What have I been seeking, and when did my search begin? Looking
back, I now see that my search for Susanna began shortly after my father's unexpected death in July 1978. Suddenly, I realized how little I
knew about my family history. I longed to know more. Like Patricia
Hampl, I have discovered that my search cannot result solely in a pro-
gression of names on a genealogical chart. My search for Susanna and
for a sense of personal identity has fused with my search for the sense
of ancestry and history that Luxembourg provides.

In August 1980, I went to Luxembourg for the first time, accompanied by my cousin Father Frank Klein. We were studying the lives of
our Klein ancestors, who had emigrated from Germany and Luxembourg to the United States in the mid-nineteenth century. Frank and I
first spent a week in western Germany—traveling to our ancestral village of Schönholthausen, then touring Bonn and Cologne.

Next we drove west, into Luxembourg. Some of our mutual ancestors (the Kleins, the Müllers) had once lived in the villages of Oberfeulen and Niederfeulen. These two villages, known as Feulen, are nestled in the rolling hills, a few kilometers from Ettelbruck, in the
central part of the country.

Although I had never been in Luxembourg, I recognized its landscape as akin to the landscape of my childhood in the American Midwest, and I felt a strange sense of being at home. At the same time,
however, my experiences during my first visit to Luxembourg taught
me just how foreign I was to the country, its people, and its culture. I
had walked into unfamiliar territory.

AUGUST 10, 1980
      In Niederfeulen, Luxembourg! This afternoon we drove from
      Cologne. When we reached the Luxembourg border, we hit the

green grass, golden wheat fields, and rolling hills. It was almost sunset, and a mist was settling over the valleys.

In Feulen we found a pensione—a beautiful, big place where we
were told, "Sorry, no rooms tonight, try again tomorrow night." We
reserved rooms for the rest of the week and were just about to leave
when a couple came in and told the landlady that they couldn't
keep their reservation for tonight. So we got rooms after all. Tomorrow our Feulen search begins.

AUGUST 11, 1980   10 A.M.

In St. Roche parish church at Niederfeulen, with the cows bellow-
ing in the background outside. Stained-glass windows, three altars,
and a beautiful carved pulpit with little statues of Sts. Matthew,
Mark, Luke, and John on it. The church walls are whitewashed inside, and the carpet is red and maroon. The large choir loft has old
wooden chairs for kneelers.

5 p.m. Outside the pensione in the sun, a cool and pleasant late
afternoon. After Frank and I saw the church, we stopped for lunch at
the local bar. Next, we went to visit Magdalena and Henri Bonert,
who are cousins on the Müller-Penning side. They spoke no English, and we conducted the entire conversation in a mélange of
French, German, and Lëtzebuergesch. I understood about half of
what was said! Tomorrow we're going to meet our cousins the
Steiwers, who have a letter written by Jacob Klein late in the 1800s
and a letter written in 1936 that tells of Jacob's death.

AUGUST 12, 1980

Frank and I drove the half-mile to the parish cemetery in Oberfeulen. It's an old cemetery; on some limestone markers, the names
are entirely washed off. I found the names Hottua, Klein, Welter,
and Koob, among others. Each grave plot was carefully decorated
with flowers (often geraniums or marigolds) and edged with stone
borders. These are family plots, no doubt with generations buried
on top of one another.

I thought about Dad as we were driving back from the cemetery
tonight. What I'd give to be able to tell him about this trip! At times
I miss him so much that I can almost believe I could call him to
sight before me. I picture him smiling and happy, sitting in his
livingroom chair with his hands in his lap (he's pushing at one
fingernail) and telling stories. I do think he knows what I'm doing,
and I hope he is happy.

It's raining now and will be cool by morning. Mme. Steichen, the woman who runs this pensione, has several pretty cats, among them a gray tiger like mine and a cute little black and white kitten. I'm enjoying them.

AUGUST 13, 1980

A busy day, and a good one. In the morning we drove to the village of Tadler where the pastor, Father Theodor Terres, took us to see the grave of Michel Klein, out in a little country cemetery a mile from the town. A tiny grave, marked by an old stone cross, with all the writing worn off.

The pastor said that the story goes that an old woman would come to visit the grave and that, after she stopped coming, the people who owned the plot next to it would plant flowers on the little grave and care for it. Evidently Frank and I were the first visitors to the grave in a very long time. I felt sad standing there at the grave of my great-great-grandfather, and I thought of the little grave of his wife, Mary Müller Klein, in Granville. She joined her sons there after they had immigrated to the U.S. around 1870. I'm sure Mary often thought about her husband's grave on the edge of Tadler and wondered if anyone would care for it.

In Tadler, we also saw the little house where Mary and Michel Klein lived during their marriage. Once part of a larger house, their section is now used as a barn. It used to have two rooms downstairs and a sleeping loft that one had to go outside and climb up to. I could imagine little Nick and Jake Klein playing there, and Mary so frightened when Michel died so suddenly. Their third son, Theodore Klein, Frank's grandfather and my great-grandfather, was born six months after his father's death. Frank and I also saw the Tadler church where Nick and Jake Klein were baptized. The patron saints are St. Donatus and St. Willibrord.

Then, after lunch in Ettelbruck, we went to visit Margaret Krieps, another cousin. Mrs. Krieps' house is tiny, and she lives frugally. Mrs. Krieps had dressed up for our visit—a clean gray vest and skirt with a red sweater underneath, and a clean green-print hubbard apron. Her great treasures seem to be the family pictures on her walls. She brought out some German liqueur and served it to us, and she showed us a record book which the Krieps family kept when they ran a store. Inside the front cover was the address of Theodore Klein in Granville, Iowa.

Then we walked down the street to meet more cousins, the

Steiwers. Their new house is carpeted and filled with antiques, some from the old Müller house. We had a good talk with Antoine and Maria Steiwer, even though they could speak only French and I could barely speak any. When their daughter Laure came in, the conversation went more smoothly. They opened a bottle of champagne and fed us a delicious meal of meat, bread, cheese, and desserts.

Antoine told how, during World War II, he was part of the Resistance. At one point, he had to leave home and hide out in the nearby forest for a year because he had hidden 24 Luxembourgers who had resisted being conscripted into the Nazi Army. Maria had to divorce Antoine to avoid being sent with her little son, Jacques, to a concentration camp. Eventually, after the war, the family was reunited.

Antoine mentioned that Herr Steichen (owner of the pensione where we are staying) had collaborated with the Nazi occupation forces and that Mme. Steichen had been even worse than her husband in turning townspeople over to the Nazis as spies. Today, the Steichens are pretty well ostracized by the townspeople of Feulen.

I am amazed that the Steichens are so despised 35 years later, though I can understand the resentment that people like the Steiwers must feel. To have to spend a year hiding in forests, wondering about your family and not knowing whether or not you'd be caught and executed—not to be able to trust your own townspeople.

AUGUST 16, 1980

This afternoon my cousins, the Lindens, took me for a drive up to Vianden and on to Esch-sur-Sure and other towns. Beautiful countryside, set into huge forests on large hills—the Ardennes. We stopped to tour a power plant and see a dam that provides electricity for an entire region. Erny, Nick, and Nico Linden seemed to enjoy showing me around, and I liked traveling with people who knew the area.

Last night Frank and I went to the celebration of the Feast of the Assumption here at the church in Niederfeulen. There was a procession from the church for about 1/2 mile to a grotto out near the edge of the town. Everyone in the procession carried a little lighted candle, and people sang religious songs to Mary in Lëtzebuergesch all the way from the church to the grotto. Magdalena Bonert walked with me, and what a beautiful singing voice she has, strong and in tune. Every once in a while she'd sing along with the priest when

hc'd do the little lead-ins to the chants like "Ave Maria" that people
would say in response as we walked along.

When the procession reached the grotto, there were about twenty
more people waiting there. The whole grotto was lit by candles—
probably several hundred—and large bouquets of roses and of garde-
nias were all around the statue of Mary.

At the grotto, there were several more songs. The priest led the
prayers, but he had to be prompted by his assistant, Paul Colling,
because the older man was having problems remembering exactly
what he was supposed to be doing. During the ceremony, there were
about 75 people present, and I could see more people standing outside their houses off in the distance, watching the ceremony. After
about 45 minutes at the grotto, the group dispersed. Paul invited
Frank & me over to tour "L'École Nationale de L'Incendie"—the
National Firefighters School—and to try some Luxembourg beer.

About ten men were there. Everyone toasted one another with
Henri Funck beer and talked in a mélange of Lëtzebuergesch,
French, and English. That went on till nearly midnight; then Frank
and I walked back here to the pensione. I slept well, perhaps because I'd done a good deal of walking during the day, and I was tired.

At L'École, Paul Colling pointed out that it had first been a tuberculosis sanitarium. Then, after WWII, it was a prison for Nazi collaborators. Next, it became a reform school for wayward girls, and
finally the training school for Luxembourg's firefighters.

One of the men we talked to, a Mr. Schreiner, had once been to
the U.S. and had, in fact, worked for a while on a farm near Remsen,
Iowa. But he didn't like the prairie flatlands, so he returned to Luxembourg and remained here ever since. At the grotto after the service, another man came up to me and said he had been in Kansas
and Virginia once for a farmers' exchange program.

AUGUST 17, 1980

Today we drove north to Clervaux, where we saw the castle and
toured the "Family of Man" exhibition of photographs organized by
Edward Steichen. We also went through a museum commemorating
the siege of the Ardennes during World War II. I saw uniforms and
military paraphernalia from U.S. troops, and some from 3rd Reich
troops. Many plaques honored General George Patton, Jr. It felt like
a shrine. I never realized just how much admiration and gratitude
the people here have for Patton and for the U.S. liberation forces.

AUGUST 19, 1980

Today Frank and I will drive to Heidelberg to see the castle and look around at the city. Then tomorrow, it's off to the airport at Frankfurt early in the morning.

Yesterday before leaving Niederfeulen, we stopped at the records office to get copies of birth, marriage, and death certificates. Then we went to say goodbye to Magdalena and Henri Bonert and to Margaret Krieps. We found Margaret shaking out pillows on her porch. She was wearing an old brown wool skirt, a shiny blouse, and a hubbard apron. Big boots on her feet—up over her ankles. And socks— brown and pushed down to where they met the tops of her boots. She asked us to come in, and she gave us some more German liqueur. Then she said she had "des cadeaux" for us. Into the back room she went, and she came out with a little plastic apple filled with kirsch liqueured candy. I could tell she was so proud to give it to us. And then she went into the cellar and got up some brandy she had made. She put some into a bottle and gave it to Frank, "pour le papa."

Then we all said goodbye, and Frank and I drove up to the Shell station to get gas. I wanted to introduce myself to the proprietors, the Hottuas. Mr. Hottua (Nick) sat there impassively, puffing on a big cigar. But Mrs. Hottua was friendly, especially when I told her that the name of my great-great-great-grandmother was Angela Hottua. There is an Angela Hottua today, and my name, Suzanne, is one that has been passed down through the Hottuas in every generation.

AUGUST 22, 1980   5:30 A.M.

Back in Madison, WI, after a safe trip.

I've been wanting to write down my experience with Mme. Steichen because that has been one of the things that has most intrigued me during the trip. How could she stay in a town where everyone so obviously hated her & wanted nothing to do with her? Then, on the other hand, what choice did she have but to stay there? Where else could she go?

Always, Mme. Steichen seemed friendly. Every morning, she'd come in to serve breakfast & say, "Bonjour—dormiéz-vous bien?" She'd be wearing a housedress with a dark blue sweater and a hubbard apron. White, somewhat curly hair, clear blue eyes, pale complexion. Always the same navy blue slingback pumps on her feet. Always smiling. Setting food out on the table—good bread, meats and cheeses, delicious plum & prune jams, flowered china cups and saucers for coffee. And generally a bowl of cornflakes or rice krispies for us to help ourselves from. And a white pitcher filled with very creamy milk. Then she'd look at the whole table spread, smile and say, "Bien," and quietly go out, closing the door behind her.

Sometimes I'd try to talk with her about her cats, especially about a pretty little kitten—white with some black spots, still with blue eyes, and with a crooked tail that had once evidently been broken. A real sweet kitten that loved to curl up in my arms & purr. "La petite chat" was how I'd refer to this kitten when I talked with Mme. Steichen. Sometimes at breakfast I could hear meowing, and once Mme. Steichen explained that "la petite chat" was in a "cache" behind one of the walls in the dining room—a little dark place where it liked to hide. Several times, another of the cats would sneak into the house when the door was opened, and Mme. would have to shoo it out. That cat she called "Pussy."

So she and I got along well, talking about the cats. I thought that this subject would give us a common ground & perhaps help me understand her better. Somehow, I just couldn't believe that she could still be the horrible person whom the Steiwers called a Nazi collaborator during WWII.

Then, about the middle of our stay in Niederfeulen, Frank and Paul Colling accidentally ran over the little kitten, killing it. They acted very offhand about it, announcing it to me while we were all in the livingroom at the Steiwers'.

Frank said that Mr. Steichen had carried off the kitten into the barn, and that Mme. Steichen seemed to forgive them for running over it. So when we got home from [the] Steiwers' and Mme. Steichen opened the door for us, I told her I was sorry, and I asked if the cat were dead. "Yes," she said, looking very tired & sad. I kept saying, "Je regrette" and trying to think of some other words to say in French, but nothing would come to me.

"C'était un shock," she said, and she said also, "Je oublierai." [It was a shock. I will forget.]

I began to cry. Somehow that kitten had come to represent the fragile friendship built up between Mme. Steichen & myself. As the week went on, I was able to converse with Mme. Steichen, but neither of us mentioned "la petite chat" again.

On August 20, 1980, during our flight back to Chicago from Frankfurt, Frank and I had time to reflect on our experiences of the past two weeks. Our time in Luxembourg had taught us so much about our ancestral lines, and we were amazed and grateful for the warm welcome our cousins had given us. Frank and I shared some embarrassment over having found lodging at the Maison des Vacances, the one place in Feulen that our cousins avoided. But how could we have known? In fact, Frank pointed out, perhaps because we had stayed there, we'd had a chance to understand more about the history of Luxembourg and its people than if we had stayed elsewhere.

As we talked, I browsed through *Les Deux Liberations du Luxembourg, 1944–1945*, a history of the two liberations of Luxembourg given to me by my cousin Antoine Steiwer. The book, which outlined troop movements and battles during the Ardennes offensive, ended by emphasizing the need for Americans, Germans, and Luxembourgers to join efforts to defend a common heritage and civilization: "Aujourd'hui Américains, Allemands, Luxembourgeois—pour ne parler que des acteurs du drame décrit dans cet exposé—se sont unis pour défendre un patrimoine commun: la civilisation, telle qu'elle est comprise dans le monde occidental."

Upon my return to the U.S., I received a news clipping from my mother, along with a holy card given out at the funeral of my great-aunt, Theresa Welter O'Connor Lieb. She had died on August 16, 1980, while I was still in Europe. I knew I'd miss Aunt Theresa, my Grandma Bunkers' youngest sister. Aunt Theresa had lived down the street from our house when I was growing up, and she had worked for many years at Beck's Store in Granville.

As a girl, I liked to stop by Aunt Theresa's house and listen to her tell family stories. She made the names of many Welter, Linster, and Bunkers ancestors come to life. More important, she filled in some of the blanks about my grandparents, Frank and Lillian Bunkers, and about my father's childhood. In March 1980, I had sat down with Aunt Theresa and turned on my tape recorder. I asked her many questions about the Welter, Linster, and Bunkers families. She told me the family stories again, and both of us enjoyed our conversation. I didn't know it would be our last one.

In late August 1980, new Ph.D. in hand, I moved from Madison, Wisconsin, to Mankato, Minnesota, where I would soon begin teaching English at Mankato State University. A small place by comparison with Madison, Mankato looked like one of those sleepy little Midwestern towns in a Sinclair Lewis novel. The university campus looked more like a large high school than a university to me. It was deserted. Classes would not resume until mid-September, and most faculty were enjoying a brief respite between summer school and fall quarter.

During my first weeks in Mankato, I moved boxes of books into my office in Armstrong Hall, and I began preparing my freshman composition courses. I settled into my run-down apartment in a large house on the edge of town, next to the local sanitation company.

My cats, Alice, Vincent, and Teddy, were my constant companions. I ate a lot of macaroni and cheese, for I had been living on a student loan all summer while finishing my dissertation, and my first paycheck from MSU would not arrive until early October.

During those weeks, I had time to reflect on my trip to Luxembourg and to muse about Susanna. What might it have been like to have been pregnant and unmarried in 1856? Had Susanna been forced to take her baby daughter, Barbara, and flee Luxembourg? Had an unhappy life there led Susanna to a place called Iowa, in the middle of a prairie, several thousand miles from her home? How could I learn more about Susanna's life? And what might her life have to do with mine?

A few months earlier, I had come across the words to a song written by Ernest M. Woll and Joseph Winandy. Legend had it that the song, "My Luxembourg across the Sea," was popular with nineteenth-century emigrants who had sailed for America but who still longed for their homeland. Although I did not know the melody to this song, its lyrics moved me. Might Susanna have known this song? Might she have been moved to tears by its final lines?

MY LUXEMBOURG ACROSS THE SEA

Across the mighty ocean, as the sun is sinking fast,
And the fleeting shadows tell the knell of day,
My thoughts are fondly dwelling over happy days, long past
In my home in Luxembourg, so far away,
I behold the Moselle valley with the swiftly flowing stream,
And the vine-clad hills, the rushing waterfalls,
And the little hillside cottage, set in choicest foliage green,
Oh! what cherished childhood scenes they do recall.

My Luxembourg, for you I'm sighing
And I'm longing for my home, so dear to me,
To that sweet spot my thoughts are flying,
To my dear Luxembourg across the sea.

In my fancy, I can see again my kind and loving dad
As he used to sit by the old rustic mill,
And the sweetheart of my boyhood days, whom I hoped to wed,
She's now sleeping in the churchyard on the hill,

But the dearest of all visions and the one I love the best,
'Tis of mother dear, her whom I long to see,
God bless you, darling mother, my true heart will never rest,
Till we meet again at home across the sea.

My Luxembourg, for you I'm sighing.
And I'm longing for my home, so dear to me,
To that sweet spot my thoughts are flying,
To my dear Luxembourg across the sea.

As I reflected on my journey across the sea, I wondered how it had changed me. What had I learned from the time spent in my ancestors' native village? How had my interactions with my newly found cousins influenced my ways of looking at Luxembourgers? How had the fact that I had stayed in the Maison des Vacances—the one house in Niederfeulen that was off-limits to my relatives—influenced their perceptions of me? How had my impressions of Mme. Steichen, so at odds with my cousins' impressions of her, affected how I looked at the aftermath of World War II in the lives of Luxembourgers today?

What was the truth of my experiences? Could I find out, and, if so, could I put it into words? Perhaps the best I could do would be to take to heart the words of Adrienne Rich in *On Lies, Secrets, and Silence*:

> In speaking of lies, we come inevitably to the subject of truth. There is nothing simple or easy about this idea. There is no "the truth," "a truth"—truth is not one thing, or even a system. It is an increasing complexity. The pattern of the carpet is a surface. When we look closely, or when we become weavers, we learn of the tiny multiple threads unseen in the overall pattern, the knots on the underside of the carpet.

How could I become a weaver? How could I begin to look more closely at the tiny, unseen threads in my family's history? What would I find if I looked at the underside of the carpet? Perhaps some of the answers lay closer than Luxembourg, buried in the stories of those, like

my father, now at rest in St. Joseph Parish cemetery in Granville, Iowa.
During Easter week 1981, I set out in that direction.

EASTER SUNDAY

It is April
And I am journeying
Across Wisconsin.
The Greyhound passes
"Viroqua Country Kitchen, 6 mi."

"For Sale, 80 acres" defines
Burnt-gold fields
Along the highway.
Cornstalks, weathered and tall,
Lean against barbed-wire ridges.
Leafless trees bend outward
For warmth, renewal.

I am traveling
Toward the flatlands,
The black soil,
The Iowa plains.
I am passing
Over farmland,
Through rolling hills,
Along the thawing Mississippi.
Near where the Floyd
Empties into the Missouri,
I pause
To drink in
The Midwestern spring:

Sparrows perching
On telephone lines,
Calves trailing freshened heifers
Through the furrows,
Gravestones gleaming
Copper and silver
In the setting sun.

—Suzanne Bunkers, 1981

In the Name of the Father

Men's stories, women's stories. How they are about
blood and roots and earth, how they must be
repeated each generation or they are lost forever.
—John Edgar Wideman, *Fatheralong*, 1994

In nomine Patris, et Filii, et Spiritus Sancti. Amen.
> *In the Name of the Father, and of the Son, and of the Holy Spirit.*
> *Amen.*

Introibo ad altare Dei.
> *I will go in to the altar of God.*

Ad Deum qui laetificat juventutem meam.
> *The God of my gladness and joy.*

Judica me, Deus, et discerne causam meam de gente non sancta:
ab homine iniquo, et doloso erue me.
> *Do me justice, O God, and fight my fight against a faithless*
> *people: from the deceitful and impious man rescue me.*

Quia tu es, Deus, fortitudo mea: quare me repulisti, et quare tristis
incedo, dum affligit me inimicus?
> *For You, O God, are my strength: why do You keep me so far*
> *away; why must I go about in mourning with the enemy op-*
> *pressing me?*

—from *The Ordinary of the Mass*

Latin. Its exquisite cadences filled my ears every time I went to
Mass. Next to the side door, about halfway to the back of St. Joseph
Church, was our family pew—a few feet from a life-size statue of Saint

Anthony and just below a gigantic wall-mounted statue of the Fourth Station of the Cross, "Jesus Meets His Most Afflicted Mother."

Before I was old enough to be enrolled at St. Joseph's Catholic grade school (or "Sisters' School," as we called it), I'd sit in our family pew every Sunday morning. In front of me, Saint Anthony would hold out his fingers in blessing, while above me, the Blessed Virgin Mary would gaze lovingly at her son as he carried his cross toward Calvary. During Lent, our family would again fill our assigned pew each Friday afternoon during Stations, listening as Father Dalhoff or Father Becker intoned: "O Mary, Mother of Sorrows, help me by thy powerful intercession. While considering the sufferings and death of thy dear Son, let me share in the sorrow which pierced thy tender heart."

Devotion to the Blessed Virgin Mary was at the center of my religious life, for Mary was the Virgin Mother of the Son of God. A symbol of purity, patience, resourcefulness, ingenuity, and love, she represented much more than the Stabat Mater at the foot of the cross. If I prayed to Mary to intercede with Jesus on my behalf, my prayers had a much better chance of being answered. My favorite prayer to the Blessed Virgin Mary was "The Memorare." I learned it by heart and recited it every day:

> Remember, O most gracious Virgin Mary, that never was it known that anyone who fled to thy protection, implored thy help, and sought thy intercession, was left unaided. Inspired with this confidence, I fly unto thee, O Virgin of virgins, my mother! To thee I come, before thee I stand, sinful and sorrowful. O Mother of the Word Incarnate, despise not my petitions, but in thy mercy hear and answer me. Amen.

In religion class, I'd learned that, because of the fall of Adam and Eve, I'd been born in the state of original sin, with a big black spot on my soul. The Sacrament of Baptism had wiped away that spot and saved me; the Sacraments of Penance and Holy Communion could keep me in the state of sanctifying grace. I'd also learned that Jesus' mother Mary was the only human being conceived and born without original sin on her soul so she could become the virgin mother of Our Saviour, Jesus. The feast day of the Immaculate Conception, celebrated as a Holy Day of Obligation on December 8, commemorated Mary's unique status.

A second Holy Day of Obligation, August 15, commemorated Mary's Assumption into Heaven. Because she had been born without sin, Mary did not have to die like other human beings. She was simply assumed up into Heaven to rejoin her Son, who had ascended there after his resurrection from the tomb on Easter Sunday morning. I was taught not to try to understand either Mary's Immaculate Conception or her Assumption. They were "mysteries of faith," unfathomable though true, verified by proclamations from Our Holy Father the Pope, who could not err in matters of Catholic faith and doctrine.

In miraculous appearances to Bernadette at Lourdes as well as the three children at Fatima and elsewhere, The Blessed Virgin Mary had told Catholics that they could demonstrate their devotion to her by praying the rosary. Children were especially encouraged to say the rosary. In *The Secret of the Rosary*, St. Louis De Montfort tells the story of two sisters who lived in Paraguay. One day they were saying the rosary when a beautiful lady suddenly appeared, took the little sister by the hand, and led her away. The older sister searched everywhere, to no avail, then went home to tell their parents about her sister's disappearance. For three days, no trace of the little sister could be found. On the third day, however, she happily returned home and told her family that she'd been visiting the Blessed Virgin Mary's house, where she helped take care of Baby Jesus. The parents sent at once for a Jesuit priest, who taught them and their daughters devotion to the Most Holy Rosary. De Montfort concludes this story by speaking directly to children:

> Dear little friends, this beautiful rosebud is for you; it is one of the beads of your Rosary, and it may seem to you to be such a tiny thing. But if you knew how precious this bead is! This wonderful bud will open out into a gorgeous rose if you say your Hail Mary really well. . . . So, dear children, imitate these little girls and say your Rosary every day as they always did. If you do this you will earn the right to go to heaven to see Jesus and Mary. If it is not their wish that you should see them in this life, at any rate after you die you will see them for all eternity.

Who could tell? Maybe "the BVM," as we called Mary, would appear to one of us someday. Many nights my family would gather in the living room to pray the rosary. We'd bring pillows from our beds, lay them on the hardwood floor, kneel down on them, and lean our elbows on the cushions of the sofa and armchairs. Mom would shut the curtains on the picture window directly across from the couch so that anyone driving by our house would not see our backsides pointing out at them.

When Linda and I got old enough to learn all the Sorrowful, Joyful, and Glorious Mysteries by heart, Dad and Mom would let us take turns leading the rosary. Despite our good intentions, sometimes my sister and I found it hard to lead the rosary with a straight face. Once Mom gave me a sharp jab in the ribs when I began reciting the Apostles' Creed in a Southern drawl. Another time, Linda got a kick in the shins from Dad when she launched into the Hail Holy Queen in a British accent.

After the rosary, it was time for bed. Dad would stop in our room to tell us bedtime stories and listen as Linda and I recited "Now I Lay Me down to Sleep" and "Our Father, Who Art in Heaven." Dad made up other prayers for us. My favorite was "Jesus of Nazareth." As Linda and I would recite, "Jesus of Nazareth, King of the Jews, preserve me this night from a sudden and unprepared death," Dad would trace the letters INRI (Hebrew for "Jesus of Nazareth, King of the Jews") across our foreheads. Another favorite prayer, also taught to us by Dad, went like this: "Jesus, watch over Suzy tonight, Linda tonight, my two grandmas, one grandpa, Mommy, Daddy, Denny, Dale, and everybody else in the world." When our youngest brother, Danny, was born in 1963, his name was inserted into the prayer right after Dale's. As Dad made the Sign of the Cross, he'd bless Linda and me with holy water from the font just above the Guardian Angel light switch. Then he would walk out into the hall, gently closing the bedroom door.

For us, Catholicism wasn't something that "happened" on a Sunday morning or a Friday afternoon. It was part of the fabric of daily life in Granville, where everyone was Catholic and where there was only one church and only one school. When I started Sisters' School, I learned that, like other Catholics, I had been specially chosen by Our Saviour, and that, if I were good, I could someday join Him in Heaven. My Catechism lessons had begun.

Why did God make you?
  God made me: to know Him, to love Him, and to serve Him in this world, so that I may be happy through Him in this life, and with Him forever in Heaven.
How do you know God?
  I know God through the teaching of His Church.
What should you do if you have the dreadful misfortune of offending God?
  If I have the dreadful misfortune of offending God, I should at once ask God's pardon by making an Act of Contrition, and go to Confession soon.

What should you do if God sends you disappointment, pain, or
suffering?
    If God sends me disappointment, pain, or suffering, I should
    be patient and say: "Lord, Thy Will be done. I accept this for
    my sins."
Why does God will or permit poverty, suffering, and other evils in
the world?
    God wills or permits poverty, suffering, and other evils in the
    world as a punishment for sin, or to try the just and increase
    their merit.
What is our obligation when the Church teaches a doctrine of Faith
or Morals?
    When the Church teaches a doctrine of Faith or Morals, we are
    bound to believe it.
What should you do to remain pure?
    To remain pure I should:
        1. go to confession and Holy Communion frequently;
        2. be devoted to our Immaculate Mother;
        3. keep away from bad books and magazines, bad pictures,
    bad shows and movies, and bad people.
—from *Catholic Faith: A Catechism*, 1938

Even as a second grader, I realized how crucial it was for me to learn
my Catholic Catechism, obey the Ten Commandments, and attend
Mass on Sundays and Holy Days of Obligation. I learned how important it was for me to do God's will and remain pure. As a seven-year-
old, I dreamed of two things: making my First Holy Communion and
becoming an altar boy.

To prepare for making my First Holy Communion, I needed to make
a good First Confession. At school, Sister Agatha taught me about venial sins and mortal sins. Venial sins were little sins like accidentally
eating a piece of candy during Lent or talking back to my mom or dad.
Venial sins could land me briefly in purgatory after death, but they
could not keep me out of heaven forever.

Mortal sins were another story. If I committed adultery or murdered someone, I could land in hell for eternity. But I would never com-
mit any of those kinds of sins. I planned to stay on the straight and narrow. Each school day during religion class, Sister Agatha would lead
the other second graders and me through an examination of conscience, helping us to memorize the Act of Contrition. We would need
to know it by heart when we made our First Confessions in the spring:

Oh my God, I am heartily sorry for having offended Thee, and I
detest all my sins because of Thy just punishments. But most of all,
because they offend Thee, my God, who art all good and deserving of
all my love. I firmly resolve, with the help of Thy grace, to sin no
more and to avoid the near occasions of sin.

Sister Agatha emphasized the importance of making a good examination of my conscience in order to make a good First Confession.
Each night, I took out my new little black prayer book and opened it to
the page titled "Examination of Conscience." I memorized the Seven
Deadly Sins of Pride, Covetousness, Lust, Anger, Gluttony, Envy, and
Sloth. I read that, when making my confession to the parish priest, I
was really "at the feet of Jesus Crucified, Who wishes to hear from
your own lips a sincere confession of all your sins, and is ready to grant
you absolution if you really are repentant." Each night, when I exam-
ined my conscience, I would consider which of the Ten Commandments I might have broken that day:

First Commandment: Had I doubted that mine was the true religion?
Second Commandment: Had I taken God's name in vain?
Third Commandment: Had I missed Mass on a Sunday or Holy Day of
   Obligation?
Fourth Commandment: Had I disobeyed my mother or father?
Fifth Commandment: Had I been violent toward another person?
Sixth Commandment: Had I deliberately taken pleasure in impure
   thoughts or committed any willful impure actions?
Seventh Commandment: Had I stolen anything or cheated anyone?
Eighth Commandment: Had I told any lies, either lies of commission or
   lies of omission?
Ninth Commandment: Had I coveted my neighbor's wife?
Tenth Commandment: Had I coveted my neighbor's goods?

Lying in bed after my prayers were said, I'd puzzle over what to confess during my First Confession. Should I say I'd lied? About what?
Should I say I'd disobeyed my parents? If so, how many times? I hadn't
missed Mass or cheated on my weekly spelling test. I hadn't committed adultery or coveted my neighbor's wife. What if I couldn't think of
anything to confess?
   When I shared my concern with my baby-sitter Kathy, a fifth grader,
she advised me to do what she always did when she went to confession: recite the same list of sins every time. That way, she explained, I
would always have something to confess; and, if I went to confession

with the same priest each Saturday, I'd get the same penance: three Hail Marys. Kathy told me that it would take me only a few minutes to complete this penance after my sins had been forgiven, if I'd be sure to make this confession:

> Bless me, Father, for I have sinned. It has been one week since my last confession. During that time I have disobeyed my parents five times, I have told three lies, I have argued with my brothers and sisters two times, and I have daydreamed during Mass once. I am sorry for these and for all my sins.

This list of sins sounded about right. I thought it covered almost every sinful thing I'd ever done, and I figured that a fifth grader ought to know what she was talking about. I decided to follow Kathy's advice. On the morning of my First Confession, I entered the tiny, dark confessional, took my place on the wooden kneeler, and devoutly made the Sign of the Cross. Then I waited for the priest to slide open the little door that covered the latticework through which I would whisper my sins. When my turn came, I recited just what Kathy had suggested. Bingo! Father Wagner gave me three Hail Marys for my penance.

The next time I went to confession, I recited the same list of sins and got the same penance. For about a year that system worked. Then one Saturday afternoon I walked to church for confession in a state of high anxiety. The day before, I'd been playing with my friend Chris in her dad's feed and supply shop. We were supposed to be watching the phone while he ran an errand, but we decided to have some fun in the back room. We were jumping around on stacks of fifty-pound bags of dog and cat food when I misjudged a jump and fell off one stack, pulling two sacks of dog food down with me.

A glossy magazine had tumbled out from between the sacks. *Nudist World*, read the title on its cover. The picture showed a group of absolutely naked men and women playing volleyball on the beach. Once Chris and I had gotten over the initial shock of seeing all those unclothed body parts, we sat down with the magazine to take a better look. Up to that time, the closest I'd come to seeing a naked person other than myself was on the underwear pages of our J. C. Penney catalog. But *Nudist World* had naked people on every page. They were jumping up and down at the volleyball net on one page, riding horses on another, drinking sodas around a swimming pool on a third. Did people actually go around naked doing those kinds of things?

"This must be the hired man's magazine," Chris whispered. "My dad would never look at something like this!"

"Mine neither," I said. "Holy Cow! Did you know that people took off all their clothes and did this kind of stuff?"

Chris shook her head. Just then, the front door of the shop flew open. We stashed *Nudist World* under a couple of bags of dog food and ran out the back door just as Chris' dad walked in the front one.

That night when I made my examination of conscience, I had the funny feeling that I'd done something wrong by looking at that magazine. But was it a sin? And, if so, how would I confess it? I didn't want to get a lengthy penance. If I stayed on my knees praying for hours after going to confession, everyone would know I'd done something really bad. But I did have to confess it, I felt it in my gut. I slept on it, but the next morning I didn't feel any better. I had to go to confession that afternoon. What could I tell Father Wagner?

"Bless me, Father, for I have sinned. It has been two weeks since my last confession. These are my sins. I disobeyed my parents ten times, I argued with my sister five times, I stole pieces of my brother's bubble gum twice, and I did something bad once." I held my breath.

"My child, what do you mean, 'I did something bad once'?"

I took a deep breath. "Well, Father, I did something . . . something . . . impure."

"Impure in thought or in deed?"

"Impure in deed, Father."

"With yourself or with others?"

What? I was puzzled. Did looking at *Nudist World* count as doing something impure with myself or with others? Well, it must have been doing something impure with myself, since I had looked at those naked people. Then again, Chris had been looking, too. So did it really count as doing something impure with others?

"My child," Father Wagner said again, "did you do something impure with yourself or with others?"

"I . . . I don't know, Father." My heart pounded. The silence grew long on the other side of the little window. Then it grew even longer. Finally, Father Wagner sighed.

"Well, whichever it was, my child, in the name of God, you are forgiven. For your penance, say ten Our Fathers and five Hail Marys. Now make a good Act of Contrition. Then go in peace, and sin no more."

"Yes, Father."

I got out of that little box as fast as I could. I sped through my penance at the back of the church before any of my friends could show up to make their confessions. I'd learned my lesson. I vowed not to think, say, or do anything impure—with myself or with others—ever again.

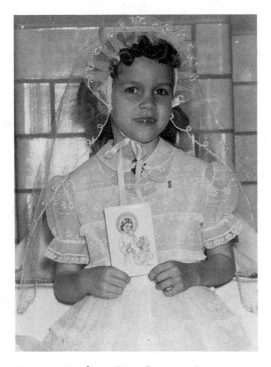

Suzanne Bunkers, First Communion,
March 16, 1958.

During the winter months leading up to my First Communion in March 1958, Sister Agatha would sometimes bring a roll of unconsecrated hosts to religion class. My classmates and I would kneel in the aisles alongside our desks, and Sister Agatha would help us practice learning how to receive Holy Communion. The key, she said, was to close your eyes, open your mouth, then stick out your tongue—not too far but just far enough so that the priest could place the tiny circle of unleavened bread on it. Then, Sister said, close your mouth very slowly, being careful not to accidentally catch the host with your upper lip. That could knock it out of your mouth and onto the communion rail or, worse, onto the floor. And the Body of Christ did not belong on the church floor!

I practiced fervently during the week leading up to Sunday, March 16, 1958, my First Holy Communion. That morning I put on my frilly white dress, my lace-edged white anklets, and my new white patent-leather shoes. The night before, my mother had wound up my hair in pink rubber curlers. Now my hair sprung up and down on my shoulders, and my bangs curled daintily on my forehead, just below the gathered lace of my veil. In my white-gloved hands I carried my First Communion prayer book and rosary.

There was only one small complication. For the past week, my top front tooth had been loosening gradually. When I told Mom, she warned me not to pull it before my First Communion. A big hole in my smile would ruin my First Communion portrait, which would be taken after Sunday Mass. Every day, I'd push at my tooth with my tongue, checking to see how loose it was. On Saturday morning, while watching *Mighty Mouse* on TV, I tested it once again. This time the tooth fell out onto the couch. I clapped my hand over my mouth and ran to the bathroom. I hiked myself up over the sink and opened my bloodied mouth before the mirror. There it was—the biggest hole I could possibly imagine.

I tried to keep my mouth shut during lunch, but Mom noticed that my tooth was missing. She sighed and rolled her eyes. All I could do was put the tooth into Dad's favorite shot glass and set it on the windowsill so Teena, my tooth fairy, would find it that night. Mom and Dad advised me to keep my mouth shut during First Communion pictures the next morning.

I tried, but it was impossible not to smile. When the photographer lined up the entire class before the main altar, I was relieved to be in the second row, where my missing tooth would be less noticeable. Later on, however, when I stood in the lunchroom with my classmates Sheila Ballard, Juliann Graff, and Mary Jo Sanders for a "Bunkers cousins" picture, I smiled broadly. But I didn't feel too bad about it. Next to me was my cousin Juliann; she was also missing one of her front teeth.

I knew that if I learned my prayers I could fulfill my dream of making a good First Communion, but I also knew that I'd never be able to fulfill my dream of becoming an altar boy. The closest I could come was to pretend. So, in third grade, I offered to clean school for Sister Marietta, the nun who taught the grade school boys how to serve Mass. Sister Marietta schooled the boys in the fine points of genuflecting, waving censers filled with pungent incense, carrying the cruets containing water and wine, and walking gracefully in ankle-length acolyte garb.

Sister Marietta kept the new altar boys after school so she could teach them to recite, by rote, the Latin responses to the priest's entreaties during Mass. While they recited, "Ahd *day* oom kwee lay *tee* fee kaht, you ven too tem *may* ahm" in their loudest voices, I scrubbed the blackboard, my back to them, reciting those same Latin words under my breath. If Sister Marietta would chide a boy for forgetting or mispronouncing a Latin phrase, I would chuckle inwardly. I knew it all by heart.

But the nearest I could ever get to the altar was with a dust cloth whenever I'd help Sister Gertrude or Sister Matilda clean church late in the afternoon. When I was dusting the communion rail or replacing burnt-out vigil lights with new ones, I'd recite the altar boys' responses from the Ordinary of the Mass in impeccable ecclesiastical Latin. I would bow, genuflect, beat my breast (*"Mea culpa, mea culpa, mea maxima culpa"*), then run my mop along the hardwood floor. I would volunteer to go into the sacristy and collect the dirty vestments so I could peek into the cupboards that hid the priest's embroidered finery and the acolytes' flowing cassocks. Sooner or later, I figured, the Catholic Church might change its rules.

On my way home after school, I would stop off to visit my mother's parents, Frances and Teddy Klein. They had built a new house next door to ours when they retired from the farm in 1956. The same blueprints had been used for both three-bedroom ramblers, the only difference being that Grandma and Grandpa's house was sky blue and ours was pale green. I liked it that we had identical houses. I always knew where everything was at Grandma and Grandpa's house because everything was in the exact same place at our house.

I'd ring the front doorbell, then walk in. Grandma would usually be reading the *Catholic Digest* in her armchair, but as soon as I arrived, the two of us would sit down at her spinet to play duets. Grandma didn't read music; she played by ear. If I hummed a few bars of a song, she could play the entire thing, on the black keys as well as the white ones. Having just begun piano lessons, I was still having trouble finding middle C and making my fingers hit the white keys when I tried to play "Row, Row, Row Your Boat."

Grandma loved teaching me to play the old songs she knew so well, songs like "Beautiful Ohio," "Smile a While," "Three O'clock in the Morning," and my favorite, "Doodle De Doo." Soon, seated next to her on the piano bench, I could pound out the old songs with ease, taking the right hand's, the left hand's, or both hands' parts.

While Grandma and I played, Grandpa would rock in his wicker chair, praying the rosary or reading from his prayer book. Grandpa prayed more than anyone I'd ever known. Once, I recited to him the Latin prayers I'd learned while cleaning school, and I confided my hopes of becoming a Mass server. Grandpa wasn't too encouraging, but he had another idea: why not become a nun, a Bride of Christ? The

Klein family had a long history of producing priests and nuns, but none of Grandpa and Grandma's seven children had had a religious vocation. Maybe their granddaughter would.

Grandpa and I talked about this possibility nearly every day while playing canasta or euchre at the kitchen table. For my ninth birthday, he ordered me a rosary from the Vatican. Pope John the XXIII had blessed it himself, and each bead of the rosary carried with it a five-hundred-day indulgence. If I prayed the entire rosary devoutly, I could earn seventy-five years' indulgence. I'd never have to spend a single day in purgatory! That tiny set of pink beads soon became my most prized possession.

I liked Grandpa's idea. I had learned about religious vocations at school, and I was eager to become a Bride of Christ. But how could I do that? First, I talked my sister, Linda, and my cousin Patsy Feller into playing nun. We dressed up in old white bedsheets with strings of rope around our waists and Mom's dishtowels tied on our heads. We carried our rosaries and little bottles of holy water. Then we talked the little neighbor kids into playing school in our basement. There, as "Sister Mary Veronica," I began conducting reading, spelling, arithmetic, and religion classes. I began going to 7:00 a.m. Mass with Grandpa Klein on school days and writing religious poems. "Dear Jesus," composed when I was nine, was one of my best efforts:

> You died on that hard cross
> Just because You love me,
> When I see You hanging there,
> I think how good you must be.
>
> I love You very much, Christ,
> To look at You that way,
> I could never, never think of
> All I want to say.
>
> You thought of all my sins
> When the men were after You,
> I can never be, Dear Lord,
> As kind, as nice, as true.
>
> Now I must finish, Lord,
> I know I soon must end,
> I just know I will love You
> In life and death. Amen.

In sixth grade, I joined a group of my classmates in a special musical group, Schola. We learned to read Gregorian chant so we could sing at funeral Masses. I had always been fascinated by Catholic funerals, and now I could attend every one at St. Joseph Church. After Mass, I could follow the casket and the mourners to the cemetery for the burial. I would get goose bumps when the priest would intone, "Let us pray for the one among us who is the next to leave our midst." Dad sang at Sunday High Mass as a member of the St. Joseph Parish Men's Choir. Now I could do the same at funeral Masses. I felt honored each time I climbed the steps to the choir loft and heard Sister Felicitas pound out the first chords of the Requiem.

My favorite chants were the "Dies Irae" early in the Mass and the "In Paradiso" at the end. The "Dies Irae," a mournful chant, commemorated Judgment Day, the "Day of Wrath" facing the soul of the departed. But the second chant, "In Paradiso" was a joyful hymn sung during the benediction, just before the casket was wheeled out of church. "In Paradiso" commemorated the departed's welcome into Heaven by the choirs of angels and holy martyrs. I liked it that the Catholic Mass of Burial ended on this hopeful note. I felt good after each funeral, knowing that I'd done my part to help send the soul of the departed on its way to Paradise.

> *Stories aren't written as a series of intellectual decisions. It is an intuitive sort of thing. The intellect controls, selects, and rejects, yet the story doesn't come from the intellect. It is brewed in the unconscious.* —Janet Campbell Hale, *Bloodlines: Odyssey of a Native Daughter*, 1993

Like Janet Campbell Hale, I believe that stories don't come solely from the mind; they also come from the heart. Stories have always been important to our family. Ever since Rachel was a toddler, I've been telling her "Suzy-and-Linda stories," tales about the adventures of my younger sister and myself when we were little girls. There's one about the time Linda ran away from home after Suzy tricked her into believing that a doll in a laundry cart was a new baby sister. There's another about the time Suzy's punishment for calling her sister names was to write "I will not call Linda a wet turd" fifty times on the blackboard in the basement. Rachel knows many "Suzy-and-Linda stories" by heart, and she's passed some of them on to her cousins and friends. Now, during sleepovers and family get-togethers, the children beg me to tell "just *one more* Suzy-and-Linda."

Stories can be powerful things, often more about wishes and dreams than actual events. Yet stories always contain a kernel of truth; and, if they are good stories, they can become a cherished gift from the teller to the listener. My dad was one of the best storytellers I've ever known, and his stories are one gift that can be passed on through his children to the grandchildren who will never know him. Many of the stories Dad told us kids were about his childhood. They were often sad stories, for Dad had not had a very happy life.

One story had it that his family was so poor that, for Christmas one year, the four boys each got a pocketknife, while the two girls each got a handkerchief. This tale, retold annually as a bedtime story during the weeks just before Christmas, never failed to leave me in tears as I tried to imagine a little child receiving only one tiny Christmas gift. I prayed that history would not repeat itself.

Another story, "Buddy Lee," was a perennial favorite. It went like this:

> One wintery day in the mid-1920s, Lillian Bunkers took her young son Tony along to get groceries. Lillian, recently widowed, was poor, and she was hoping to trade some of her laying hens' eggs for flour, sugar, and other provisions for herself and her six children.
>
> As mother and son walked through the grocery store's aisles, little Tony spotted a pretty doll up high on a shelf. It was a Kewpie doll with a smile painted on its face. A dusty sign propped up next to it read, "Buddy Lee." Tony pointed up. "I want that doll, Mama."
>
> Lillian took her son's hand and pulled him away. "No, I'm sorry, Tony. I just don't have any money to buy it for you." She walked toward the front of the store to pay for her groceries.
>
> "Please, Mama? Please, can I have that doll? Please?" Tony's eyes filled with tears.
>
> "No, son, I don't have any money to buy a doll."
>
> Tony sat down on the floor. He began crying quietly as his mother paid for the groceries, thanked the grocer, and turned to leave the store.
>
> The grocer watched as the little boy stood up, then silently followed his mother to the door. "Wait just a minute, Tony."
>
> The grocer walked slowly to the back of the store, reached up onto the shelf, and pulled down the doll.
>
> "Say, Tony," he called out, "Buddy Lee is looking for a good home. Would you like to have him?"
>
> Tony nodded.

On porch: Anna Linster Welter holding Viola Bunkers. In and on car (l. to r.): Ray Bunkers, Larry Bunkers, Dick Bunkers. Standing in front of car (l. to r.): "Dutch" O'Connor, Bernice Bunkers, Tony Bunkers.

When Dad reached this point in the story, his voice would waver. Then he'd continue: "So that day I got Buddy Lee for free, and I took him home. Buddy Lee was the only toy I had."

In a boxful of old photographs discovered in Grandma Bunkers' bedroom closet several years after her death, I come across a tiny black and white photograph of several children posing in and around an old car in a farmyard. I send the picture to my dad's sister, Bernice Feller, and ask her if she can tell me who is in the picture.

Bernice writes back: "That's Dick standing on the fender and Larry leaning out the back door window right above Tony, then me and Dutch and Ray above us, looking out the front door window. Grandma's on the porch, no doubt holding Ole, and that's our 1926 Chevy. Oh, to only be all together once again."

I look more closely at the photograph. My great-grandmother, Anna Linster Welter, is the woman standing on the porch of a farmhouse, holding a baby, my aunt Ole. In the driver's seat of the Chevy, my uncle Ray scratches his chin from behind the steering wheel. My uncle Larry leans jauntily out a back window of the car, while my uncle Dick stands atop a rear fender.

Three smaller children stand in front of the car, next to the running board. The tallest, my aunt Bernice, smiles at the camera. The second-tallest, her cousin "Dutch" O'Connor, looks to his left past Bernice and toward the smallest child, a little boy in winter coat and stocking cap, who stands next to the running board, clutching a doll and smiling shyly at the camera. It's Dad, and he's holding Buddy Lee.

In her book of essays, *The Sewing Room*, Barbara Cawthorne Crafton writes about how difficult yet necessary it is to learn how to view our parents as people in their own right rather than as extensions of ourselves: "It is hard for us to imagine our parents as people separate from us, they are so important to us as symbols of our nurture and our security. We look at their photographs when they were young, before we came along, before they were married even, and their young faces look back at us with an inexperience we cannot recognize as belonging to our mothers and fathers."

When I look at old family photographs, I try so hard to imagine. I imagine traveling back in time to ask my grandmother Lillian Welter about her and Frank Bunkers' wedding on that sunny day in June 1908. I imagine warning my grandfather Frank not to go out into the barn alone on that chilly day in November 1926. I imagine lifting little Tony up onto my lap and admiring Buddy Lee.

The eleven-by-fourteen-inch mat is dog-eared and watermarked. Its top left corner is torn, and the portrait bends slightly with the concavity of a memorial that has lain atop a closet shelf or in a dresser drawer for many years. The small oval photograph is centered amid sepia-toned floral arrangements. Already the mums are starting to wilt, the bows to droop.

Staring out at me is a handsome man—his hair parted in the middle and gently waving to the sides. He looks directly at me and, as I return his gaze, I glimpse reflections of my three brothers and of my father in his blue eyes, broad nose, firmly set jaw. Neither smiling nor frowning, he stares straight ahead, inscrutable.

My grandfather, Frank Bunkers. He was born in New Vienna, Iowa, on March 16, 1883, the fifth child of Henry and Barbara Simmerl Bunkers, who had married in 1875 and who farmed near Dyersville, close to Henry's parents, Theodore and Elizabeth Bunkers. When Frank was still a boy, his grandparents moved to a farm in northwestern Iowa, just south of Remsen. Frank's parents and their family soon followed, settling on a farm ten miles north of Remsen, a mile north and a mile west of Granville, Iowa.

Frank Bunkers' funeral portrait.

As a young man, Frank began courting Lillian Welter, the daughter of Matt and Anna Welter, who ran the local saloon. On May 25, 1908, the clerk of court of Sioux County, Iowa, issued a marriage license to Frank P. Bunkers, age twenty-five, and Roseline Lillian Welter, age nineteen. On June 2, 1908, Frank and Lillian were married at St. Joseph Catholic Church in Granville, and the young couple began farming on their own near Granville. Three sons, Larry, Dick, and Ray, were born there.

Then, about 1914, the family moved to a farm in northwestern Minnesota, just outside Mahnomen. Frank and Lillian's fourth child, Vincent, was born there in 1915. But, as Mahnomen County death records reveal, the baby died of chronic diarrhea only two days after his birth. In 1917, their fifth child, Cletus, was born. He lived a little more than a year, dying in 1918 of whooping cough. On August 13, 1919, their sixth child, a daughter, Bernice, was born. She survived. Then, on November 16, 1921, Frank and Lillian Bunkers' seventh child, Jerome Anton Bunkers, soon nicknamed Tony, was born. All four births at Mahnomen were on the family's farm, and the birth records list no doctor or midwife, only Frank Bunkers as "attending physician."

Farming in Minnesota was hard, and by 1925, shortly before the birth of Viola, the youngest child, the Bunkers family returned to Granville. That year Frank took over Henry and Barbara Bunkers' farm, which had been worked by Frank's brother Otto. On January 29, 1925, while butchering a hog, Otto's knife slipped, severing a major artery in his thigh. Otto bled to death. Now it was up to Frank to farm the homeplace, with the help of his three oldest children, Larry, Dick, and Ray.

It went as well as could be expected until the morning of November 24, 1926, the day before Thanksgiving. Frank was out in the barn, trying to corner a horse that had broken loose from the post. From outside, his sons heard him swearing at the animal as he rounded some bales of hay in pursuit. Then they heard only silence.

When they hurried into the barn to check on their father, they found his body on the floor. At the age of forty-three, Frank Bunkers was dead. The official cause of death was listed as "heart failure" in the parish records, and Frank was buried in the St. Joseph Parish cemetery the Saturday after Thanksgiving.

Whenever my father told me about his father's death, the story grew more detailed and vivid. I could see my grandfather Frank chasing that huge black horse around the dusty barn. I could watch him clutch his chest and fall. I could see my uncles standing in tears over their father's body. I could envision my father, who had turned five just the week before, shivering on the farmhouse porch as the undertaker's wagon arrived to take his father away.

Many years later, when I came across these two newspaper clippings, I remembered my father's story; and, for the first time, I felt in my gut the reality of my grandfather's untimely death:

GRANVILLE NEWS

The community was shocked Wed. morning when it was learned that Frank Bunkers had died suddenly. Heart failure was the cause of his death. He leaves a wife and six children. The funeral was held from St. Joseph's church Sat. morning at 9:30 o'clock.
—*Alton Democrat*, December 3, 1926

"THANK YOU"

We wish to express our heartfelt thanks to the relatives, neighbors and friends who so kindly assisted us in the hour of bereavement of our beloved husband and father, Frank. Also to thank the Rev. J. A. Gerlemann for his comforting words and all who sent spiritual bouquets. Your kindness in our hour of sorrow will be always remembered.

—Mrs. Frank Bunkers & children, in the *Alton Democrat,* December 3, 1926

For me, "Grandpa Bunkers" has always been a sketchy character in my father's stories, existing only in Dad's memory and my imagination—a character defined by his absence, not his presence. No one spoke of Frank Bunkers at family gatherings; he seemed to exist only in old photographs and on tombstone inscriptions.

Dad could never talk about his father without breaking into tears, and I'm convinced that the early loss of his father affected him in ways that I might never be able to understand. That loss changed the landscape of my father's life forever, and I doubt that he could ever recapture the sense of security and family that he had known for only his first five years.

Knowing the story of Grandpa Bunkers' death, I worried that my father, too, would die young, before all five of his children were grown. And that is what did happen. My youngest brother, Danny, was only fifteen when our father died. I had just turned twenty-eight. Yet the night my brother Dale phoned me to say, "He died," I didn't feel grown up at all. I felt like a child playing circus, an amateur acrobat whose safety net had just been ripped out from under her, leaving a gaping hole into which she could, at any moment, fall.

SERVICES HELD FOR JEROME "TONY" BUNKERS

Jerome "Tony" Bunkers, 56, Granville, died Thursday in an Orange City hospital after suffering a heart attack. Services were held at 10:30 a.m. Saturday in St. Joseph's Catholic Church at Granville. The Rev. Edward Hoffmann officiated. Burial was in the parish cemetery.

Mr. Bunkers was born Nov. 16, 1921, at Mahnomen, Mn. When still a youth, he came to the Granville area and made his home with the Vincent O'Connor family until he was married. He married Verna Klein June 14, 1949 at Granville.

He served as acting postmaster from August 16, 1947 to May 1, 1949 and as postmaster from then until Jan. 15, 1950. He was a rural mail carrier from then until his retirement July 5, 1975.

Mr. Bunkers served in the U.S. Navy during World War II. He was a member of Wasmer Post 222, the American Legion at LeMars; the

Disabled American Veterans; the Veterans of Foreign Wars, Granville; the National Rural Letter Carriers Association and the National Association of Retired Federal Employees.

He also coached Little League baseball at Granville for many years and was a longtime member of the men's choir at St. Joseph's Church.

Survivors include the widow; three sons, Dennis of Cedar Falls, Dale and Dan, both at home; two daughters, Miss Suzanne of Madison, Wisc., and Mrs. Dan (Linda) Kennedy of Polk City; two brothers, Larry and Raymond, both of Worthington, Minn., and two sisters, Mrs. Bernice Feller of Stillwater, Minn., and Mrs. Clarence (Viola) Thorman of Bloomington, Minn.

—*Capitol-Democrat*, August 4, 1978

AUGUST 1, 1978

10:30 p.m. Just finished writing thank you's for Dad's funeral. I asked my aunts—Angie, Clarice, and Ann—to help Mom and me. We spent about three hours working on them. People were very nice about sending cards, flowers, and memorial money. It made me stop and think about the positive aspects of life in a small town—everyone gathers around to help and console when a person dies.

Now that the cards have been written, I have to attend to the legal matters and notify the Disabled American Veterans, social security department, rural carriers life insurance office, and others that Dad has died and that the survivors want to apply for benefits. Mom is worried about money, naturally, and I know she'll feel better when all this is settled. I feel good that I'm able to help in a tangible way. Doing this mechanical stuff also keeps me from sitting around feeling depressed.

Everything is so quiet. I expect to hear Dad's voice coming from somewhere, but it never comes. I find myself turning down the volume on the TV so as not to wake him up during the afternoon soap operas. I expect to see him walk through the living room grumbling about something. Finding his dirty clothes in the clothes chute made me cry yesterday—50 cents and his pocketknife still in his pocket and his dirty sox on the floor. And the little brown bag of his clothes that the funeral home sent back with us after we picked out the vault and the casket.

AUG. 4, 1978

It's still hard to believe Dad's dead. Even this morning, when Danny and I stopped at the cemetery, it was hard to grasp the fact that he really is buried there. I keep thinking about all the water in the grave when it was dug and whether the water seeped right in when the casket was put in. The funeral director said the water would be pumped out first, but the casket went into the ground so soon after we left the cemetery that I wonder if the water really was pumped out. Probably better that I assume it was.

Tonight Mom was looking for Dad's keys but couldn't find them. She thought they were in the pocket of the pants he wore to the hospital. Finally, she found them in a drawer. She was telling me about helping Dad put on his good pants the night he had to go to the hospital. I could imagine her helping him, only a little while before his death.

I've thought about how scared Dad must have felt that nite when he knew how sick he was. I wonder if they could have saved him if they'd gotten him to the hospital just a little bit earlier? Mom and the boys must wonder about that too, but we can't do anything about it now. Dad refused to go to the hospital, and they had to call the Granville rescue unit. Dale told me Dad talked all the way to the hospital, then started having breathing problems. His heart stopped, but the doctors got it going again. For a while they thought they could save him. But his heart weakened, and he died a little after midnight on the 27th. The facts seem so bare. But to know that it's all happening to someone in your family makes it so horrifying.

Dad was only 56. I wonder how much of his health he could have preserved if he had started taking care of himself a little earlier? I should have known how bad off he was the last couple times I was home. He couldn't walk even a block without being worn out, and his lips had little white spots on them from the nitroglycerin tablets he was taking for his angina. I never thought when I was here a month ago that I'd never see him alive again.

AUG. 7, 1978

Mom cried when I left for Madison today; she said she felt sad because she was so dependent on me. It was hard to leave, but I knew it was time for me to go back and pick up the pieces of my own life. And it's important for her to do the same thing—even though it seems so hard, even impossible, right now.

AUG. 21, 1978

I just looked at Dad's obituary. The name, date, everything is there, but I still expect him to be home in Granville. I feel like I could

crack up over this. At first I felt really in control—all through the
funeral, etc. Now I feel so helpless and angry at this happening to
him. I don't really feel anger toward him, but I'm definitely mad.
Toward God, whomever—I guess I can't even say. I find myself thinking, if only he'd gone to the hospital sooner. If only this, if only
that. He was too young to die! It isn't fair! I'm so goddamned mad!

AUG. 27, 1978

Sunday. I'm visiting Mom in Granville again. Tomorrow she and
I will go to Sioux City to see the social security people about
benefits. Tuesday a man from the D.A.V. is coming and also a man
from a monument company in Worthington, Minnesota. Guess
I'll be the one to help Mom handle this stuff. I don't mind, but it's
so depressing.

I miss Dad a lot. The worst is that sure knowledge that I'll never
see him again. When I'm home, I see his fishing equipment in the
garage, his clothes in his closet, his winter caps in the coat closet,
his shaving kit in the hall closet—and I get choked up every time. I
wish I could do something to make everyone, including myself, feel
better—but there's nothing.

AUG. 27, 1978

Mom and I went up to the cemetery and sowed grass seed on Dad's
grave. We commented on it being one month since he died. I wanted
to scream and cry as hard as I could. Instead I fought to control myself and keep from crying. I don't know whether that was better or
worse than crying would have been.

I came home and began thinking about how each person in a family is responsible for every other person and no one can really escape
that responsibility, only try to by denying his/her links to the family. So now I feel responsible for Mom, and I suppose she feels the
same way about Grandma and Grandpa. It never ends.

SEPT. 18, 1978

I had my first dream about Dad last night. He was sitting in an armchair smiling, and he motioned me toward him. I put my arms
around his neck and kissed him and told him I loved him and would
always love him. Then he nodded and smiled but didn't say anything.

SEPT. 24, 1978

I find myself thinking about Dad, always the same thought: it was
too soon. I wanted more time with him. I wonder if everyone is

grieving the same way I am? I feel a need to ask everyone in my
family if they have the same thoughts. Every day I remember good
times I had with him—I don't seem to remember the bad right now.
Just knowing he's not at home but instead is rotting away under the
ground where he'll be frozen and where the water will run right
in on him (those coffins aren't airtight—I don't care what they
say). He did a lot of good and he showed a lot of love to his kids,
even if he did have a cynical, bitter attitude about his own childhood. I'm amazed that there was so much good in him after so
much unhappiness.

SEPT. 27, 1978

Last night I had my second dream about Dad. He was standing
there, and I ran up and hugged him again and again and told him
I loved him. I knew that was the last time I'd see him before he
died, and he knew it too, but we weren't sad. It just felt so good
to hug him.

NOV. 1, 1978

I was reading a biography of Sarah Orne Jewett today, and I came
across this letter she wrote to Annie Fields, dated March 24, 1882:

> Today is my father's birthday. I wonder if people keep the day
> they die for another birthday after they get to heaven? I have been
> thinking about him a very great deal this last day or two. I won-
> der if I am doing at all the things he wishes I would do, and I
> hope he does not get tired of me.

NOV. 17, 1978

Yesterday was Dad's birthday. I tried to keep real busy. I've been
dreading the day and hoping I wouldn't fall apart when it came. The
actual day was much less traumatic than the weeks before when I'd
been thinking about it all the time and feeling sad.

I've noticed a subtle change in my grief lately: I cry less often and
I feel a little calmer. At times I'm still overwhelmed by this sense of
shock and loss, and I can't think or talk. I feel as if I'm all alone in a
world of silence, and I'm trying to keep myself alert when I feel like
just slipping away. I almost called home late last night but didn't. I
didn't want Mom to think I forgot Dad's birthday, but I thought we
might get too depressed if I did call. So, the day came and went, and
I'm still kicking.

I've felt an affinity for W. S. Merwin's poetry ever since I first read it as an undergraduate English major. I like the way Merwin uses nature imagery to explore the essential mysteries of life and death. "For the Anniversary of My Death" is my favorite Merwin poem; without becoming sentimental, it speaks of the one anniversary that can rarely be determined in advance. Merwin's poem is a contemporary version of the sentiments expressed by Sarah Orne Jewett in the excerpt from her letter that I copied into my diary a few months after my father's death.

Like W. S. Merwin, Sarah Orne Jewett tells her stories of life and death through the use of nature imagery. That's what draws me to *The Country of the Pointed Firs*. I especially like the characters with which Jewett peoples the seafaring village of Dunnet Landing, Maine. There is Almira Todd, the kindly woman who takes in the story's narrator and nurtures her. There is Mrs. Todd's brother, William Blackett, who lives with and cares for their elderly mother. There is Joanna Todd, disappointed in love and now a recluse on Shell Heap Island. There is old Elijah Tilley, grieving for his dead wife while knitting a blue stocking. In this story, the narrator, a disillusioned writer, learns from these individuals to trust her own perceptions of the world around her.

Willa Cather was so drawn to Sarah Orne Jewett's work that she wrote the preface to *The Country of the Pointed Firs*. In it, Cather explained the essence of Jewett's artistry:

> One can, as it were, watch in process the two kinds of making: the first, which is full of perception and feeling but rather fluid and formless, the second, which is so tightly built and significant in design. The design is, indeed, so happy, so right, that it seems inevitable; the design is the story and the story is the design.

For Cather as for Jewett, form and content must merge to make a story a *good* story.

The same holds true for me. To make my search for Susanna into a good story, I need to merge form and content by going back into the near and distant past, by turning over the tapestry of my family history and studying the knots, tangles, and imperfect stitches on its back side as well as the orderly beauty on its face.

In *Landscape for a Good Woman*, Carolyn Kay Steedman writes: "The point of a story is to present itself momentarily as complete, so that it can be said: it does for now, it will do; it is an account that will last a while. Its point is briefly to make an audience connive in the telling, so that they might say: yes, that's how it was; or, that's how it could have been."

Steedman makes sense to me. I want the stories in this book to do for now, to last for a while. I want you, the reader, to connive in the telling. I want you to read a while, then let the stories settle in. My goal is not for you to say, "Yes, it *was* that way," but "Yes, it *could have been* that way."

> When we ignore the past, we operate with flimsy, disposable identities. We fail to learn patterns in our families that might help us to understand and accept ourselves. . . . If we don't delve into our personal histories, the more remote ones become reduced to inert facts, completely unrelated to us.—Margot Fortunato Galt, *The Story in History*, 1992

Why has it become so important to me to search, not only for Susanna but also for clues about other ancestors, for bits of information that will help me put together the puzzle of where I came from, who I am? After all, no one can guarantee that by learning family patterns— and understanding them—a person can change those patterns. At the same time, I am convinced that I must make a conscientious attempt not to ignore the past because, as Galt explains, "sooner or later, past events will affect us in the present. They will shape both our personal and public lives. Like it or not, they will require attention."

As a teacher of writing and as a student of history, I also understand that any story, when told from more than one person's point of view, will be told differently. The diary entries that I wrote during those first months after my father's death embodied the truth as I saw it then. When I reread them and began typing excerpts for this book, however, I often found myself surprised. I did not recall having written some of the diary entries. Yet there they were, in my handwriting.

How does a person check one's memory against the distance that time imposes? Last year, I sent a copy of these diary excerpts to my brother Dale, and I asked him how my version of events compared with his. Dale sent back his own story of our father's final hours:

> Dad was in bed when I got home around 9:30. I was watching the "Tonight Show" when he got up and went into the bathroom. He said he didn't feel well but insisted it was indigestion and would go away. He went back to bed but got up again a little after 11 p.m. I knew he wasn't well and called the rescue unit. When Dad would lie

down, he couldn't breathe easily, so he sat in an upright position until the rescue unit arrived. When Dad was being loaded into the rescue unit, he was again sitting in an upright position. As the rescuers placed Dad into the rescue unit, our eyes met. What I saw in Dad's eyes was fear, and I believe he may have known he was never coming home again.

What do I remember most about the days just after my father's death, all these years later? Today, this is my most vivid memory. It was mid-afternoon on July 28, 1978. The sun beat down on my youngest brother, Danny, and I as we walked from our home in Granville up to the high school lunchroom, where Dad's wake would be held that night. We wanted to see whether the funeral home had already brought Dad's body there. At home, all of us had signed Danny's favorite baseball so he could put it into the casket with Dad. Now, Danny and I wanted a few moments alone with Dad.

We tiptoed into the lunchroom. The casket was on the far side of the room, propped open. A woman was quietly arranging the floral displays that surrounded it. When she saw us, she nodded and excused herself.

My brother and I walked closer to the casket. My head began to pound, and I couldn't breathe. I dropped down onto the kneeler in front of the casket. Danny knelt down next to me, the baseball in his hand.

Dad wore a baby-blue leisure suit with a crisp white shirt. His blue-and-black-flowered tie had been knotted neatly around his neck. Entwined in his hands was his black rosary. His gold-rimmed glasses were set unevenly upon his nose. His cheeks had been rouged, and his lips were pursed. Had they been sewn together?

I lifted my hand over the satin lining to touch his chest, first fingering the silk tie, then patting it down. When I tapped my finger against it, Dad's chest felt hard. The skin on his hands was puckered and cold. I reached up to run my hand lightly over his short, bristly hair. It was auburn, with just a few gray hairs on the sides.

How can you be dead? I shook my head in disbelief. You hardly have any gray hair. Tears welled in my eyes. Dad began to blur.

Danny stood up, leaned over the casket, and pushed the baseball down along Dad's side, sliding it nearly under him.

"I don't want anybody to find it and take it out," Danny whispered. "I want Dad to have it."

Danny leaned against me, and huge sobs ran through both of us. We

Tony Bunkers, 1975, Granville, Iowa. Photo by Dennis Church.

knelt there for a long, long time, until we had cried ourselves dry. Then
we stood up and turned to leave the lunchroom for our walk home.

When I looked over my diary entries from those final days of July
1978, I felt certain I would find an account of this scene. But there was
none. Perhaps it was just too painful for me to write about my father in
his casket, there in the school lunchroom. Maybe that's why I didn't,
couldn't, write about it then. Yet the first time I saw my father dead
has burned itself into my memory. It cannot be erased, though there
have been many, many times during the past seventeen years when I
have prayed to forget it.

If my brother Dan were to read the passage above, would he remember it the same way as I have? I can't say. He and I have never spoken
about that day since it occurred—not because either of us does not
care, but, I suspect, because both of us care too much. Even after all
these years, the memory of my father lying in that casket has power. I
know it's dangerous to let that memory surface too often: the scab can
easily be scratched open, and the wound bleeds again.

4. Forget Me Not . . . Remember Me

*Our mothers are our most direct connection to our
history and our gender. Regardless of how well we
think they did their job, the void their absence
creates in our lives is never completely filled again.*
—Hope Edelman, *Motherless Daughters: The Legacy
of Loss,* 1994

She was born in Grafton, North Dakota, but she lived most of her life in Minnesota, in towns like Bird Island, Wilmont, and Worthington. My first memory of her is that of a short, stocky, white-haired woman who had the softest skin I'd ever touched. When I'd go to visit her, I would eat her homemade applesauce and watch her tat or crochet intricate borders for pillowcases that she had fashioned as gifts for family and friends. In a cage hanging above the dining room table was her little yellow canary, Pinky, to whom she would talk gently. This was my grandmother, Lillian Welter Bunkers Thorman, and I am her goddaughter and namesake.

When I was growing up, I didn't know a lot about the early life of Grandma Bunkers, as everyone called her. She was in her sixties when I was born, and I didn't see her very often, for she lived fifty miles away in Worthington, Minnesota. I knew Grandma Bunkers was a good-hearted woman. She sent weekly letters to my family, and she never forgot to send me a birthday card addressed "To my goddaughter," with $1.00 in it.

It wasn't until 1980, over ten years after Grandma Bunkers' death, that my conversation with her younger sister Theresa O'Connor Lieb unveiled some of the long-forgotten facts of Grandma's life. I found out, for instance, that my grandmother's first name was actually Roseline, but that she went by Lillian, which she preferred. Grandma's

Wedding of Frank Bunkers and Lillian Welter, June 2, 1908, Granville, Iowa.

ancestors, the Welters and the Linsters, had immigrated to the United States from Luxembourg and the Luxembourg Province of Belgium around 1850. They had settled near Fredonia, Wisconsin, a small village just north of Milwaukee. Grandma's parents, Matt and Anna (Linster) Welter, had come west, gotten married in Alton, Iowa, and for a short time had homesteaded in Grafton, North Dakota.

But life had proved too hard there, so Matt and Anna Welter returned to Iowa, where they opened the Welter Saloon in Granville. Their daughters and son (May, Lill, Theresa, and Silverius) waited tables and set pins. Eventually, Matt and Anna Welter retired to Bird Island, Minnesota.

As a young woman, Lillian Welter attended the Normal School at Humboldt, Iowa, where she trained to become a teacher. Like many

Matt and Anna Linster Welter family. Standing (l. to r.): Anna, May, Lillian.
Seated (l. to r.): Silverius, Matt, Theresa.

young women at that time, however, she gave up her teaching am-
bitions when she married Frank Bunkers in June 1908. Lillian Welter
Bunkers then settled into the life of a young farm wife near Granville, Iowa.

Grandma Bunkers' married life was not easy. Her first child, Larry,
was born two years after her marriage to Frank Bunkers. During the
next fifteen years, Lillian gave birth to seven more children, two of
whom (Cletus and Vincent) died as babies. Six children (Larry, Dick,
Ray, Bernice, Tony, and Viola) survived to adulthood.

In November 1926, when her youngest child, Viola, was just a year
old, Lillian's husband, Frank, died of a heart attack. At the age of
thirty-eight, Lillian found herself a widow with six children to support. A dog-eared photograph from that era shows a weathered Lillian,
in housedress and work shoes, posing in the farmyard with her
children—her five-year-old son, Tony, who would grow up to be my father, standing with his stomach thrust forward and a quizzical expression, like his mother's, on his face, as if both mother and son were trying to figure out how life had gotten them into that predicament.

The next years were hard ones for Lillian Bunkers and her children.
Henry and Barbara Bunkers' family farm, which Frank and Lillian had
rented, was passed on to one of Frank's surviving brothers. Lillian and
her children needed to find somewhere else to live. Her three oldest

Lillian Bunkers and her children, late 1920s. Back row (l. to r.): Ray, Dick, Lillian, Larry. Front row (l. to r.): Bernice, Viola, Tony.

children—Larry, Dick, and Ray—tried unsuccessfully to farm on their own. The three younger children—Bernice, Tony, and Viola (called "Ole")—stayed with their mother, who moved from Granville, Iowa, to Wilmont, Minnesota, after her first husband's death.

In August 1932, Lillian married her second husband, Joe Thorman, who had been her suitor before she had married Frank Bunkers. Joe, himself a widower with several children, was large and burly, with a reputation as a strong-willed man. In later years, Lillian would tell how, in the middle of winter, Joe would shut off the woodstove, open the windows, and take a nap in his undershirt. She would also tell how, to buy groceries for the family, she would have to sneak into the hen-house, quietly gather some eggs, and send her children into town to the grocer's without her husband finding out what she had done. Had Joe discovered it, Lillian would have been punished.

Soon after her marriage to Joe Thorman, Lillian began sending Bernice and Tony back to Granville to spend summers with her younger sister, Theresa, and her husband, Vincent O'Connor. By the mid-1930s, Bernice and Tony were living with the O'Connors full-time. They grew up with the O'Connors' children, Orville (nicknamed Dutch) and Rita.

Years later, when I was taping a family history interview with Theresa, she summed up her perspective on her sister Lillian's second marriage in this way: "Yeah, she had it rough with him. He was just really a mean person. She didn't have much happiness in her second marriage. . . . Lill used to come here real often. When things got too rough for her up there, she'd come down here [on the bus]. She'd call from Alton, and we'd go and get her, and she'd spend three-four days, and then she'd go back. She would have [left] if she'd have had the financial means."

Then Theresa told me how it was that young Tony had come to live permanently with her, her husband, Vin, and their family rather than with his mother and stepfather, Lillian and Joe Thorman. It was the end of the summer, and Theresa and Vin were taking Tony back to Wilmont when she heard him crying in the back seat of the car.

"Tony, why are you crying?" she asked.

"Because he put me down the well," Tony sobbed.

"Who did?"

"Old Joe. He tied a rope around my waist and put me down the well. Told me to clean it up."

Theresa turned to her husband. Vin stopped the car, and they drove back to Granville. From there Theresa sent her sister Lillian a letter, explaining that Tony would be staying with the O'Connors, not returning to the Thorman farm in Minnesota.

"He stayed right here, and he was happy," Theresa recalled. "Vin treated him like our own. Vin was a prince of a man, a good person. At Christmas Tony would get just like our own kids. We used to pay Dutch and Tony a penny an egg case to make an egg case, and then they'd save that up, and Tony bought an old car, and he and a Kokenge kid drove it to Alton so they could go to high school."

Photographs given to my family after Theresa's death in August 1980 provide glimpses into this extended family. One photograph, taken at Theresa and Vin O'Connor's house in Granville about 1944, shows Tony in his Navy uniform, home on leave. He poses with his mother, Lillian, and his younger sister, Ole, in the driveway, all three smiling. Ole, wearing a pinafore that reminds me of Dorothy Gale's in *The Wizard of Oz*, links arms with her mother. Lillian, wearing a housedress, smiles warily; her graying hair flies untamed. She looks tired, older than her fifty-five years. Tony grins broadly.

My great-aunt Theresa's photographs and family stories have helped me appreciate the deep emotions that ran through my father whenever he used to talk about his family. Now I can understand why Dad would cry when he recalled the death of his father, Frank, and why, as an adult, Dad would feel such a need to be close to his mother again.

Now I can understand what had once shocked me as a child: Dad's

Viola Bunkers (l.), Lillian Bunkers Thorman, Tony Bunkers, June 1944, Granville, Iowa.

story of Joe Thorman's death from a heart attack during a family dinner on Christmas Day 1949. Dad told me that his stepfather's body had been laid out in a bedroom. When Dad was told to take his turn going into the bedroom to pay his last respects, Dad walked up to the bed, looked down at Joe, and whispered, "You son of a bitch. I'm glad you're dead."

It is 1995, seventeen years since my father's death. I am browsing through his autograph book, remembering the first time I saw it, back when I was ten. Back then, I giggled at the clever, if corny, rhymes written by Dad's adolescent friends. I skipped over his mother's inscription, which didn't seem cute or clever, just dull:

Wilmont, Minn.
April 16, 1935

Dear son Jerome
Upon a hilltop
Carved in a rock
Three little words
Forget me not.

—Your loving mother

"Forget me not."

I imagine my father as a teenager, in his room at his aunt and uncle's house in Granville, reading the little rhymes that friends had written in his autograph book. Dad might have smiled at Herbert Schumacher's verse: "When you get married and have twins, don't come to me for safety pins." Dad might have blushed at Elaine Hodapp's recipe:

Granville, Iowa
March 12, 1937

Dear Tony—
    4 ounces of love,
    4 lips pressed tight together,
    1/2 ounces of squeezing
    1/2 ounces of teasing
    Bake well with a young girl in your arms,
    And serve hot—in the dark.

And I suspect Dad would have agreed with Kitty Luken's message:

Dec. 9, 1935
Granville

Dear Tony,
    True friends are like diamonds,
    Precious and rare,
    False friends are like autumn leaves
    Found everywhere.
    Always remember me as a true friend.

    Though ups and downs and smiles and frowns
    Make life's design 'tis true,
    May fate reserve its soaring curves
    Of ups and downs for you.

    P.S. Try and learn to play truth and consequences.

Somehow, though, I suspect that Dad might have gotten tears in his eyes when he came upon the second inscription his mother had written further back in his autograph book:

Wilmont, Minn.

Dear son Jerome,
What shall I write
What shall it be?
Only two little words
  "Remember me"

Your loving mother

What might it signify that Lillian wrote not just one inscription, but also a second, in her son's autograph book? When I was younger, I didn't know what to make of them. Now I believe my grandmother was sending my father a message, a message more poignant and heartfelt, given her children's separation from her. Only Ole, who had been a baby when her father, Frank, had died, remained in the same house with my grandmother and her second husband, Joe.

I looked at a prayer scribbled inside the back cover of my grandmother's prayer book, handed down to my father after her death and to me after my father's death:

PRAYER TO ST. ANTHONY

When all other friends have failed,
  Pray to St. Anthony.
If a sorrow fills your heart,
Or you fail at all you start,
When bad habit plays its part,
  Pray to St. Anthony.

If you're broke or unemployed,
  Pray to St. Anthony.
If your dreams are all destroyed,
  Pray to St. Anthony.
If your soul is just a strain
And your faith is on the wane,
If a goal you've got to gain,
  Pray to St. Anthony.

If you've lost a treasure dear,
  Pray to St. Anthony.

When a loved one will not hear,
    Pray to St. Anthony.
If the doctor's done his best
And it shows you by his test
That you're through, you know the rest,
    Pray to St. Anthony.

This your pledge day in & out,
    Pray to St. Anthony.
If you tire or if you doubt,
    Pray to St. Anthony.
Time will prove he'll grant your prayers,
He has a power great and rare,
Trust in him & do your share,
    Pray to St. Anthony.

I knew Saint Anthony of Padua well, for I had often knelt in our family pew at church, praying to him to help me find something I'd lost. Saint Anthony extended his fingers in blessing, promising to keep me safe. But I had never seen the prayer to Saint Anthony that Grandma had copied into her prayer book. What might lines like "If your dreams are all destroyed" or "When a loved one will not hear" have meant to her?

In her reflection upon visiting the basilica of Saint Anthony in Padua, Italy, the Rev. Barbara Cawthorne Crafton marvels at the faith of the believers, those who make the pilgrimage to invoke the saint's help, leaving behind photographs, knitted baby bonnets, and "hundreds of letters requesting the saint's help in new lost causes." Crafton concludes: "It is official: there is now nowhere else to turn. Perhaps Saint Anthony can help."

I knew that Grandma Bunkers believed in the power of prayer. I had seen her rosary hanging over her bedpost. I had noticed that same small prayer book on her nightstand, with "Mrs. Joe Thorman, Wilmont, Minnesota" written inside the cover.

Grandma had glued black satin fabric over the prayer book's original cover. Inside, a rose petal encased in plastic, "a relic of Saint Theresa," was taped to the front page. On the back side of that page, in my grandmother's handwriting, was this prayer:

O most beautiful flower of Mount Carmel, fruitful vine, Splendor of heaven, Blessed Mother of the son of God, immaculate Virgin, assist me in this my necessity. O Star of the sea, keep me & show me herein you are my mother of God. O holy Mary, Mother of God, Queen of heaven and earth, humbly beseech thee from the bottom of my heart to succor me in this necessity there are none that can withstand your power. Oh, show me herein you are my mother. O Mary, conceived without sin, pray for us who have recourse to thee (3 times). Sweet Mother, I place this cause in your hands (3 times).

I had studied the lives of the saints enough to know that Saint Theresa of Lisieux was to be revered. Born Marie Frances Theresa Martin in Alençon, Normandy, France, in 1873, she entered the convent of the Carmelites of Lisieux in 1888. There she lived a pious, contemplative life and wrote a play about the life of Saint Joan of Arc. Theresa remained in the convent until her death from tuberculosis in 1897. Pope Pius XI canonized her in 1925. In her autobiography, *The Story of a Soul*, Theresa promised to send a shower of roses down to earth after her death. According to Catholic tradition, she kept her promise, and the symbol of Saint Theresa, "The Little Flower," is the rose.

Now I realize that, as with many female saints in the Catholic tradition, the life of Saint Theresa of Lisieux embodies both powerlessness and power. Biographer Monica Furlong notes: "Thérèse of Lisieux, sweet, childlike, obedient, tragic, has been until recent times a cherished icon of Catholic womanhood . . . she has been cast in one of the favourite moulds of traditional female sanctity, the mould of virginity, of suffering, of drastic self-abnegation." Yet Furlong concludes, "[Thérèse] might be seen, paradoxically, as a model for the power, endurance, and resourcefulness of women, a power which, even when intolerably constricted, crushed and punished by circumstances, reasserts itself with the tenacity of a weed (or little flower) growing on a wall."

What would have made this saint so appealing to my grandmother that in 1947, the golden jubilee of Saint Theresa's death, Lillian Welter Bunkers Thorman taped the rose petal relic into her prayer book and added a handwritten prayer that addressed both Saint Theresa and the Blessed Virgin Mary? What was "the necessity" for which my grandmother prayed to St. Theresa for succor? What was the "cause" that she prayed to place into the Blessed Virgin's hands? I believe that my grandmother's prayer book contains some clues to how she survived her unfortunate marriage to my father's stepfather.

My great-aunt Theresa's family stories also gave me insights into the psyche of my grandmother Lillian, who by all measures was a battered wife during her second marriage and who had felt helpless to protect her children from their stepfather. How much anguish, I wondered, would I have felt when I realized I'd have to give my children up to keep them safe? What would I have written in my fourteen-year-old son's autograph book, knowing that he and I had been separated, perhaps for good? Would I ever be close to him again?

And, as Lillian's granddaughter, I don't know how much I can read into two four-line rhymes inscribed by my grandmother in her teenage son's autograph book. What layers of meaning and emotion might have underlain Lillian's requests to Tony, "Forget me not" and "Remember me"?

On the holy card bearing the relic of Saint Theresa is this biblical verse, Ecclesiastes 39:17–19:

> Open up your petals, like roses planted near running waters; send up a sweet odor like Lebanon. Break forth in blossoms like the lily, and yield a smell, and bring forth leaves in grace, and praise with canticles, and bless the Lord in His works.

Yes, prayer can be a double-edged sword. It can help a person withstand trials and tribulations, yet it can help trap a person in the very situation that causes those trials and tribulations. Now, as I remember Grandma Bunkers' life, I wonder if this was the predicament she faced.

For the first eighteen years of my life, to live in Minnesota was my dream. To a girl who had grown up landlocked in northwest Iowa, the "LAND OF 10,000 LAKES" represented much more than a slogan on a license plate.

Like my father, I loved to fish, and when I was about ten, Dad asked me if I'd like to start a nightcrawler business. Together we lettered a sign, NIGHTCRAWLERS, 15 CENTS A DOZEN, and hammered it into the grass next to the curb out front. On muggy summer nights following Iowa thunderstorms, Dad would grab two flashlights and coffee cans and take me across the street to Mrs. Schmidt's ditches. There, he and I would hunt worms until the black mud covered our hands and stuck under our fingernails.

The secret to catching nightcrawlers, Dad told me, was to make sure they didn't know you were coming. That meant stepping very lightly over the rain-soaked ground, then shining the flashlight quickly over a wide area. You'd want to keep the flashlight's beam just a little higher or lower than the place where you'd spotted the worm. Slowly, you'd bend over, peering carefully to figure out which end of the worm was dug into its hole and which end was its head. Then, you'd grab for the end nearer to the hole. Once you'd gotten a firm grip on it, you shouldn't pull too hard too fast. If you did, you'd snap the worm in two. But if you pulled very slowly, then waited until the worm relaxed its muscles before pulling again, you'd eventually get it out of its hole in one piece. Then you could slide it into the writhing mass of worms already in your coffee can and go after another worm.

Dad bought an old refrigerator to put in our basement. That became the Bunkers Nightcrawler Business Office. Soon my sister and brothers joined me in the business. Dad's fishing buddies became our regular customers. Whenever Earl Muehl or Jim Jacobs would call to order five or six dozen worms, we kids would run down to the basement to sort the juiciest-looking nightcrawlers out into a coffee can before our customer arrived. We'd always throw in a few extra worms for our best customers, and for many years we earned our spending money from this lucrative business venture.

I lived for the summers, when my parents would take my sister, brothers, and me fishing in Minnesota. We'd start out at Lake Okabena in Worthington, then work our way up toward Lake Shetek, Round Lake, and Lake Sarah. Unaware that, as Iowans, we were sometimes the butts of Minnesotans' jokes, we would innocently bait our hooks with nightcrawlers and cast out our lines, angling for the mighty bullhead.

One summer we traveled to Sauk Centre, Minnesota, where we spent a week at the Sunset View Motel and Resort. It was there that I had my first adolescent crush. His name was Denny, his family was from Iowa, too, and he won my heart by buying me a Snickers bar. I invited him along when my family toured the Sinclair Lewis Boyhood Home and Museum. Even though I had no idea at the time who Sinclair Lewis was, I decided that he must have caused quite a ruckus in his hometown. Twenty years later, when I finally read *Main Street*, I could understand more about what Lewis had meant when he described Carol Kennicott's ambivalence toward small-town Midwestern life.

But back then I wasn't concerned about all of that. The next summer, when my parents took us kids further north—up to Ashby, to fish Pelican and Pomme de Terre Lakes—I marveled at the sophistication of Minnesota folk. It seemed that everyone knew how to water-ski, how to catch gigantic walleye and pike, and how to lie back and enjoy the evening breezes along the lakeshores.

I vowed then that someday I would live in Minnesota. My fantasy was to marry the son of the couple who owned the resort where my family stayed. He and I would keep up the cabins, sell minnows and nightcrawlers at the bait shop, and chew the fat with the vacationers, who would, for the most part, be nice people from Iowa who had come to Minnesota to escape their humdrum existence. I hung on to this fantasy, or a similar one, most of the time I was growing up.

Every summer, my younger sister, Linda, and I would go to Grandma Bunkers' house for a week's vacation. Dad and Mom would drive us the fifty miles from Granville through Sheldon, Ashton, and Sibley, Iowa, to Bigelow, Minnesota, then on to Worthington. Once there, Linda and I would help Grandma take care of the modest house she shared with her son, our uncle Ray Bunkers, who worked on the city's dredging crew. For sisters from a tiny Iowa town of 350 residents, Worthington was a huge metropolis. Linda and I were amazed that we could walk down for a swim in Lake Okabena or spend our 25 cents allowance at the local dime store.

Sometimes our cousin, Patsy Feller, whose family lived up the street from us in Granville, would go along for a vacation at Grandma Bunkers' house. If we were lucky, our cousins Sandy, Charlene, and Dean Bunkers, from Wilmont, would drive into town to visit. Their mother, Dagney, had been killed in a terrible car accident along with several of her coworkers from the Campbell's soup plant in Worthington. Our cousins and their father, Larry Bunkers, were still reeling from their loss.

A special treat would be the arrival of our cousins Tom, Dick, Harry, Jerry, and Laurie Thorman. They and their parents, Ole and Clarence Thorman, lived in Minneapolis. If Ole could get time off from her waitress job at Bridgeman's, the family would drive down to Worthington.

1125 Eighth Avenue. Grandma Bunkers' house. It was an older, two-story structure with white shingles and red trim on its window frames. Large pine trees shaded the tiny front yard, and a crab apple tree grew out back. Grandma's neighbors were the Hauges, the Thompsons, and the Fiolas. One block away on the corner stood the brand-new St. Mary's Catholic Church, controversial among its parishioners because the gigantic crucified Christ at the front of the church had been chiseled from green marble. "A *green* Jesus?" People shook their heads.

Grandma had renters living upstairs in a tiny apartment that Uncle Ray had fixed up to bring in some additional monthly income. Some nights, as we lay whispering on the hide-a-bed in Grandma's living room, Linda and I could hear muffled footsteps and laughter from the young couple in the apartment above us. Once, when Grandma and Uncle Ray were between renters, Linda and I sneaked up there to take a look around. We sat on kitchen chairs under the eaves, drinking "tea" (a concoction of sugar and water) and playing "renters." It was the fascination of the forbidden. We knew we were breaking the rules, but we didn't care.

Only later, when we had come back downstairs, been caught by Uncle Ray and forced to confess that we'd disobeyed him by sneaking up to the apartment, did we regret our transgression. But only for a moment. Linda and I knew Uncle Ray wouldn't be too hard on us. He tried to act tough, but he was a soft touch, especially when Linda, his god-daughter, would ask him to tell her the story, just once more, about how he had lost the middle finger on his right hand.

That story never came out the same way twice. Once Uncle Ray told us that a great big dog had bitten his finger off. Another time he told us that a train had run over it. Once he even told us that he had sold it to buy a pack of cigarettes while in the Army!

But Dad explained what had really happened: Uncle Ray had broken a glass and cut his finger clean across. It had been lopped off at its base, leaving him with a big open space between his index and ring fingers. Linda and I thought it was pretty exotic, and we loved to tell our friends about our uncle who was missing his middle finger.

Often, during the late 1950s and early 1960s, our family would drive up to Worthington. By then, Grandma was retired. But for several years after her second husband's death, she had worked in a nursing home, cleaning rooms and helping to care for the residents. Now Uncle Ray, a lifelong bachelor, supported himself and his mother.

Grandma had been left poor both times she was widowed. The first time, in 1926, she had six children to raise, and the family had to leave the farm where they had been living. The second time, in 1949, she had to contest her husband's will because she had been left out of it. Family legend had it that the house at 1125 Eighth Avenue had been part of the settlement.

I knew that money—or the lack of it—had always been a central concern in my father's family, from the time his father, Frank Bunkers, had died, through the Great Depression and World War II, and up to the present. Dad had once told us kids how, when he and his brother Ray were in the service during World War II, both of them sent home a portion of their monthly pay, some for their mother to live on, the remainder for her to put away for them to use after the war. Dad and Ray had been bitterly disappointed upon their return to find out that their mother had given the money they'd sent her to their older brother, who was trying to make a go of farming.

Years later, Dad still must have resented what his mother had done. Once he pulled a crumpled letter out of a drawer and handed it to me. Written sometime in the mid-1940s by the dean at Westmar College in LeMars, Iowa, the letter informed my father that he had been admitted for study there. But, Dad told me, the money he had been sending his mother to save for him while he'd been in the Navy was gone; even with G.I. benefits, Dad could not afford to go to college. Instead, he began working at the post office in Granville, where he worked until he retired.

I wondered if Dad or Uncle Ray had ever confronted their mother or their brother to ask that the money be paid back. Maybe they knew it would be pointless, and maybe it was forgotten as the years passed. Whenever the entire Bunkers family gathered at Grandma's house in Worthington for Thanksgiving or Christmas dinner, I would never have known that there had ever been a rift, if, indeed, there had been. The only feeling I remember from watching my father and his siblings at family gatherings is a genuine happiness at once again being with one another—and with their mother.

It was the summer of 1968. Martin Luther King Jr. and Bobby Kennedy had been assassinated. The Democratic convention in Chicago had erupted into chaos. My sister, Linda, and I were spending a week at Grandma Bunkers' in Worthington, taking care of her while our uncle Ray worked. Grandma, almost eighty, was bedridden. I knew that Grandma liked to sew, and I hoped to interest her in the patchwork quilt that Linda and I were piecing on the living room floor. But Grandma slept away the days, calling for my sister and me only when she needed help to get from the bedroom to the bathroom.

Three years later, in 1971, as a college student in an introductory creative writing class, I wrote this story about those dog days of summer in August 1968:

> The radio is still broadcasting the pre-game interview with Harmon Killebrew. No one has thought to turn it off, and now it seems I'm the only one who hears it. My sister Linda and I sit on kitchen chairs waiting for Dad and Aunt Bernice to arrive. Jipper is barking at the back door to be let in. Standing next to the livingroom sofa, Uncle Ray unfolds a clean white sheet and slowly lowers it over Grandma's body. Now only her loosely laced black shoes stick out from under the sheet.

What time is it? The clock above the stove says 12:45 p.m. She's been dead almost half an hour. Her coffee cup is still sitting right there on the table.

Grandma! Uncle Ray's home for dinner. Want me to pour the coffee? Linda, go see if Grandma can make it out here all right. She's really weak.

God, why didn't I notice earlier how weak Grandma really was? Uncle Ray, Linda and I brought her home from the hospital four days ago. Were her eyes all hazed-over then? Were her hands that jittery? Did she talk with that funny slur? I can't remember.

I walk into the livingroom, closing my eyes as I pass by the lumpy form on the sofa. Linda grimaces. We both look at Uncle Ray crying at his desk. What can I say to him? The closest I ever got to Uncle Ray was to kiss him and thank him for the dollar he used to give me every Christmas. What do you say to someone whose mother has just died right in front of him and you?

How's dinner, Uncle Ray? Linda made the gravy—that's why it's so darned lumpy. Grandma, why don't you eat some apple sauce, if you can't get that hamburger down? Linda, pour Uncle Ray some more coffee.

I had my first bite of chocolate cake in my mouth when Grandma leaned a little forward on her chair. Her fork fell to the floor and rattled over against the refrigerator.

Uncle Ray—Linda—grab her! Here, let's get her into the livingroom. Put her on the sofa.

We put Grandma on the sofa, but I doubt if she ever knew it. Her eyes opened wide as we lowered her, and her mouth dropped open. She was dead. She didn't even get to finish her coffee.

And here we sit. I called home, and Mom answered the phone. I was so glad. I couldn't have told Dad. Linda and I are supposed to call Dad and Uncle Ray's other brothers and sisters. I hate to tell them over the phone that Grandma's dead when she's lying right over there. I can even see the outline of her nose under that sheet.

Gravel crunches as a car jerks into the driveway next to the window. Car doors slam. God, I don't want Dad to walk in here and see Grandma lying there like that. What am I going to say to him?

Dad, Dad, you'd better sit down and have some coffee.

On Easter weekend 1995, Rachel and I went to Mason City, Iowa, to spend time with Linda, her husband, Dan Kennedy, and their family.

While we were there, Linda agreed to take a look at the story about Grandma Bunkers' death that I'd written twenty-four years ago. A few seconds after she started reading, she looked up.

"Suzy, this isn't the way it was. Grandma died early in the morning, don't you remember? We were watching a polka program on TV, and Uncle Ray was telling you and me to get dressed for Mass. That's when Grandma needed help to get from her bedroom to the bathroom.

"So we all grabbed hold of her, but when we got as far as the hide-a-bed in the livingroom, her legs gave out, and she fell backwards onto the bed. You got on the phone and called the priest to come and give her Extreme Unction. Then Patsy, you, and I went out and sat on the front porch."

Morning? Breakfast? Polka show? Patsy? I stared at Linda. Why, she wondered, had I changed the story? Why, I wondered, had she? Linda's memory of Grandma's death was so different from mine, I had to find out whose memory was playing tricks on her. I dug out the diary I'd been keeping the summer of Grandma's death.

JULY 29, 1968.

> Packed for going to Grandma Bunkers. Jim came up and we played Yahtzee and goofed off.

JULY 30, 1968.

> Tuesday. Jenny came over and slept. Linda's in Minnesota. Had a real good long talk with Jen.

JULY 31, 1968.

> Went up to Grandma Bunkers for a few days. Plan on having a dead and yukky time. Great, huh?

AUGUST 1, 1968.

> Grandma wasn't feeling very well and we took her to the doctor. Better now. Linda got here tonite.

AUGUST 2, 1968.

> Larry's wife Esther came over and helped us take care of Grandma. Esther's really nice to us all.

AUGUST 3, 1968.

> Went shopping and got a navy blue turtle neck shell. I'm sewing a quilt for school.

AUGUST 4, 1968.
> Grandma got sick and died at about 7:45 a.m. We had to see her
> die—it was gruesome and pretty sad.

AUGUST 5, 1968.
> Had a wake at Worthington for Grandma. Alot of people there—she
> looked real young.

AUGUST 6, 1968.
> Another wake at Granville. Later Pat Feller, Jim, and I went to
> Alton Drive In and smoked! Fun!

AUGUST 7, 1968.
> Buried Grandma today. So many relatives were here. No one knows
> how to pay for the funeral.

AUGUST 8, 1968.
> Thursday. Started sewing again. Relatives went home. At nite Jim
> and I messed around.

AUGUST 9, 1968.
> Jim came up for dinner and stayed a while. His folks are gone. Had a
> good time goofing off.

AUGUST 10, 1968.
> Another dead day. I can't wait to go to Ames. I hope I'm popular and
> like it there.

So, Linda was right: Grandma had died early in the morning. Now I
remembered. After I phoned her parish priest, I called Mom. She went
up to church to call Dad and Bernice out of High Mass and send them
to Worthington.

When they arrived, they found Linda and me out on the front porch.
Dad looked at us. "Is she gone?"

We nodded.

He and his sister rushed into the house. There they found their
mother's body on the hide-a-bed, under that white sheet. When I heard
Dad moan and Bernice scream, I understood: they'd thought we'd told
them Grandma had gone to the hospital.

Was our cousin Patsy Feller there when Grandma died? I don't know,
and my diary doesn't mention her. But I'd like to think she was. I'd like

to think Patsy went up to her mother, Bernice, and put her arms around her. Whether that actually happened, I don't know. Still, it helps if I imagine it did.

AREA OBITUARIES

Mrs. Lillian Thorman, 79, of Worthington, Minn., died at her home Aug. 4. Mrs. Thorman had been suffering from a heart condition for the past year.

Lillian Welter was born Aug. 7, 1888, in Grafton, N. Dak., the daughter of Matt and Anna Welter. She was married to Frank Bunkers in Granville June 2, 1908, and they resided at Granville until his death on Nov. 24, 1926.

On Aug. 27, 1932, she married Joseph Thorman at Wilmont, Minn. Mr. Thorman died Dec. 25, 1949.

Survivors include five children, Larry and Ray Bunkers of Worthington, Minn., Jerome Bunkers of Granville, Mrs. Lawrence Feller (Bernice) of Granville, Mrs. Clarence Thorman (Viola) of Minneapolis, Minn., a brother, Silverius Welter of Minneapolis, Minn.; and a sister, Mrs. Theresa Lieb of Granville, also eight step-children, 19 grandchildren, and six great-grandchildren.

—from *The Alton Democrat*, August 8, 1968

FROM *THE REQUIEM*

In Paradiso, deducant te angeli,
In tuo adventu, se suscipiant te martyres.
Et per ducant te in civitatem sanctam, Jerusalem.

May the angels lead you into Paradise.
May the martyrs welcome you,
And lead you to the holy city, Jerusalem.

The priest
Plays
A circular game,
Tips
His censer,
Forces
Musk ripples
Onto the air,
Thumbs the casket top,

Through dust
To dust.
Candle flames
Gasp.
The grey shell
Rolls
Down linoleum aisles.
On the face
Of the old woman
Inside,
A loose smile
Has pasted itself.

May the choirs of angels welcome you,
And with Lazarus the beggar
May you find eternal rest.

Chorus angelorum te suscipiant.
Et cum Lazaro quondam paupere
Eternam habeas requiem.

—Suzanne Bunkers, 1974

There is, in anyone who mourns, an odd pride in the fact of mourn-
ing, an impulse to cultivate grief as a fitting tribute to the beloved
dead, like the ancient Egyptian practice of shaving one's eyebrows
to show bereavement. But a person cannot do that for long with-
out ceasing to be himself, without climbing into a casket of his or
her own making, in a useless pantomime of the death of another.
—Barbara Cawthorne Crafton, *The Sewing Room*, 1993

On her eightieth birthday, Grandma Bunkers was buried next to her
first husband, Frank Bunkers, in the St. Joseph Parish cemetery in
Granville, Iowa. A few weeks later, I left home for college at Iowa State
University in Ames. That autumn, I started working as a server on the
cafeteria line at the Iowa State Memorial Union. I was caught up in the
whirl of classes, social activities, and new friends. I wrote home often,
since phone calls were an expensive luxury reserved only for family
birthdays, but I didn't spend a stretch of time with my family until
that Thanksgiving.

When I got home, I could see that Dad was not feeling well. He'd
been on sick leave from his job as a rural mail carrier for more than

a week. He spent a lot of time sleeping and complaining that his chronic inner ear imbalance was acting up again. When Dad was up and about, he was generally irritable and unhappy. The rest of us tip-toed around the house, trying not to upset him further. I couldn't see it at the time, but now I believe that Dad was suffering from depression precipitated by his mother's death a few months earlier. I think Dad had grieved so much that he'd climbed into his own casket, in what Barbara Cawthorne Crafton calls a "useless pantomime of the death of another."

When I came home for Christmas break in December 1968, Dad seemed worse. By the following March, when I returned home from college for spring break, he was so weak and depressed that he couldn't get out of bed. I sat by his bedside, trying to talk him into putting on his bathrobe and coming out to the kitchen for a cup of coffee. For several days, my mother and I debated what to do. We knew Dad wouldn't get better unless he was hospitalized, but every time we broached the subject with him, he told us he couldn't afford to go to the hospital. Finally, I persuaded my mother to phone Uncle Ray, who drove down from Worthington and loaned Dad some money. Mom and Uncle Ray bundled Dad up in the car and drove him to the county hospital, thirty miles away in Cherokee.

A few days later, I went back to college. Mom wrote me that Dad was undergoing treatment and could not have mail or phone calls. Soon, to everyone's relief, he was feeling well enough to be dismissed from the hospital. When I came home in June at the end of my first year of college, he seemed to be back on an even keel. In August he even felt well enough to take us all for a week in the Black Hills. It was our first family vacation in three years.

But I never again trusted that Dad was well for good. In 1971, he was only fifty, but his physical health was declining. The kidney disease that he had contracted while serving in the Navy during World War II flared up again. He began having serious heart problems and was eventually diagnosed with an aneurysm. He spent time in Veterans Administration hospitals in Knoxville, Iowa; Sioux Falls, South Dakota; and Omaha, Nebraska.

During those hospital stays, he sent me periodic letters:

Letter postmarked Sioux Falls, S.D., October 18, 1972:

Dear Suzy,
Just a few lines today. Just ate dinner and don't get much to eat.
Lost 4 lbs so far. Also am confined to the ward in P.J.s. Got the same

Dr. and he is really nice to me so far but can't understand him too good. Saw him this A.M. and he said they are going to send records to Mpls as I may need heart surgery. How are things going with you two. Mom said we have a duck hunter in the family by the name of Dale. Guess he got a teel and ate it for supper Mon. nite. Got a real nice roommate here from South Sioux City. He is in bad shape, hasn't worked for 11 years, heart and his legs are like hamburger in a roll. Got T.V. and watch the ballgames. Vince Kokenge was here Monday. Ray, Larry, & Esther here Sunday. Want to write to Linda also so better close.

Love,
Dad

Letter postmarked U.S. Postal Service, NE, October 31, 1972:

Dear Suzy,
Just wrote a few lines to Linda so will get off a few to you also. Hope you had a safe trip home. Mom got home at 7:30. Dale sold the pens and I hear he reordered. Some hustler, eh!

Not much news around here. Won 75 cents Mon. nite at Bingo. More tests are coming up for this week. Had a change over of student and intern Docs today, guess they change every 2 months. Finally got Playboy but don't send anymore magazines, we have lots of them around here.

No more on quitting work. Paul Goergen wrote they are raising hell with rural carriers, consolidation, etc., and Granville is also on the list, when he did not say.

Getting lots of rest, only saw 13 so called Socs & Docs to be today. Looked like Broadway in the hall.

Not much else for now. Will write later.

Love,
Dad

Letter postmarked U.S. Postal Service, NE, November 7, 1972:

Dear Suzy,
Decided to write a few lines and one can call the other, no use of writing twice. More tests today and yesterday, didn't get to see any Dr. so far, really don't care either. If it would not be for compensation I'd tell them to go to hell but for $100 a month you got to keep your mouth shut.

Ray, Mom, Danny, Bernice, & Lawrence were here Sunday for about 3 hrs. Danny was up on 7 and the nurse let me know about it.

Told her my wife didn't know. Suppose you voted today, I didn't so if someone wins by one vote I'll take the blame.

Ole wrote yesterday, nothing really new except 2 boys are studying welding, one carpenter work under G.I. bill. Do you plan on coming Sun. or are you going to watch football game? Bud the big guy gets to go home today for 2 months so will be alone again. All for now. Read to Linda.

Love,
Dad

Eventually, Dad got well enough to come home. Though his spirits seemed good, his physical health continued to worsen. A few years later, when he began having occasional blackouts on the mail route, his supervisors let him know it was time to retire. So, in 1975, at the age of fifty-three, Dad stepped down from his job as a rural letter carrier, the only job he had held for over twenty-five years.

That summer I drove home to Granville from Madison, Wisconsin, where I was living at the time while going to graduate school. One steamy night, after a downpour, Dad, Danny, and I hunted nightcrawlers in the ditches across the street from our house. The next day Dad, Mom, Danny, and I drove to Worthington, met up with Uncle Ray, and headed to Round Lake to fish. The bullhead were biting, and we got the limit by shortly after noon.

As we loaded our fishing gear back into the car for the drive home, Dad struggled to get his breath. He slumped down in the back seat and slept while I drove the family back to Granville. Once home, he went to bed and did not get up until the next day. That was when I knew my father had very little time left.

Just when you think you've told it all, there's always more that can be told. But how much? That's the question. I'd known for a long time that the Bunkers family had a history of problems with alcohol. I'd heard that one of Grandma Bunkers' uncles, Nick Linster, who helped bartend at his brother-in-law Matt Welter's saloon in Granville, had often been found lying on the floor, his open mouth under the tap of a full keg of beer. Nick Linster had died as a fairly young man; the St. Joseph Parish records list the cause of his death as "Drunkenness."

I'd also heard, from my great-aunt Theresa, that my grandfather Frank Bunkers had had a drinking problem. When I interviewed her about family history, Aunt Theresa recalled one afternoon out on Frank and Lillian Bunkers' farm near Granville. Theresa had been vis-

iting for the day, helping Lillian take care of her children. At sunset the
two women saw a horse and buggy pull up at the end of the lane. They
watched as Frank Bunkers tumbled out and staggered up to the house,
where he passed out on the front porch. Theresa told me that some
folks around Granville had wondered whether something more than a
massive heart attack had caused Frank Bunkers' untimely death.

As Theresa talked, I recalled how my parents, Linda, and I had spent
some of those hot summer evenings in the early 1950s when our family was still living in the little white house across from the church
in Granville. We would walk up the street to Hank and Harriet
Schwarzkopf's gas station on the corner. Inside, we would sit in the
dark mahogany booths, Linda and I munching on beernuts and playing
with bottle caps.

Hank and Harriet, in their early thirties like my parents, wore bib
overalls every day and chain-smoked unfiltered Camels. Their only
child, Darlene, a year or two younger than Linda, would sit with us,
drinking a Dr Pepper or 7-Up while our parents and other customers
sipped cold beers and chatted. Once I overheard my dad telling someone that Hank and Harriet were always "in the bag," but I didn't know
what that meant. A few years later, after our family had moved to the
other side of town, Harriet Schwarzkopf died of liver failure, or so
rumor had it. Hank was killed in a motorcycle accident not long after,
and Darlene went off to live with an aunt and uncle. Linda and I never
saw her again.

Sometimes on those hot summer nights, Dad would take the whole
family for a ride to cool everyone off. We'd cruise the streets of
Granville. That wouldn't take long, since the entire town was only
four blocks long and four blocks wide. From our house on Long Street,
we'd drive south two blocks to Highway 10. Then we'd take a left for
three blocks, past the old kindergarten schoolhouse, the Conoco station, and St. Joseph High School, to the corner kitty-corner from the
cemetery, where Schwarzkopfs' gas station stood. Then we'd take another left and drive two blocks down past St. Joseph Church, grade
school, and playground. In one more block we'd pass the VFW Club.
Then we'd turn left onto Main Street, which was only one block long.

Anchoring Main Street's four corners were Beck's Store, Van
Bergen's bowling alley and bar, Budden's "66" gas station, and the
Granville branch of the Hospers Savings Bank. On both sides of Main
Street were various businesses. Next to Beck's was Bachmann's Sun-
dries, a little drugstore and soda fountain run by Nora Bachmann's son
Bob. Next to it was the Electric Shop, as we called it. That was where

Patsy Feller's dad, Lawrence, worked as an electrician. A bit further down the block was the U.S. Post Office, where Dad worked. Next to it was the Feed and Supply Store. Then came Beck's Produce, where Patsy Feller's mother, Bernice, worked candling eggs. Finally, there on the corner was the bank. On the other side of Main Street, just up from Slagle's lumberyard, were Budden's "66" gas station, Neuroth's butcher shop, Perlot's Cafe and Dance Hall (formerly Welter's Saloon), Korbach's Plumbing, and Van Bergen's bowling alley and bar.

Our first stop would be at Perlot's. As the oldest child, I'd run inside to get each of us kids an orange sherbet push-up, an ice cream sandwich, or a vanilla cone. I'd carry the treats to the car and hand them in through the open window to Linda and Denny in the back seat, then to Mom and Dale in the front seat. I'd hop into the back seat to enjoy my treat.

Then Dad would drive the half block past Beck's to the VFW Club. While Mom stayed in the car with us kids, Dad would go inside for "just one nickel beer," as he put it. In the meantime, we'd watch people coming in and out of the club, and Mom would tell us anecdotes about some of the more inebriated ones. Some nights Dad would stay inside the VFW Club for only five minutes; other nights he'd linger until Mom sent me to get him. I'd stand outside the door, press the buzzer, and jump up and down so my face would show in the one-way mirror. Then someone would let me in, and I'd give Dad the message: "Time to go home." He would usually nod, chug the rest of his Schlitz or Blatz, and follow me out the door.

When I was ten, Dad took a second job to earn some extra income. For a while, after working days as a rural mail carrier, he pumped gas at the local Conoco station in the evenings. Later, on nights when he wasn't helping coach my softball team or my brother's baseball team, Dad began bartending at the VFW Club.

Sometime during these years, I'm not sure when, it dawned on me that Dad drank a lot. But he didn't seem to drink much more than most of his buddies, the fathers of my friends. When he got off the mail route, just before noon, Dad would stop in at the VFW Club for a beer. After he took his afternoon nap and put up the next day's mail at the post office downtown, he'd stop back at the club to play cards with friends and have another beer or two. The 6:00 p.m. whistle would be his signal to come home for supper.

It seemed that everyone in Granville drank. Much to the chagrin of our Dutch Reformed neighbors ten miles away in Orange City (the county seat), Sioux County had recently voted to go wet after years of voting dry. Liquor-by-the-drink was the result.

In Granville, even children were allowed to drink under certain conditions. Parents gave their children sips of beer without batting an eye. At high school graduation parties every spring, many parents, mine included, let their children try mixed drinks. At home, our refrigerator was always well stocked with cold beer, and Dad's liquor cabinet held fifths of whiskey, scotch, vodka, gin, and brandy.

It wasn't until I was in college (where I was doing some underage drinking on my own) that I began to question whether Dad might have a problem with alcohol. I couldn't know for sure. By then, after his many hospitalizations, he was taking a number of medications for angina and an aneurysm as well as for his periodic bouts with depression. I'd learned in a Family Health course that alcohol, when taken in combination with any of those medications, could have dire effects on a person. That seemed to be what was happening to Dad, but I had no idea how to help him. All I could do was study for the final exam for my Family Health class, on which we were tested over the characteristics and dynamics of an alcoholic family system. I wondered if mine fit the bill.

Eventually, in the mid-1970s, Dad tried to help himself. After thirty years of smoking two packs of Winstons a day, he quit smoking. He quit drinking at the same time. But by that time, though only in his early fifties, he was old beyond his years. His doctors briefly considered surgery to repair his aneurysm, which could burst at any moment and kill him. But the doctors decided that Dad's chronic kidney disease precluded successful surgery. All they could do was continue to treat him with various medications. During his last two or three years, Dad kept a bottle of nitroglycerin tablets in his shirt pocket, popping them under his tongue frequently to get temporary relief from the angina that he suffered daily.

In late July 1978, a few days after Dad's death, while getting paperwork together to help my mother apply for survivors' benefits, I came upon a copy of his medical records in his lockbox. Dated December 1974, the records listed Dad, aged fifty-three, as suffering from congestive heart failure, hypertensive cardiovascular disease, hypertension, sinusitis, chronic nephritis, and a possible old stroke. The records state that, after Dad's doctor had treated him with a succession of drugs like lasim, aminophyllin, digoxin, and morphine, Dad "symptomatically became better."

Today, as I open the thick manila folder and review those medical records once more, I'm amazed at everything that was wrong with Dad by the time he was fifty-three, just eight years older than I am now. I'm even more amazed that he lived as long as he did.

A Sense of Place

I expect one's sense of place is deeply psychic; I doubt
we are moved by or drawn to mountains, deserts,
rivers, woodlands, coast lines, or amber waves of
grain alone and in a vacuum, but imperceptibly
respond to them in combination with whatever
human circumstances connect us to them.
—Elizabeth Hampsten, *Mother's Letters,* 1993

After I returned from my first trip to Luxembourg, in August 1980, my mother suggested that I contact our cousin Barbara Jacobs and ask if I could talk with her about the Bunkers family history. After all, my mother pointed out, Barbara Jacobs was the daughter of John Graff and Catherine (Kate) Bunkers Graff, the older sister of my grandfather Frank Bunkers. Barbara Jacobs was the granddaughter and namesake of Barbara Simmerl Bunkers. And, Mom reminded me, Barbara's husband, Jim Jacobs, had been one of my dad's fishing buddies. Nearly every fall Dad, Jim, and Dad's brother Ray would drive up to Baudette to fish the Lake of the Woods on the U.S.-Canadian border. I decided to give Mr. and Mrs. Jacobs a call the next time I was in Granville.

Mrs. Jacobs was eager to talk, and she invited me to her and her husband's home for coffee. There, she offered me a delightful surprise: the Graff-Bunkers family Bible. As she and I studied the faded entries in the Family Records section, we came across this notation: "Barbara Simmerl Youngblut, born January 1, 1856 in Luxembourg, Europe, died February 4, 1943, in Des Moines, Iowa."

Youngblut. Where had that name come from? At no point in my search in the Feulen records had I encountered the name "Youngblut" in the Simmerl ancestry. Another entry in the Family Records section of the Graff-Bunkers Bible, however, provided an explanation. Barbara Simmerl Youngblut's parents were listed in this way:

Father	Mother
——— Youngblut	——— Youngblut
b. 2–11–1823	b. 4–6–1830
d. 5–11–1893	d. 5–20–1906

Now for my next question: had this Mr. Youngblut been Barbara
Bunkers' stepfather? Could her mother, Susanna, have married him
after she and her daughter arrived in the United States in 1857?

Mrs. Jacobs' eyes sparkled. "Yes, I do believe that's so. I remember
now hearing that our grandmother's mother hadn't been married and,
you know, she married a Mr. Youngblut from the Waterloo area after
she came to this country."

As I gently prodded her memory, Mrs. Jacobs recalled that the
Youngbluts had had many children and that some of the Youngbluts
probably still lived in the Waterloo area. I finished coffee with Barbara
and Jim Jacobs, then drove seven miles to the Alton, Iowa, library to
study old issues of the *Alton Democrat*, hoping to find some news
item that would shed light on the subject. My hunch proved correct. In
the February 12, 1943, issue of the *Democrat* appeared this obituary:

> Barbara Simmerl Bunkers, born Jan. 1, 1856 in Luxembourg and died
> Feb. 4, 1943 at Des Moines where she lived with Miss Munda
> Bunkers since Oct. 20, 1941. She came to the United States at an
> early age and on July 20, 1875, at Dyersville married Henry Bunkers.
> They farmed at Granville until 1916, then retired. Of her twelve chil-
> dren, five survive: John, Garretson, S.D.; Tony, Madison, Mn.; Emil,
> Dell Rapids, S.D.; Nora (Mrs. Joe Bachmann), Granville; Miss
> Munda, Des Moines.
>
> Mr. Bunkers preceded her in death Feb. 15, 1924. Her children Joseph
> died in 1911, Elizabeth in 1915, Otto in 1925, Frank in 1926, Clara
> (Mrs. Art Full) in 1933, Henry in 1936, Catherine (Mrs. John Graff)
> in 1941. Fifty grandchildren survive. Also two sisters, Mrs. Sophia
> O'Connor of Waterloo, and Mrs. Suzan O'Connor of Milwaukee.

Now I had yet another important clue: Sophia and Suzan O'Connor
were Barbara's half sisters and the daughters of Susanna, who, according to the entry in the Graff-Bunkers family Bible, had died in 1906.
Susanna had been buried, I surmised, in the Waterloo area, since no notice of her death appeared in either the Granville or the Luxemburg,
Iowa, parish records.

Henry and Barbara Simmerl Bunkers and family, circa 1900, Granville,
Iowa. Back row (l. to r.): Anton, John, Catherine, Henry Jr., Elizabeth, Frank.
Front row (l. to r.): Otto, Barbara, Clara, Henry, Emil. Seated in front (l. to r.):
Elnora, Edmunda, Joseph.

It was not too likely that Sophia or Suzan O'Connor, Barbara's half
sisters, would still be alive nearly thirty years after Barbara's death. But
their descendants could quite likely be living in the Waterloo, Iowa, or
the Milwaukee, Wisconsin, area. How could I find them?

Once again, my cousin Barbara Jacobs came to my aid. On one of her
trips to the Mayo Clinic for a periodic cancer checkup, she'd met a
Mrs. Kayser from the Waterloo area and had asked her if she knew of
any Youngbluts or O'Connors there. When Mrs. Kayser sent Mrs. Jacobs the name and address of Mrs. Marie Hellman of Waterloo, Barbara
Jacobs forwarded the information to me. In early January 1983, I wrote
Mrs. Hellman a letter. A week later I received this reply:

Henry and Barbara Simmerl Bunkers family portrait, circa 1910, Granville, Iowa. Back row (l. to r.): Frank, John, Anton, Henry Jr., Joseph. Middle row (l. to r.): Emil, Catherine, Clara, Elizabeth, Otto. Front row (l. to r.): Barbara, Edmunda, Henry, Elnora.

Waterloo, Iowa
January 12, 1983

Dear Suzanne,
Received your letter of inquiries about the Susanna and Frank Youngblut family. I am going to forward your letter to my niece Charlotte Witry (Paul O'Connor's daughter), who is also doing a family tree.

I called her today, and she was quite pleased as she's been looking for some information on Aunt Barbara's family. You will probably be hearing from her sometime in the future.

Barbara Simmerl Bunkers, about age 85, circa 1940, Granville, Iowa.

Kate Graff had a daughter, Charlotte, that is my age, that I remember as a young girl that I would like to get in touch with. Would you know her whereabouts?

I'm also curious as to how you heard about me. Was it through someone in Mankato?

Sincerely yours,
Marie Hellman

Less than three weeks later, I received a thick packet of genealogical charts, along with this letter:

1137 Mitchell
Waterloo, Iowa
Jan. 30, 1983

Suzanne L. Bunkers
901 East Main
Mankato, Minn. 56001

Dear Suzanne,
Here it is—a letter from a Youngblut!
Friday I had lunch with three cousins and heard about your Genealogy research. Studied your letters etc. to Marie Hellman. They contained much of interest to me, and many new facts.

*Sisters, July 1954 (l. to r.): Uniden-
tified, Sophia Youngblut O'Connor,
Susan Youngblut O'Connor, Mary
Youngblut LaVasseur.*

I hope that I have copied records from my files that will be of special interest to you. From this François and Susan Simmeral Youngblut sheet I can go on and give you almost complete up to date histories of the seven families, if you are interested.

Each summer the descendants of the John Youngblut family have
a reunion at Gilbertville or Jesup. I bring my books and they are
great by giving me information of the past year.

I'm sorry but I haven't done any research on the Simmerals. I did
my mother's family (Phillips) before I started Youngblut and Robert.

I will look forward to hearing from you and trust that we can
help each other more in our interesting search.

Sincerely,
Mabel Slater

Barbara Jacobs was as thrilled as I was that we had found our Youngblut cousins and that they, too, were interested in piecing together the
puzzle of our mutual ancestor Susanna's life. During 1983 and 1984, I
began sending these cousins the information I had gathered about the
Simmerl family in Luxembourg. I vowed that on my next trip to Luxembourg I would locate information about Susanna Simmerl's husband,

Frank Youngblut, whose name, as I learned from Mabel Slater, had originally been spelled "Jungblut" and who had been born in the village of Aspelt, in the southern corner of Luxembourg.

It was time to immerse myself in Luxembourg immigration history. I needed to understand not only why Luxembourgers left their native land but also why they came to the United States, where they settled, and what their lives were like in the "New World."

Church and civil records in Luxembourg, dating back to the mid-1700s, had indicated that most Luxembourgers lived in peasant villages and worked the land. These Luxembourgers were not wealthy landowners; in fact, most were "journaliers," or day laborers. By the middle of the nineteenth century in Luxembourg, a small amount of mining was under way in the southern part of the country. Most Luxembourgers, however, eked out a living through some form of agriculture. As historian James Newcomer explains,

> In 1847 more than 12 percent of the population were absolutely indigent, a condition that was to persist for decades, though it would be alleviated somewhat. Harvests were still uncertain, and a poor harvest was still followed by near starvation. Nourishment was poor, and living conditions were primitive. There was no great wealth; even those who were rather well off were not affluent. The poor employee was subject to the grinding demands of employers who still squeezed from the worker the last ounce of energy and the last sou. Poverty impelled emigration, which grew to major proportions.

It was into this world that my ancestors—the Welters, the Linsters, the Ahrends, the Grethens, the Simmerls, the Hottuas, the Müllers, the Kleins, the Youngbluts—were born. And it was this world that many of them left when they left their homeland and immigrated to the United States. Historian James H. Shenton notes, "Between 1820 and 1880 more than ten million immigrants poured into the United States, with the greatest activity in the two decades between 1840 and 1860, when almost four and a half million arrived." These immigrants came primarily from countries in northwestern Europe (e.g., Ireland, Germany). During the next wave of immigration, from approximately 1880 to 1924, nearly 27 million white immigrants, primarily from other parts of Europe (e.g., Russia, Austria-Hungary, Italy) came to the United States.

In *Moving Europeans*, historian Leslie Page Moch explains,

> Eighty years of mass migrations began with the 1840s, when two important trends emerged. On the one hand, the demand for labor in-

creased in the farmlands and cities in North America and the sugar and coffee plantations of Latin America, partly because the slave trade had been abolished. On the other hand, Europe's "hungry forties," the potato famine, and political struggles exacerbated suffering and unemployment. Emigration pushed into high gear as 200,000 to 300,000 Europeans departed per year in the crisis-ridden late 1840s.

Moch's analysis indicates that emigration from Europe to other continents continued unabated after mid-century:

> An estimated 13 million embarked between 1840 and 1880, and another 13 million departed in the last 20 years of the century. In all, about 52 million migrants left Europe between 1860 and 1914, of whom roughly 37 million (72%) traveled to North America and 11 million to South America (21%). Three and a half million Europeans, primarily British, moved to Australia and New Zealand.

Because political and economic control of Luxembourg had changed hands so many times, and because the grand duchy did not actually exist as an independent state until the mid-nineteenth century, it is difficult to establish accurate figures regarding the number of Luxembourgers who left their country for other lands. On passenger ship manifests, naturalization documents, and U.S. census records, Luxembourgers have often been listed as Prussians, Germans, or Belgians. Research that focuses specifically on Luxembourger immigration, however, has made a substantial effort to ascertain and account for such numbers.

Why did Luxembourgers leave their homeland during the nineteenth century? As historian Nicholas Gonner explains in *Luxembourgers in the New World*, numerous factors influenced Luxembourger immigration. Gonner cites the primary factor as the "progressive and permanent impoverishment of the population in general," involving "not so much a lack of money as a decline in the quality of life." In their recent new edition of Gonner's 1889 study, immigration history scholars Jean Ensch, Jean-Claude Muller, and Robert Owen analyze the factors influencing emigration from Luxembourg during the mid- to late 1800s. Conditions that pushed Luxembourgers outward included an increase in population, a decrease in infant mortality, and substantial industrialization during the 1870s. Although the poorest of the poor,

> unable to afford even the gradually decreasing rail and ocean passage of the nineteenth century, had to remain at home, the lower middle

class, afflicted with poor harvests and high taxes, found the means to leave. To do so made economic sense for many: the proceeds of the sale of their land and homesteads in the Grand Duchy permitted them to buy in North America as much as ten times the amount of acreage which they possessed at home. For a migration which consisted of persons who either had been or were to become farmers, this was no small consideration.

Ensch, Muller, and Owen go on to state that in addition to the possibility of having land to farm in the U.S., individuals also emigrated from Luxembourg during the 1800s to avoid being forced into military service in the Dutch, Belgian, and Prussian armies. The lure offered by letters sent from immigrants already in America to their relatives and friends still in Luxembourg was another reason for immigration, as was the desire to avoid punishment for crimes or offenses. Susanna Simmerl's status as an unwed mother was another contributing factor, illustrating the theory explained by historian Donna Gabbacia in *From the Other Side*: "Not all the problems immigrants hope to solve by migrating are economic or political in origin."

Even though some Luxembourgers had emigrated before 1840, the decades that followed witnessed a rapid increase in the numbers booking passage on ships sailing from Antwerp, Belgium, and Le Havre, France, to New York City, Baltimore, and New Orleans. Early Luxembourger immigrant communities sprang up in the states of New York and Ohio. By the mid-1840s, Luxembourg immigrants had traveled further west, to such places as Chicago, Illinois; Port Washington, Holy Cross, Belgium, and Fredonia, Wisconsin; and Dubuque, St. Donatus, and Luxemburg, Iowa.

During the 1850s, an ever-greater number of Luxembourgers left their homeland for the United States. Economic depression and famine, combined with political unrest, the partitioning of land, and increasing mortgage rates made the prospect of settlement in the "New Land" appealing. Yet by 1858, immigration had virtually ceased, partly as a result of improved economic conditions in Luxembourg and partly because of increasing pre–Civil War unrest in the United States. Immigrants to America during the 1850s continued to settle in Ohio, Illinois, Wisconsin, and Iowa, as well as in newer Luxembourger communities like Rollingstone, Caledonia, and Luxemburg, Minnesota.

The period from 1860 to 1890 saw a resurgence in emigration from Luxembourg to the United States, followed by a decrease toward the end of the nineteenth century. All told, during the sixty-year period

Luxembourger settlements in Iowa are indicated by italics.
Map by Pat Conrad.

from 1831 to 1891, more than 72,000 Luxembourgers left their homeland for a variety of destinations; in 1890, according to Newcomer, a
total of 212,000 people remained in Luxembourg. Gonner estimated
that 29,700 people emigrated from the grand duchy from 1831 to 1888.

In 1889, when the population of the United States was estimated at
60 million people, Gonner estimated that one U.S. resident in 2,500
was a Luxembourger. Although some Luxembourgers settled in large
cities like New York, Chicago, New Orleans, and Detroit, the majority
settled near rural Midwestern towns. There, like their ancestors before
them, they farmed. Susanna Simmerl was one of those immigrants.

What might Susanna's life in the U.S. have been like? Could I gain
insights by studying the lives of other Midwestern American women?
These two questions were the impetus for my study of unpublished diaries by nineteenth-century Midwestern women.

I spent the summer of 1983 living in Chapel Hill, North Carolina,
taking part in a National Endowment for the Humanities Summer
Seminar, "Forms of Autobiography." As it turned out, my professor,
James Olney, had grown up in Marathon, Iowa, a little town about an
hour east of Granville on Highway 10. In fact, he still had relatives

living in Marathon. When I explained to James that my interest in
women's diaries had had its genesis in my search for information about
my own ancestors, particularly Susanna, he encouraged me to keep
searching, both in the United States and in Luxembourg.

So it was that in early June 1984 I packed for my second journey to
"the old country." My cousin Father Frank Klein, also traveling in Europe, rented a car and met my plane in Paris. Once again we set out for
Feulen, with plans to visit historical sites along the way.

JUNE 9, 1984   8 P.M.

I'm alone in a little courtyard at our hotel in Nemours, France.
Frank went off to Mass. I decided not to go out for dinner but to eat
bread, cheese and wine—same as for lunch. This time alone feels
good. When I came on this trip, I don't think I was aware of how
little time alone I'd be spending during the next month. I'm used to
a fair amount of time alone, and I can sense that I need it on this
trip just as I would if I were at home. So I need to build in some
opportunities to have some.

I'm feeling calmer this trip than when I came to Europe in 1980.
I feel more at home in France than I did in Germany, for one thing.
Also, I have more of an idea what to expect. Just being able to understand some of the language and to be able to carry on a basic
conversation has put me more at ease.

JUNE 10, 1984   SUNDAY

Today we toured Le Cathédrale de Chartres—magnificent! Huge,
beautiful, ornate structure with incredible stained-glass windows
and statues carved throughout the building. We got there just in
time for Mass at the main altar—celebrated in French and Latin. All
the old Latin prayers (Sanctus, Pater Noster, Agnus Dei) came back
to me, and I sang along and went up for Communion. Frank and I
walked around the inside of the cathedral, where a supposed "relic"
of the Blessed Virgin Mary (part of the gown or veil she was wearing
when Christ was born) was displayed. We saw people lighting candles next to the relic and going up to touch or kiss the glass case in
which it was enclosed. Some people were even crying.

JUNE 11, 1984   MONDAY

Today is a holiday in celebration of Pentecost, and many people
have the day off. Frank and I left Clemency and came to Vezelay this

morning. This town dates back to medieval times, and Roman
architecture is evident throughout the town. Vezelay was one of
the major pilgrimage sites of the 12th and 13th centuries. The
"relics" of St. Mary Magdalene (little pieces of bone) are on display
at the basilica. The story goes that, following Christ's death, Mary
Magdalene left Palestine for Ephesus to begin a life of prayer and
fasting in penitence for her sins. In 1037, Abbot Geoffrey announced
that her relics had been found at Vezelay, and pilgrims began flock-
ing there to visit her tomb and have their sins forgiven. In 1146,
Bernard of Clairvaux launched the Second Crusade from Vezelay.
Mary Magdalene was considered one of Christ's most beloved followers, and the faithful believed that she could intercede for them
with God. She became the favorite female saint of the Middle Ages.

JUNE 13, 1984   10:45 P.M.

At Hotel de Bermont, Greux, France. This town is adjacent to Dom-
remy, birthplace of St. Joan of Arc. She died at Rouen in 1431—
burned at the stake for claiming God had spoken directly to her. She
was condemned as a witch and burned; then her ashes were scattered on the Seine River. Joan was born here in 1411 or 1412; she
had one sister, Catherine; her parents were Jacques and Isabelle. Her
father wanted Joan to marry and had more or less promised her to a
young official so he could improve his fortunes by his daughter's
successful marriage. Joan had taken a vow to remain a virgin and
she left her parents' home rather than marry.

At age twelve Joan heard voices—those of St. Michael, St. Catherine and St. Margaret. People doubted her, but she said God had
told her to go to Charles, the heir to the French throne, and tell him
to stop waging war.

She was eventually accused of treason, imprisoned, then handed
over to the British and judged a traitor—convicted of the crimes of
schism, idolatry, and invocation of devils. Joan was burned at the
stake at Rouen, on 30 May 1431, at the age of nineteen.

At Vatican II in the 1960s, Pope Paul VI declared Joan a voice of
justice speaking out for the poor who are oppressed. Joan has been
made a saint.

How ironic that her treason was that she claimed God spoke
directly to and through her, something thought impossible for a
woman in those days of the Inquisition and the *Malleus Maleficarum* [Hammer of Witches]. Interesting, too, that the Church could

turn the situation to its advantage when it became clear that people believed Joan had been speaking for her God.

JUNE 14, 1984

Flag Day. Today would have been my parents' thirty-fifth anniversary. It's evening, and we're visiting the Meuse-Argonne American Cemetery and Memorial Romagne/Montfaucon, France. 14,246 soldiers who died in WWI are buried here, 486 of them unknown.

I'm sitting on a bench in the middle of this cemetery; white crosses and Stars of David are around me on all sides. From here I can see the pattern of the grave markers. It's like what Dad used to call "cross-checking" used by farmers in their cornfields. From here I can see the graves of Louis F. Baker (1918), Peter C. Trapp (1918), John C. Klaffka (1918), George Mack (1918), and thousands of others.

Almost all of the graves are marked with the date September or October 1918, during the Argonne offensive of 1918. Some were support personnel, listed as the medical or ambulance corps. The countryside surrounding the cemetery is green and gold—we saw farmers mowing their hay as we drove over here from the town of Verdun, 25 miles away.

Frank and I also stopped at a small German cemetery with about 900 soldiers buried there. To get to it, we had to drive through a farmer's pasture. The cows were grazing next to the cemetery, where only small brown crosses marked the graves. Two Stars of David were among the grave markers, which surprised me. I hadn't even thought of Jewish soldiers being in the German Army of WWI.

10:30 p.m. In bed in my room at Reichlange, Luxembourg, in a hotel run by Frank's cousin, Marie Gengler. This is an old, old house that dates back to the 1600s. It was once a wealthy family home for the Genglers, and now Marie runs it as a bed and breakfast.

JUNE 15, 1984

Afternoon. I'm in Ettelbruck at the George S. Patton Museum in the downtown area—two rooms in one of the official city buildings. Both rooms are filled with American Army and Nazi troop memorabilia from the Battle of the Bulge in late 1944–early 1945. One room has a 3' x 5' portrait of Patton on the wall, lots of photographs of the Ettelbruck/Feulen area taken at the time of the battle, and case after case of army memorabilia, ranging from spent cartridges to grenades, gas masks, knives, compasses, helmets, canteens, even pots and pans.

The Proclamation that Eisenhower issued when U.S. troops liberated Ettelbruck hangs on one wall. It's in both French and German,
and it thanks the Luxembourgers for their support during the war
and tells them they must obey the Government's orders to help
keep the peace: "Vous *devez* donc obéir les ordres de votre Gou-
vernement et les miennes dans tous leurs detail, de meme que
maintenies, de meme que maintenir la paix . . ."

In the second room are all sorts of Nazi memorabilia—including
pistols, machine guns, something labeled a *pazerbuchse*—a huge
tube-like contraption—a gun evidently. A display of cards with German soldiers' songs is on another wall—songs like "Marie-Helen"
and "Kleine Dorothée." There is also a small poster of Adolf Hitler
standing over a field full of bodies in the winter. He's smiling, and
the caption reads "Ich fuhle mich so frisch. Es kammt der Fruh-
ling." Dated 24.2.41.

Another display case has U.S. medical supplies—talc for men,
dried eggs, lemon juice powder, and booklets like French and German phrase books. Also envelopes from two letters to a Pvt. An-
drew Hruska 3362324, c/o C. 159th Engr (c) Bu. APO NY—dated
Sept. 13 and Oct. 9, 1944.

Finally, there's a series of photographs of the destruction and re-
construction of the Ettelbruck/Feulen cities and countryside.

JUNE 16, 1984

Niederfeulen. Saturday night at the Steiwers' home here. I have my
own room in Laure's portion of the house. Actually, it's an entire
house in itself—built onto the original house—with kitchen, livingroom, bath, and two bedrooms.

I came here late this p.m. and joined Laure and her parents for a
meal of bread, jam, applesauce, coffee, and cocoanut milk. After
supper, Laure and I took a walk out of town on the old road to
Heiderscheid. Came back about 9 p.m. and we talked an hour
more. Then I excused myself to come to bed. I need to be alone for
a while.

Laure's very glad to see me, and wants to talk a lot. She's eager to
converse in English, asks me about many vocabulary words, and
wants to keep the conversation going, no matter what. Her father
and mother know French, so we sometimes talk in that language.
It is nice to be able to speak in English after doing all French for a
week. Some of the days and places seem blurry now. I remember
a succession of hotel rooms but not the towns they were in.

I'm interested in seeing what Laure thinks about things. We had a good talk about being single women, and about carving out lives for ourselves. I still wonder at how she lives at home with her parents. Tomorrow Laure's brother Jacques, who is a philosophy teacher in Brussels, will come for dinner and so will Frank, so we'll all have a chance to meet.

JUNE 17, 1984

Sunday morning. I just woke up and am lying in bed looking out the window at the houses of Niederfeulen and the countryside. I want to take a walk later on, just out into the countryside, perhaps to the Oberfeulen chapel and cemetery.

Last night I asked Laure more about the Steichen family. We were near the Maison des Vacances and saw Mme. Steichen out working in her yard. I asked Laure if everyone in town hated that family, and Laure said that most people ostracized them. Laure said that perhaps Mme. Steichen had had a "catharsis" since the 1940s. Still, the family stays pretty much to itself; once the younger son ran for a post in the town, but no one would vote for him.

While we talked, we watched Mme. Steichen in her yard, digging up the ground and carrying off dirt to put around plants. She was wearing the same blue housedress-apron that she'd worn when I was here four years ago.

Laure confirmed my sense that, after WWII, the Steichens remained here because there was no place else for them to go. Everyone in Luxembourg knew that they had been Nazi collaborators. If they left Luxembourg, they could only really go to Germany, and they'd have nothing there. So, what else was there to do but to remain here and live as outcasts in their own home village?

Evening. Today I met Jacques, the Steiwers' son, who is a philosophy teacher in Brussels. I liked him very much—open, friendly, easy to talk to—he's well-read and well-traveled, sophisticated. He has a 17-year-old daughter, Natalie, and he's now divorced. He's 8 years older than Laure, so I guess he's about in his early to mid-forties. Blond, about 5'10", and has eyes my own color.

Jacques, Laure, Frank and I drove to Esch-sur-Sure and took a long walk through the woods this afternoon. Good chance to talk to both Jacques and Laure and to get some exercise.

JUNE 19, 1984

11 p.m. Reichlange. Tonight Frank and I went to a concert in Niederfeulen with Nick and Erny Linden. We heard a band called

the "Blue Lake Symphony" from Twin Lake, Michigan. They played some Sousa marches, some classical, and some popular songs. Very well-received by the audience. When I heard them play "Irish Tune from County Derry," I realized it was "Danny Boy." It made me think of Dad singing that song so often in years past, and I can remember him singing it to Danny. Poignant memory. I'm so glad Dad used to go around singing songs like "Irene, Goodnight," "Danny Boy," and "Red River Valley." Now when I hear them, I can remember him by them.

JUNE 21   THURSDAY   LUXEMBOURG CITY

I'm spending some time today searching in the archives at the palace of justice. Thus far I've been able to learn more about Frank Jungblut, whom Susanna Simmerl married after she came to the U.S. This is painstaking work because I have just bits and pieces. Mr. Perrard of the office was patient and helpful; he spoke broken English while I hobbled along in French.

Later on, Frank and I drove out to the American Military Cemetery on the outskirts of the city, where General George Patton is buried. Over 5,000 men are buried there amid pine, oak, beech and larch trees and wild roses and lilacs. Most of the men buried here died in the Battle of the Bulge in 1944–45, fought across northern Luxembourg. Again, as at Verdun, I was struck with the enormity of the situation—thousands of white crosses and stars of David.

Afterwards we drove to a nearby German soldiers' cemetery where 8,000+ soldiers are buried, many of them unknown soldiers. A grim cemetery, especially on a foggy, drizzly day, as it was today. Not like the crisp green grass and white crosses and immaculate grounds of the American Cemetery, yet a somber and appropriate memorial. The soldiers in these two cemeteries a few miles apart no doubt killed one another.

My time in Europe is half over today. Already I'm fantasizing about coming back to live all summer next year. I want to live here and learn the language and culture.

JUNE 22, 1984

My last day in Luxembourg. From here I'll take the train to Paris.

I had a good day at the archives in Arlon, Belgium, just across the border from Luxembourg City. I found a lot of good information on my ancestors, the Linsters: the marriage record of Anna Linster's parents and births of several children, Anna among them. I'm glad that Jean-Claude Muller gave me the tip that Honolingen, Belgium,

was Hondelange, Luxembourg, in the 1800s—technically part of
Belgium, but in the Province of Luxembourg. The people who lived
there considered themselves Luxembourgish, and Anna Linster's
family was of this group.

When we returned to the house here, I had a phone call from
Liliane Stemper-Brickler, who had information on the Simmerls.
She mentioned that the latest newsletter of the Luxembourg Society
of Wisconsin includes a passenger list for the ship *William B.
Travis*, which arrived in New York City from Le Havre on 6 May
1857. Susanna and Peter Simmerl are listed as passengers.

Just this morning Anita Becker had given me a copy of that very
newsletter. It has to be more than coincidence. When it's time for
me to find out these things, they come to me, then and not before.
It's been a feeling I've experienced often—that feeling from the gut
that tells me something is right/wrong, timely/untimely. All I have
to do is trust these gut feelings more and relax into them.

I hope I can live here all next summer. I feel such an affinity for
the country, the land, the people. I also know I can become fluent in
French if I can practice it. Time to close for now, with the hope of
returning here soon.

From Luxembourg City, I took the train to Paris, where I spent the
next two weeks, then flew home. Upon my return from Europe on
July 5, 1984, a letter from my cousin Frank Klein awaited me. Frank
wrote that Nick Linden had had a stroke the day after I had left Feulen
for Paris.

Nick Linden—dead. I knew it, but I didn't want to believe it. I
thought about Erny, his widow, and Nico, his son. Though I didn't
know the Linden family well, I felt close to them. They had been so
kind to me during both of my visits to Luxembourg, treating me not as
a stranger but as a member of the family. I wanted to stay in touch with
Erny and Nico—and to see them again. After all, they were family.

Nick Linden's death took me back to the death of Larry Bunkers, my
father's oldest brother, on May 21, 1984. When I saw Uncle Larry in his
casket, all I could think was how much he looked like my dad lying
in his casket six years before. When Larry's daughter Sandy wrote to
thank me for doing a reading from scripture at her father's funeral
Mass, she noted, "Always nice to see one another, too bad it's usually
funerals." Sandy was right. The days of gathering at Grandma Bunkers'
home in Worthington were, indeed, over.

The sad news of yet another relative's death reached me upon my return to the United States that summer. My elderly cousin, Barbara Graff Jacobs, had died on July 5, 1984, the same day I was flying home from Paris. Barbara, eighty-one, had been suffering from cancer, yet her spirit was indomitable. Like my cousins in Luxembourg, Barbara and her husband, Jim Jacobs, had welcomed me into their home in Granville and shared information about our common ancestry. Had it not been for them, my search for our Youngblut relatives might not have taken wing. The next time I visited my mother in Granville, I stopped at Barbara's grave in the parish cemetery and offered a silent prayer of thanks.

Back in Mankato in mid-July, I felt restless and confined. I needed to be in a place with a larger spirit. So I drove to Madison, Wisconsin, rented an efficiency apartment on Lake Mendota, and spent the rest of July and August 1984 living down the block from the State Historical Society of Wisconsin. When I wasn't reading women's diary manuscripts, I combed the society's historical records for further traces of my ancestors.

Although I had already learned from U.S. census records that Susanna and Barbara Simmerl had to have immigrated to the United States before 1870, I hadn't known the circumstances surrounding their immigration until that second visit to Luxembourg in 1984, when Liliane Stemper-Brickler had called my attention to the current issue of *Lëtzebuerger Sprooch*, the Luxembourg Society of Wisconsin newsletter, which included arrival gleanings from ship manifests.

To my amazement, in that very issue of *Lëtzebuerger Sprooch*— among the Beckers, Welschers, Kellners, and Russlers on board the *William B. Travis* when it docked in New York City on May 6, 1857— were the names "Pierre Simmerl, aged 25," and "Susanna Simmerl, aged 21." I quickly ordered a copy of the manifest for the *William B. Travis*, which had sailed from Le Havre, France, in spring 1857 and arrived in New York City several weeks later. Pierre Simmerl is listed as passenger 132. Susanne Simmerl is listed as passenger 133. A total of 151 passengers (119 adults, 24 children, and 8 infants) are listed as having exited the ship upon its arrival in New York City.

I realized that both Peter and Susanna Simmerl's ages had been mistakenly recorded in the ship's manifest. According to church and civil records in Luxembourg, Peter Simmerl would actually have been thirty and Susanna Simmerl twenty-six in 1857, when they left Luxembourg for the United States. But in those days, it was not unusual for people's dates of birth and ages to vary from one church or civil record to another.

The important thing was that I now had a date: May 6, 1857. Now I knew when Susanna Simmerl and her older brother Peter had arrived in the United States, but I was puzzled not to find Barbara's name on the ship's passenger list. Why not? The names of other children on board were listed under their parents' names.

Maybe I would have to rethink my assumption that Susanna had taken her infant daughter and sailed for America, no doubt to escape the shaming to which she, as an unmarried mother, would have been subjected in her native village. Surely, I reasoned, Susanna must have hoped to find a more hospitable climate in the United States, where, with her child, she could make a fresh start.

I continued to cling to this "heroic mother" theory despite my intuition that certain things just didn't add up. For instance, the 1870 U.S. census records for Liberty Township, Dubuque County, Iowa, contain these listings:

Simmerl, Angela	W	F	64	teacher's widow	b. Lux.
" Peter	W	M	41	painter	b. Lux.

The same census records listed young Barbara as a thirteen-year-old domestic servant in the neighboring household of the Simon Weler family.

When I checked the records for Gilbertville, I found that the 1880 U.S. census for Cedar Township in Black Hawk County, Iowa, lists the occupants of house #521 as follows:

NAME	RELATIONSHIP	AGE	BIRTHPLACE
Youngblud, Frank		57	Luxembourg
Youngblud, Susana	W	48	Luxembourg
" John	S	19	Iowa
" Josephine	D	17	Iowa
" Frank	S	15	Iowa
" Anna	D	12	Iowa
" Mary	D	10	Iowa
" Sophia	D	5	Iowa
" Susana	D	3	Iowa

Susanna Simmerl had come to America with her brother Peter in May 1857. But how and when had her mother, Angela, and her daughter, Barbara, immigrated? Why did census records list young Barbara as a domestic servant on a farm near Luxemburg, Iowa, and not as a child living with her mother, Susanna, on the Youngblut farm near Gilbertville?

Additional Iowa church and civil records for the 1870s and 1880s noted that, on July 20, 1875, nineteen-year-old Barbara Simmerl married twenty-seven-year-old Henry Bunkers at Dyersville, Iowa. Their first child, Henry H. Bunkers, was born on May 14, 1876, in Dyersville, Iowa. Eleven more children (Elizabeth, Catherine, John, Frank, Anton, Joseph, Otto, Clara, Emil, Elnora, and Edmunda) were born to Henry and Barbara (Simmerl) Bunkers between 1877 and 1900. Henry and Barbara Bunkers moved west in the late 1880s to farm near Granville, Iowa. Henry Bunkers died at Granville, Iowa, on February 15, 1924. Barbara Simmerl Bunkers died at the home of her daughter Edmunda Bunkers in Des Moines, Iowa, on February 4, 1943.

I remembered childhood walks through the Granville cemetery with my father, Tony Bunkers. We would stop to pray at the graves of his parents, Frank and Lillian Bunkers. Sometimes Dad would cry when he repeated the story of his father's unexpected death at the age of forty-three. Because as an adolescent Dad had gone to live in the Granville home of his maternal aunt and uncle, Theresa and Vin O'Connor, he knew little about his Bunkers ancestors. But during those cemetery walks he told me what he could.

After stopping at Frank and Lillian Bunkers' graves, Dad and I would walk over to the main Bunkers family plot, where my great-grandfather, Henry Bunkers, was buried next to my great-grandmother, Barbara Simmerl Bunkers. A small gray obelisk stood next to Barbara's grave. Inscribed on it was the name "Angela Simmerl" and the date of death, 1897.

"Who was she?" I asked.

"I don't know," Dad replied.

That was where matters had remained until late July 1978, when I once again stood in the Granville St. Joseph Parish cemetery, this time before my father's freshly dug grave. The next day, I asked the pastor at St. Joseph's if I could look at the parish burial records.

There I found the record of Angela Simmerl's death: "Simmerl, Angela. Died July 15, 1897. Old age. Age 90. Funeral July 17, 1897. Granville, Iowa. Grandmother of Barbara [Simmerl] Bunkers." The name "Simmerl" had been penciled in on the death record, no doubt by the priest who had officiated at Angela Simmerl's funeral.

Now, many years after my father's and my walks through the cemetery, I did know who Angela Simmerl was; and I wondered why she was buried in Granville, Iowa, next to her granddaughter, Barbara, rather than in Gilbertville, Iowa, next to her daughter, Susanna.

That question opened the door for many more questions. Had I been named after my great-great-grandmother Susanna?

"How did you give me my name?" I asked my mother.

"Oh," she smiled, "I liked that song 'Oh, Susannah,' and I named you Suzanne."

So that was how I came to bear the name of my great-great-grandmother, although my parents had not even known it was a "family" name. Intrigued by the mystery I was beginning to unravel, I began to feel that perhaps my name was Suzanne for a reason.

Often, as I listened to music late into the evening, I'd catch myself musing about Susanna's life. I'd wonder how she grew up and who fathered her first child, Barbara. I'd wonder what it must have been like for Susanna to arrive in America, what her life with a new husband and several more children must have been like. I'd wonder who and where my Youngblut cousins were—all of us descendants of Susanna Simmerl, in whose name I would continue my search.

6. Annunciation

Ever since I have known I was going to have a child
I have kept writing things down on these scraps of
paper. There is something I want to say, something
I want to make clear for myself and others. One lives
all one's life in a sort of way, one is alive and that
is about all that there is to say about it. Then
something happens.
—Meridel Le Sueur, "Annunciation," 1940

Meridel Le Sueur has said, "If you go far enough down into the root, you'll come to the root of all." Going down to the root has been Le Sueur's goal for more than seventy years. Born in Iowa in 1900, Le Sueur values her Midwestern heritage, and she writes stories that reflect her belief in what she calls "re-membering"—recovering our lost cultural past by rediscovering and retelling forgotten stories.

By the age of twelve, Meridel Le Sueur knew she wanted to be a writer, but she saw that women were discouraged from writing about such subjects as sexuality and reproductive control. In searching out the works of Midwestern women writers such as Zona Gale, Meridel discovered a cache of information about the hidden lives of women. She began to write. Later, she would remark, "It was the silence of women that first got me to writing."

In 1927, when most Americans were struggling to survive the shock of the postwar years and the collapse of many reform movements, Le Sueur decided to have a child, a decision she saw as a "choice for life" in a deadened world. During her pregnancy, Le Sueur wrote notes to her unborn child, and these notes later became the basis for her story "Annunciation." Meridel Le Sueur gave birth to her first child, Rachel, in 1928.

Scribbling on scraps of paper, the narrator of "Annunciation," who lives in a dilapidated boardinghouse during the Depression, concentrates on the child to come. The narrator sees herself as a pear tree with its ripening fruit. Suddenly, this story of despair becomes a story of hope, as the narrator recognizes that her own strength is rooted in the continuity of the mother line. "Annunciation" was a favorite choice to discuss in my women's writing classes, not only because its author came from the Midwest but also because her themes and stylistics valued women's daily experiences. Now "Annunciation" took on personal significance for me.

When I returned from Europe in early July 1984, I was excited about the possibility of returning to Luxembourg to live there in the summer of 1985. I was thinking of renting an apartment in either Luxembourg City or Niederfeulen. Either way, I could spend my days learning Lëtzebuergesch and putting together more of the pieces of what I'd started calling "the Susanna Puzzle."

After spending the rest of summer 1984 in Madison, I returned to Mankato in early September to take up my teaching duties. That fall, I began a sexual relationship with Bob Corby, whom I'd known for about a year. Bob was several years older than I, and he was a single parent, raising an eight-year-old son. Bob told me that his marriage had been troubled and that, a few years earlier, he had taken his son, left his wife, and begun a new life.

At first, Bob seemed good-natured and easygoing. One of my friends, Helga, was also friends with him. When I asked her about Bob, Helga gave him the thumbs-up. I was impressed when, on my first visit to Bob's house, I noticed his National Organization for Women (NOW) card taped to the kitchen wall above his stove, hanging alongside his large collection of carving knives.

Later on, Bob's mother, Marian, told me that she and her husband had supported Bob financially for the better part of his life. She explained that her son had "troubles." As Bob himself put it, he was "a drunk" who had recently gone through treatment for alcoholism and lost more than a hundred pounds.

Good, I thought, this man understands alcoholism, and he doesn't drink. What more could I ask for? What I didn't yet grasp was that a person could quit drinking but still continue behaving like an alcoholic and that the person's loved ones would continue to exhibit all the characteristics of an alcoholic family system.

Two months after Bob and I began our sexual relationship, I awoke one morning feeling nauseous, with searing pains in my left side. The day after Christmas, I was diagnosed as suffering from an ectopic pregnancy—what most people call a "tubal" pregnancy. A fertilized egg had implanted in one of my Fallopian tubes.

My doctor told me I needed emergency surgery to remove the blocked tube and prevent it from rupturing, which could lead to massive internal bleeding and death. I was admitted to the hospital and had surgery that same day. The next morning, my doctor came to my hospital room to debrief me on the surgery.

"Suzanne, I'm sorry to have to tell you this, but you have three strikes against you," he explained. "You're thirty-five. You have only one tube left. You have severe endometriosis. I did my best to clean it out, but I don't think you're going to be able to have children."

He left me alone so the news could sink in. Still groggy from the general anesthesia, all I could feel was relief that he had made the correct diagnosis in time.

Well, I reasoned, I hadn't been trying to get pregnant, and if I didn't have any children, that wouldn't be so terrible. I made my peace with the idea and concentrated on getting out of the hospital, recovering from the surgery, and returning to full-time teaching.

Six weeks later, when I missed my menstrual period and began feeling a little dizzy, I went back to my doctor's office. The pregnancy test was positive. At first, my doctor feared a second ectopic pregnancy, and he ordered a battery of blood tests, even scheduling a D & C in the event that it was not an ectopic pregnancy but what he called a "blighted ovum." To his and my surprise, it turned out to be a normal pregnancy.

At home alone that night, I stood for a long time in the shower, hot water streaming over me. What am I going to do? This might be my only chance to have a baby. I've got to give it a try.

Bob seemed uneasy. He reminded me that he was forty-three. He hadn't planned to have another child. He was not steadily employed, and he didn't want to leave the little bungalow his parents had bought for him in a neighboring town. Although Bob and I briefly considered marriage, I knew that given his ongoing difficulties, marriage would not be a wise step for me. As winter turned to spring, decisions about the pregnancy were mine to make.

I phoned my family members and told them the news. My sister, Linda, and brother-in-law, Dan, who had just had their first child, Matthew, the year before, were delighted. So were my brother Denny and sister-in-law Barb, whose first child, Kimberly, had been born one month after Matt. And so were my younger brothers, Dale and Dan.

I was more worried about telling my mother. Memories of high school girls who had "gotten in trouble" lingered in my mind, and I wondered how Mom would break the news to friends and other family members that her daughter was pregnant—and unmarried? When I told my mother, however, she was surprised but supportive. I was greatly relieved, but just to play it safe, I decided not to go to Granville to visit her until my baby had arrived. Instead, Mom made several visits to Mankato during my pregnancy. On one visit, she brought the baby crib in which all five of her children had slept. On another visit, she brought my pink-and-yellow-flannel baby blanket.

That spring I was being reviewed for tenure at Mankato State University. Would my being pregnant and unmarried hurt my chances? When I confided in a senior colleague, she gave me a quizzical smile. "You can't be denied tenure for having a baby. This is not the Dark Ages."

In early May 1985, I scheduled an appointment for amniocentesis so I could find out whether the baby was developing normally. In June, I bought a two-story house large enough for myself and the baby, as well as Bob and his son, Billy, in case they decided to move to Mankato and live with us.

That possibility was still up in the air when I packed for a month-long research trip to London, where I would meet Diane D'Amico, my good friend from graduate school days. She'd been writing her doctoral dissertation on Victorian poet Christina Rossetti at the same time I'd been writing mine on American writer Katherine Anne Porter. Diane and I had planned this trip together months before, and I didn't want to give it up. While she studied Rossetti, I would read women's diary manuscripts at the British Library and the Bodleian Library.

JUNE 10, 1985

It's a *girl*—and the amnio test results are O.K. What a relief! I just cried & cried afterwards—felt so tense all during the doctor's phone call and my head and heart were both pounding. It took me about 15 minutes before I could stop crying—then I felt euphoric.

I went out and bought "It's a Girl!" banners to string up in my bedroom, and I'm happy and so relieved to learn that the baby is O.K. and that it's a girl. I have been wanting a girl—even though a part of me felt sad at saying goodbye to the possibility of a boy. Now I plan to start keeping a journal for the baby. I bought one the other day and have a lot to record in it.

I called Bob and told him—he seemed happy, too. He said he wanted a girl. We both like the name "Rachel Susanna"—also like "Melinda" and "Andrea." I'm partial to "Rachel"—it sounds strong and pretty.

I wish Bob and I could have been together tonight to share the news. I still feel mostly alone during this pregnancy, and sometimes

I feel sad that it is this way. Sometimes it seems that we'll never be able to iron out all of the problems so we can be together. Time is going fast and soon I'll be off to London. I hope I'll be able to relax and enjoy the trip—it's nice to think that I'll be taking my little girl along on the trip.

JUNE 22, 1985

I'm at the British Library to get a reader's pass for the manuscript room. I just walked through the "historical documents" area, past the Magna Carta. This library is *huge*—thousands of stacks here of *old, old* books and manuscripts.

I woke up at 3:30 a.m., wondering how I'll explain to the baby about the circumstances surrounding her conception and birth. Maybe things will be more settled when she arrives. Maybe there won't be shame attached to her being born out of wedlock. I want to start a journal for her, to explain some of these things, as I see them.

I sure want her. Now, more than ever, I am determined to go ahead with birthing and raising this child. I've noticed a lot of little thumps and kicks inside my abdomen the past few days—it's nice to feel those tiny reminders that someone is in there! And it's hard to believe it's a new person, already somewhat separate from myself and responding to stimuli. I wonder often what she'll look like. I'm very happy that this baby is a girl!

JUNE 24, 1985

Evening—Diane and I are both writing postcards and spending the evening in our room. I read some of Florence Nightingale's diaries today. The central theme seemed to be a struggle to get and keep religious faith, but with many doubts. I read two tiny diaries (about 4" x 6") and 2 books where she had recorded notes (3" x 5"). She had minuscule handwriting! And she kept rigorous expense accounts. We may go to Oxford this Friday to work at the Bodleian. Diane plans to see a Rossetti relative tomorrow to talk about some of Christina's notebooks.

JUNE 25, 1985

Evening in my room—I'm tired—just read some of Charlotte Brontë's *Villette*. The baby is kicking a lot, and now I can see my abdomen jump a little with each kick. She's fairly quiet whenever I'm walking, but as soon as I sit or lie down, she kicks and begins to roll around in there. I've bought some books on pregnancy and child-birth at feminist bookstores here. I've found three bookstores—

Womanwrite, Silver Moon, and Virago—all of which have good
materials—more books from the U.S. than I'd have expected.

I bought Dale Spender's new book, *For the Record*. I'm supposed
to contact her to meet and talk re my article on women's diaries for
Women's Studies International Forum.

JUNE 28, 1985

I went over Florence Nightingale's diaries again, and now I'm
waiting in the reading room of the Library to get two biographical
works on F.N. She's more interesting to me than are the other
travel diarists I've been turning up because her diaries have some
feelings recorded.

How a person feels about what happens or what one does is
worth recording. Perhaps when a diary is started for the purpose of
being a "travelogue," the writer tends more to keep herself out of it.
I prefer to read one where there's some evidence of the writer's presence. It makes me wonder about my own travel diaries and how different they are from my regular journal. I know I restrict what I put
down in this book. And I have my other journal with me so I can
write what I feel in it.

JUNE 29, 1985

Yesterday I went to Dillon's Bookstore near here and got a copy of
Penelope Leach's *Parent and Child*. When I started reading it, I got
scared of all the responsibility for a small child and everything that
the baby won't be able to do for herself that I'll need to do. Every
book I've read so far talks about depression and exhaustion for 2–3
months after the baby's birth. I cringe when I think of how difficult
this might all be. I want to try not to worry ahead of time. Maybe
I'd be better off not to read these books on childcare right now—
I just can't help [but] imagine all that could go wrong.

The baby is getting more active every day—I feel lots of movement. Sometimes I can tell she's shifting position because the pressure on my bladder will suddenly increase or decrease. I can see my
abdomen jump when she kicks; it's funny to see my skin bounce up,
sometimes on one side, sometimes on the other. Occasionally, the
bounce is right above my navel, which is starting to turn out rather
than in. According to one book, the baby's about 10" long now and
about 1 lb. She's very thin, unable to survive outside the womb for
about another six weeks. She's about 22 weeks old right now, and
it'll be 38–40 weeks when she's due to be born.

When I think of this baby, I start to feel eager to have her and hold her and cuddle her. I think that overall, I'm happy about having a baby—especially a girl. But it is so scary to think about all of the responsibility that comes with a child. And it's scary to realize that I will have to change in certain ways once I become a mother. I'm not sure I'll like having to change.

JULY 1, 1985

Diane and I are enroute to Haworth to see the Brontës' house. Our bus is passing many small towns where houses are of brick and sheep are grazing in nearby meadows. The only jarring note so far has been a huge nuclear reactor (eight silos), which we passed near the exit to Leicester. We stopped for a lunch, then went on to Haworth and toured the Brontë parsonage and museum—fascinating to see where the sisters lived when they wrote their poems and novels. Just outside the parsonage is the cemetery and the church. I wonder what it'd be like to live right next to a cemetery? It was a very dark, dank cemetery with overhanging trees and tombstones covered with moss. Two goats were grazing in the cemetery, keeping the grass cut, evidently.

JULY 9, 1985

It's Sunday, and I'm at an outdoor cafe in the Barbicon Center—an impressive complex of art galleries, shops and museums. Last night Diane and I went to see the play "Waste." It was well done. The star was Daniel Massey, son of Raymond, who played a British politician whose career is ruined when he has an affair, the woman gets pregnant, and she dies from a botched illegal abortion. The play was set in the early 1900s, at a time when a woman had very little control over her destiny. The play, by Granville Barker, was banned when it first came out because it spoke openly of abortion.

JULY 10, 1985

It was worth the time and effort to go to Oxford. That architecture is astounding, and the Bodleian itself, especially the Humfrey Reading Room, is impressive. I remember when I'd just started grad school at Iowa State and was taking a research methods course. The professor talked about what an amazing collection there was at the Bodleian, but the name meant nothing to me then. Now that I've been there, I find it more impressive and much less mysterious and overpowering than it used to seem to me.

Diane found a huge number of Christina Rossetti's letters and family papers at the Bodleian—Diane could definitely use a whole summer to work here—she could do a fine biography to correct the errors and tunnel vision of older biographies on Rossetti.

This morning I awoke at 5:00 and was wide awake, so I got up and saw Diane off at 6:30. I felt sad yet ready to say goodbye to her. We had talked ourselves out during the past three weeks and had little left to say either about our research or our personal lives. It sure has been good to be together. I've missed the close friend-ship we had all those years in Madison, and I've appreciated hav-ing the chance to talk with her and spend some sustained time together. It seems hard to believe that Diane and I might not see each other again for months or even years. I feel almost as if we are sisters—and in a sense we are, having shared that whole grad school experience.

I am ready to go home, have been for the past 3–4 days. On Sat-urday I started to feel the urge to be at home again and to be done with being a tourist-traveler for a while. I think that's a good feeling to have—to know I'm looking forward to going home.

My new home. 317 Carroll Street, Mankato, Minnesota. My family arrived to help me move in on July 27, 1985. A week later, Bob rented out his house and moved himself and his son, Billy, in with me. As the summer months ended, my abdomen pushed further and further out-ward until my navel popped out and my feet disappeared. When fall quarter classes began at MSU, I wearily resumed full-time teaching. One afternoon in mid-October, just after I'd awakened from a nap, I felt a leaking sensation. My water had broken. It was time for labor to begin.

But my muscles were still recovering from the surgery ten months earlier, and not even the excruciating labor pains caused by Pitocin could make my cervix open any wider than three centimeters. After twenty-four hours in labor, on October 17, 1985, I gave birth to Rachel Susanna by cesarean section.

The surgery went smoothly. My doctor pulled Rachel out of me, held her up above the sheets, and announced, "It's a girl."

I saw a flash of red hair atop a fat round face. "Yes, I know. It's Rachel."

The nurse wrapped her up, popped a tiny pink knitted cap onto her head, and put her into my arms. I breathed deeply into the oxygen mask and passed out.

OCTOBER 18, 1985

8 a.m. Just had chicken broth and jello—it tasted great. It's been nearly two days since I've eaten. I got a hypo, which helped the pain in my abdomen some. It sure feels good to lie on my back again.

The nurse brought Rachel in and I nursed her—she's learning to latch on. She's such a round-faced baby—little soft face and skin and fleecy hair. I loved having her in bed with me. I'm ready to sleep after a pain pill. I kept Rachel in bed with me. Happy to have a little daughter! To think she came out of me!

OCTOBER 26, 1985

Rachel and I came home on the 21st. She's doing better after a bout with jaundice. Rachel sleeps a lot and cries very little. She wakes, feeds, has her diaper changed, and often goes back to sleep. When awake, she opens her eyes and looks around, trying to focus on me.

It's such a relief to be home and not on campus every day—just to be able to enjoy Rachel's first days together is a gift. I love her so much! I look forward to holding her and loving her and watching every little movement and gazing at her little face, hands, and feet. It's fun to bathe her and easy to change her diapers. I feel tired but it's a pleasure to get up each day. My incision is healing fast and I'm mobile and not very sore.

Mom's here to help for a week or more—all's going well. She helps with meals and laundry and holds Rachel. Bob seems somewhat dazed by it all. Hard to tell what he feels as he doesn't talk much. Billy wants more attention and I think it's difficult for him to be in the background and to learn to share the spotlight with Rachel. I think this will be a good time for him and me to grow closer. I hope so. I love him more day by day.

OCTOBER 29, 1985

We just learned from Bob's dad, Art, that Bob's mom, Marian, is in the hospital in Arizona, where they have their winter home. They think it's a brain tumor; a biopsy will be done today. Everyone is very upset; Marian has been having migraines and is disoriented now. We'll know more soon.

NOVEMBER 1, 1985

Phoenix—we flew here yesterday morning. Art wanted us all to come, since Marian's tumor is malignant and inoperable. Everyone is in a state of shock.

Bob's been in a flurry, eating huge amounts of taco chips and peanuts—jars and bags just disappear. I try to detach and not ask or say much. The whole Corby family is compulsively busy under stress. People barely cry. Instead, they jump up and get busy with something right away and shut down their emotions. I need to cry, and I will go off by myself and do it.

Meanwhile, daily life must go on. I'm nursing Rachel several times a day. I feel tired—childbirth and news of Marian's tumor are catching up to me. The word from the doctor is that Marian has 4–8 months to live. He says there's no use in radiation therapy.

NOVEMBER 4, 1985

5 a.m. Feeding Rachel and waiting for her to burp. Last night I slept from 11 p.m.–3 a.m. I was tired all day and needed the rest.

Art brought Marian out of their bedroom just when I was nursing Rachel; Marian hadn't been able to sleep. Art went back to bed, but Marian stayed up with me. She told me she was worried about Bob's lack of job, his legal troubles, etc. Marian's fear is that he'll lose everything. She begged me to promise that I wouldn't leave him. Yesterday Art asked if he could talk to me; he wanted me to tell him what to do to fix things for Bob. Art told me he could pull strings to get Bob out of trouble. Art said he'd had to do it many times in the past and was sorry I was caught in the middle. What could I say?

Rachel's doing well—she's lying across my knees on her stomach as I sit here writing. She's been nursing well—every 3 hrs. or so. When she's asleep and I talk to her, she smiles and grins. When she's awake, she looks around solemnly—alert and awake. I am so happy to have this baby. I am loving taking care of her and it feels so good to hold her and kiss her and talk to her. She is a real gift, a treasure.

NOVEMBER 7, 1985

Enroute to Minneapolis—temperature there is in the 40s—quite a change from Phoenix. We woke up early, about 7 a.m. Art drove the van, with all of us in it, to the airport. He and Marian will start driving back to Iowa today. Goodbyes were sad and fast. I hope that there'll be time to rest when we get home. I need to take Rachel back to see the pediatrician and have her bilirubin checked again. I'm looking forward to time to be home with Rachel. Billy will go to see his mom for the weekend.

NOVEMBER 16, 1985

Horrid day at home. Bob was in a foul mood again. Rachel was awake a lot yesterday evening when I was here alone with her (1:00–10:00 p.m.). Then she slept but awoke at 2:00 a.m. and couldn't get back to sleep; she seemed to have a lot of gas problems. I awoke at 3 a.m.—I could hear her crying her lungs out. I went to her room, where she was lying uncovered with a soaking diaper. There sat Bob in the rocker, intent on forcing her to "cry it out."

My heart broke. I couldn't listen to that baby in such distress, so I picked her up and quieted her and changed her. Bob stomped out of the room, slamming the door shut as loudly as he could. Rachel soon fell asleep.

By morning, he would not speak to me. He went to the basement and wouldn't come up. Then, when I was in the bathroom, he took Rachel and left the house, not saying where he was going or when he'd bring her back. I was scared—for myself and for Rachel. My breasts were filling up with milk. I had no idea whether Bob had taken any frozen breast milk along to feed Rachel. Finally after lunch he brought her home, plopped her into the bassinet, and left again.

Now it's 9 p.m. and he's still gone—no idea where he went or when to expect him back. Rachel nursed a lot, then napped with me, and then woke up and nursed some more. Now she's been asleep about 3 hrs. and is due to wake up and nurse again. Then I hope to go to bed.

NOVEMBER 17, 1985

Rachel is one month old today. I just nursed her and she was so beautiful with her eyes shut and a serene face and the fingers of one little hand curled up on my breast. I'm so thankful to have her. I love her so much.

My old neighbors, Be and Hoa Lam, invited me over to bring Rachel to see Thi this week. Their baby son, Thi, was born October 29, so I want to go and see them and take Rachel along.

Bob went on a rampage last night. When he came home about 11 p.m., I asked to talk and he refused to listen. He accused me of taking over everything, of trying to alienate him from Billy and Rachel. On and on he went. I asked him how his alcoholism and eating disorder played a part in all his rage and sullenness. He yelled that he was going to sleep on the couch and shook his fist at me and yelled, "Goddamn you! Goddamn you!" Then he slammed the door, leaving me in Rachel's room rocking her, and he stomped downstairs.

I heard a horrible racket and knew he was in the kitchen. It sounded like he had fallen over something—lots of noise. So I took Rachel and went down the stairs—scared to go and scared not to. I didn't know whether he'd attack me or not—I saw him beating a chair over the kitchen table. Another bent and broken chair was on the floor.

I yelled, "Please stop! Stop!"

He was yelling, then sobbing. He had beaten in the tabletop, bent it all down—put holes in the wallpaper, and the chairs were ruined, holes in the tablecloth. I was terrified. I thought for a moment about trying to call someone, but he was by the phone. I took Rachel and ran from the room and locked us in the bathroom. Then Bob came up and apologized and begged me to open the door. I finally did—he was contrite—promised to get some help. I slowly calmed down and put Rachel to bed. Then I went to sleep in her room—no desire to be near him. When I woke at 4:30, I nursed Rachel again and stayed in her room. Now it's early a.m. She and I are here alone. He got up real early and has been gone a while.

NOVEMBER 19, 1985

Calmer around home—I cared for Rachel all day. Bob was gone all day, I'm not sure where. He seems really sheepish and quiet when he's here. I can't seem to work, just feel exhausted and scared a lot. What to do?

Dad's sister Bernice Feller died on November 17. Her funeral is in Granville tomorrow. I wish I could go, but I can't. I'm not feeling up to the trip. Bernice has had so many strokes and heart attacks and breast cancer. It's a relief for her to be done suffering.

DECEMBER 1, 1985

Sunday at the Corbys'. There's a blizzard and sub-zero temperatures. We've been snowbound here since Thanksgiving. Everyone is trying to act "normally" despite Marian's illness. She's more disoriented and tired; she had a bad headache this morning. Art cried and felt terrible. Later he apologized to me for my entering the family at a time when everything was falling apart. I just hugged him and told him I understood.

DECEMBER 2, 1985

Marian had to be taken to the hospital last night. The snowplows had to bring the ambulance to get her, and they put her onto a wheelchair stretcher. The doctor put her on an IV with medication to sedate her, and by today she was semi-comatose. We went to see her later on and she was awake and able to recognize us all. The doctor told us that it could be a matter of days or possibly weeks. Hard to believe she could fail so fast, and so little—nothing, really—that anyone can do. She's such a sweet woman and has been so good to me.

DECEMBER 5, 1985

Home with Rachel for the weekend. Bob's at his parents' in Iowa. Marian got out of the hospital—latest CT scan shows the tumor is worse. I talked a lot with Billy in the car on our way back home the other day about death and dying. He cried and we held hands. It's hard for the little guy—I wished I could hold him and make things better for him. Rachel's awake and crying—time to go nurse her now.

DECEMBER 19, 1985

Today I realized that I didn't know what the date was! I've been tired lately. I went to an Al-Anon meeting this a.m. and I liked it. It felt good once I got there, and I think I'll go back to that group. I feel comfortable with the women who are in the group, and I feel less anxious when I am there. I know I need to detach from Bob's problems and not see if I can solve them.

I took Rachel for her two-month checkup yesterday. The pediatrician said Rachel is doing fine. She's 12 lbs. 2 oz. and 23" long, at the 80 percentile in size. She got her first shots and cried—poor little thing—I felt so sorry for her. I held her and rocked her and she whimpered a while, then fell asleep.

DECEMBER 21, 1985

Midnight. Rachel and I had an uneventful drive to Granville. She slept the entire way, never crying once. It was a big relief to me—making the drive by myself.

I'm in my old bedroom, with Rachel in bed with me. I nursed her and she fell asleep. She sucks on her pacifier and coos and sighs. I took a nap in the late p.m. while she slept—now I'm very tired and want to go to sleep. I hope she sleeps all night—that'd be so nice. Good to be here—Mom and I are enjoying Rachel, and I'm eager to see all the rest of the family, too. Eventually I'll take Rachel and make the long drive to the Corbys'. It's a relief to be away from that atmosphere for a while. I've got to admit, I needed a break.

JANUARY 14, 1986

Today's my day at home with Rachel. I got her up at 6 a.m. and nursed her, took her downstairs till 8, when she napped till 9. I wrote a letter and read the paper. Then she went into her swing and rocked; later she had more milk. The mail came, then I played with her, changed her diaper twice, fed her more, and now it's 11:30 a.m. The morning has gone by that fast. I had planned to take time to read and critique some students' papers, but so far, no use. It's amazing how time-consuming it is to care for a baby. I love Rachel and love to be with her, yet I get mentally tired sometimes from being "on duty." Now I see what Linda meant when she used to tell me about taking care of Matt full time.

Classes began January 6, and I feel the stress of return to full-time work. I've arranged with Be and Hoa Lam to take care of Rachel during the hours when I need to be on campus. On Tuesdays I get to stay home—ah!

Other days, I teach classes, grade papers, hold office hours, etc. I'm eager for the long weekend to come—no classes from Friday noon till next Wednesday. Maybe I can get caught up.

Now Rachel fell asleep in her infant seat and I'm trying to cook oyster stew and have lunch before she wakes up, but she's already stirring, and maybe if I give her a pacifier, she'll sleep a bit more. Juggling, running, resting. Rachel is such a sweet baby; when she smiles and gurgles and recognizes me, it's such a thrill.

Bob has had a lot of ups and downs. He keeps talking about getting ahold of his eating binges and going on a diet, but nothing happens. Often he's just moody or silent—no job prospects in sight, and he seems depressed about that, too.

JANUARY 28, 1985

At home with Rachel all day. Very sad day. The Challenger space shuttle blew up just after takeoff, and all seven crew members are presumed dead. Crista McAuliffe, the first teacher to go into space, was one of the seven. I feel sick with sorrow. The T.V. is broadcasting reports on the shuttle explosion. No one has any idea what happened. There's no sign of any survivors.

JANUARY 31, 1986

At the Corbys' house. Marian is very bad and isn't expected to live through the weekend. We stopped at the hospital; she was all puffy and ashen, her face sunken, and a rattle in her throat. Bob stayed there with her, and I brought the kids to the house. It's late and everyone but me is asleep. Art just apologized to me for everything going wrong with the family just as I joined it. All I replied was, "Don't worry. I understand." What can a person say? It all feels like a bad dream and it has happened so fast.

FEBRUARY 5, 1986

Marian died. She bled to death from stomach ulcers caused by the medicine to control pain from the tumor. Art got the call just as he was getting dressed to go to the hospital to sec Marian. He collapsed in a chair. I put my arms around him and tried to console him, but how do you console a man whose wife has just died?

Billy awoke and heard us and came to the livingroom. He just wailed. I put him on my lap and held him on the sofa and we both just sobbed and sobbed. I rubbed his little back and stroked his hair. God, how I wanted to make it better, but I couldn't. And I cried for my loss. I loved Marian, and she was good to me, very accepting and loving. Bob and his dad went to make arrangements for a memorial service. I am to give the eulogy.

IN MEMORY OF MARIAN CORBY

I've known Marian for a shorter time than have many of you here today; but, as I have realized, one did not need to know Marian long in order to appreciate her special qualities. Over the past year-and-a-half, she has welcomed me into the family, shared memories of her girlhood and of her and Art's early years together, told anecdotes about the family—in short, become a second mother to me.

One of my cherished memories is of the glow on Marian's face the first time she held Bob's and my baby daughter, Rachel. Marian was delighted with Rachel, just as I know she was with Billy when he was born.

Marian's illness was diagnosed only days after Rachel's birth. Ironically, as Marian was growing weaker and less able to respond to her environment, Rachel's personality was unfolding, and she was awakening to the new and exciting world around her.

During these past few months, Marian held Rachel often—cuddling her, talking to her, making her feel safe, warm, and loved. Marian helped many of us to feel this way. She expected the best in people and, at the same time, loved and accepted individuals for what they were.

Like you, I'm going to miss Marian more than it is possible to imagine or to put into words right now. One of my greatest comforts, however, lies in knowing that a part of her lives on, in the ever-increasing wonder and joy that her grandchildren, her legacy, inspire in us.

In the months following Marian's death, I began to grasp the dimensions of the problems facing our family. Bob's weight seesawed, and he seemed alternately hostile, contrite, and morose. Was it grief, or was it more than that? I loved Bob and wanted to give him the benefit of the doubt, but sometimes his behavior frightened me. I had thought the night when he broke two kitchen chairs over the kitchen table was an isolated incident, until another night, when he stormed into Billy's bedroom, lifted up the huge telescope that his son's grandparents had given him, and smashed it against the ceiling, the desk, the bed.

After each episode, Bob would apologize. He would swear that his eating binges just made him "crazy" and that, once he could get back "on the wagon" and work his 12-Step Program, he would never do anything like that again. For a while, I found his apologies earnest and convincing. But I soon realized that the "good boy" periods were growing shorter while the "bad boy" periods were growing longer.

I would puzzle over empty pizza boxes in the garbage can outside the back door, knowing that we hadn't had pizza the night before. I would stumble across an empty jar of dry-roasted peanuts that rolled out from under the front seat of the car. Where had it come from? I would notice that a six-pack of Coke I'd bought at noon had disappeared by dinnertime. When I'd cook an evening meal and put the leftovers into the refrigerator, they would have disappeared by the next morning.

How much longer could I stay in that situation? I was torn between hoping things would get better and fearing they would get worse. At an Al-Anon meeting, I was encouraged to be patient and try to focus on myself. When I'd read *One Day at a Time in Al-Anon*, I'd come across passages advocating detachment, acceptance, compassion, serenity. Daily readings like this one for February 19 made me think twice about making any drastic changes:

> Once upon a time a Frightened Woman came to Al-Anon with a shocking story. Her husband was violent and often beat her, there was never enough money for food, he tangled with the police, and time after time they were evicted for not paying their rent.

She might never have had the courage to come to Al-Anon if her husband hadn't been away in jail.

After she began to acquire a bit of confidence, she wondered whether it might not be better after all to take radical action. One day she asked her sponsor, "Shall I get a divorce?"

Her sponsor said: "This is a decision only you can make. Other wives might have given up long ago. But are you ready for a complete break? What does your heart tell you?"

Without hesitation, the woman said: "By all right and reason I know I should separate myself permanently from him, but you see, I love him."

She had found her own answer, as all of us must. Who can understand it? Who is wise enough to make a decision for another? Surely none of us in Al-Anon, for we are taught that no situation is really hopeless.

As it turned out, this one was not, either. As she overcame her fear of her husband, self-pity yielded, too. She stopped involving herself in his disasters, and taking part in arguments that used to end in violence. Her husband was compelled to face his own problems, and happily, he learned to face them in AA.

During that period in my life, I had little time to continue my research on my ancestor Susanna's life, but I thought about her often as I watched Rachel learn to sit up, crawl, walk, talk. I knew that Susanna had not been able to watch Barbara learn to do those things. By the time Rachel was a toddler, I realized that, unless I could return to Luxembourg and study additional records there, my search for Susanna would be stymied.

Not long before I got pregnant with Rachel, I had applied for a Fulbright lectureship to teach American literature in Belgium and Luxembourg. But by the time I learned that I had been selected, it was early 1986 and Rachel was only a few months old. When I called the Fulbright office to decline the award, a staff member suggested I apply the next year for a research fellowship. That way, she explained, I could travel to Europe for a shorter period, have a flexible schedule, and take my child, who would by then be a two-year-old, along with me. I talked the idea over with Bob, and in August 1986 I sent in my application.

In early 1987 I was offered a Fulbright senior research fellowship to study the lives of nineteenth-century women in Luxembourg and Belgium. Bob and I agreed that I would take Rachel with me to Europe during the first half of 1988. I suggested to Bob that he and Billy spend

Easter with Rachel and me there. The idea seemed to fly, so I turned
my attention toward preparing for the journey.

During July 1987 I had a chance to spend time in the State Historical Society of Iowa archives in Iowa City, where I studied microfilmed
copies of the *Luxemburger Gazette*, the newspaper that Nicholas
Gonner had published in Dubuque during the late 1800s. I found out
that Susanna's brother Peter Simmerl had died in 1885 at Luxemburg,
Iowa, and that her husband, Frank Youngblut, had died in 1892 at
Gilbertville, Iowa. The more I discovered, the more my emotional at-
tachment to this research project kept growing and the harder I tried to
get inside the psyche of my ancestor Susanna. One evening I took out
my journal and began to write:

> Why am I so concerned with trying to find some evidence—*any*
> evidence—that Barbara lived with Susanna, that Susanna cared
> about her firstborn? I felt so *angry* when I realized that Susanna had
> left Luxembourg only *five* months at most after her daughter's
> birth—angry at Susanna, then sorry for her, then confused at the
> mixture of feelings I was experiencing.
>
> I cried as I tried to convince myself that Barbara and Susanna
> probably never lived together except for the first couple months of
> Barbara's life. How hard it must have been for Susanna to leave her
> daughter and entire life behind in Feulen and go to Iowa. How it
> must have hurt Barbara to grow up and realize she had a mother
> somewhere but couldn't live with her. It infuriates me that Barbara
> had to be a servant in someone else's house at age 13 when her half
> brothers and sisters lived with their parents.
>
> I wanted to scream, How could you do it, Susanna? How could
> you abandon your daughter? How could you go on with your life
> and not have her with you? What lies did you have to tell—to your
> husband, your other children, your friends—to *yourself*? How did
> you ever make peace with yourself?
>
> I don't want to blame or condemn you for what I think must have
> been a wrenching experience and a life of half-truths and guilt. I just
> can't imagine ever leaving my baby behind. I love Rachel so much
> that some nights it's hard for me even to go to bed without her—or
> to go away for a week like this to do my research—to try to find out
> more about you.
>
> I wish I could know what it was like for you, what led you to
> make the decisions you did, how you lived with the effects of those
> decisions. I wish I could know more about Angela and Barbara's re-
> lationship—more about how and when they came to Iowa, more

about how Angela came to be buried in Granville next to where Barbara and Henry Bunkers would eventually be buried.

What was it like between you, Susanna, and your mother, Angela? Did she pressure you to leave home, to take Barbara, to leave her behind? Did she support you when you were pregnant? Did she shame you? Was she silent? Did she silence you?

So many questions, many of them probably unanswerable. But I am going to keep trying to put the pieces together. I'll continue to think, to toss ideas around in my mind, and to talk to other people. Someday I can, I hope, write the rest of the story.

A few days after writing that diary entry, en route back to Mankato from Iowa City, I stopped in Waterloo to meet my Youngblut cousins. Marie Hellman had generously offered to host brunch for me, her sister, Virginia O'Connor, and their cousins Elaine Thoma and Charlotte Witry. While Marie served us coffee and rolls, we exchanged bits of genealogical information. I explained that I was the great-granddaughter of Susanna's first child, Barbara Simmerl. Marie, Virginia, Elaine, and Charlotte explained the lines of descent linking them to Frank and Susanna Youngblut.

As my Youngblut cousins shared information with me, I realized that Frank Youngblut had been born when his mother was forty-six and his father fifty. By the age of eleven, Frank had been orphaned. By 1853, he had come by ship to New Orleans. But how and with whom? No one knew. Frank had worked as a laborer in Louisiana, then come up the Mississippi to Dubuque. With a small group of other young men, he took up farming near the new town of Gilbertville in Black Hawk County, and he was one of the founding members of Immaculate Conception Parish there. He married Susanna Simmerl just six or so months after her arrival in the U.S. in May 1857.

I was grateful to my Youngblut cousins for providing information that would widen my circle of inquiry. I vowed to continue my search in Luxembourg during the months ahead.

Once you have made your decision, never look back. The most tragic thing I see is people who make very painful decisions and get on with their lives, but are always looking back at what they have lost. They fail to look at what they have gained. There are positive sides to any choice, but we can spend the rest of our lives only contemplating what we have lost and never what we have gained.
—Earnie Larson, *Adult Children of Alcoholics*

After I read this passage by Earnie Larson, things seemed clearer. Finally, I could admit to myself that, for more than a year, I'd been contemplating ending my relationship with Bob. But I had not had the courage. Then January 1988 arrived. The director of the Fulbright Commission in Brussels phoned to let me know that everything was set for my arrival later in the month. Bob seemed more hostile and distant as the date of departure drew nearer. Finally, the week before Rachel and I were to leave Mankato, the lid blew off. I called my friends Cheryl and Lydia to help get me and Rachel out of the country safely.

The evening before we were to leave, Helga came over to the house to say good-bye. While she was there, Bob stopped by from his night job to get a tool. I asked him to come home the next morning, say good-bye to Rachel, then respect my wishes that he not be there when Rachel and I left.

"I don't give a shit what you want!" he yelled.

"Please, listen to me," I said.

"I told you, I don't give a shit! Goddamn you!" He rushed out the door.

Helga turned to me. "You don't deserve abuse like that."

Later that evening, after Helga had gone, my friend Lydia phoned. I told her what had happened earlier.

"You are doing the right thing," she reassured me. "You can't go on living with him. You aren't safe here." I nodded.

The next morning, January 24, 1988, in the middle of a Minnesota blizzard, Rachel and I boarded a Sabena flight from Minneapolis to Montreal. I had brought along *Ripening*, a collection of Meridel Le Sueur's writings, to read on the plane.

Once again, I turned to Le Sueur's short story "Annunciation." I knew that its name had come from the Gospel According to Saint Luke:

> *Now in the sixth month the angel Gabriel was sent from God to a town of Galilee called Nazareth to a virgin betrothed to a man named Joseph, of the house of David, and the virgin's name was Mary. And when the angel had come to her, he said, "Hail, full of grace, the Lord is with thee. Blessed art thou among women."*
> *When she had heard him she was troubled at his word, and kept pondering what manner of greeting this might be.*
> *And the angel said to her, "Do not be afraid, Mary, for thou hast found grace with God. Behold, thou shalt conceive in thy womb*

and shalt bring forth a son; and thou shalt call his name Jesus. He
shall be great, and shall be called the Son of the Most High; and
the Lord God will give him the throne of David his father, and he
shall be king over the house of Jacob forever; and of his kingdom
there shall be no end.—The Gospel According to Saint Luke 1,
Holy Bible, Confraternity-Douay Version

My daughter and I were leaving the remnants of our old life behind
and moving closer to our ancestral roots. Now, in the midst of winter,
Le Sueur's words gave me hope. I finished reading "Annunciation,"
then fell into an exhausted sleep as the plane cruised on to Brussels.

7. One Step at a Time

*The first step we take in any new endeavor is often
the most difficult because with that step we begin to
break old habits and form unfamiliar patterns. The
new is always unknown and can be a bit frightening.
As we look back at our emotional ups and downs, at
the pain we've endured in a psychologically abusive
relationship, we may loathe the way we've lived,
but it's a well-traveled path. With this First Step,
admitting that we have no power over the emotional
batterings, we start our journey away from hurt and
toward healing.*
—Kay Porterfield, *Violent Voices*, 1989

Not long before I left the United States for Brussels, the Fulbright
Commission sent me a brochure called a Culturegram. It gave a brief
history of Belgium as well as a glimpse at its contemporary political,
industrial, and social structure. The Culturegram explained that the
work ethic was strong in Belgium, that Belgians tended to be more private than Americans, that family and culture were very important to
Belgians, and that Belgium was a traditionally Roman Catholic country where most people held strong opinions about religion but where
only a minority practiced their faith.

The Culturegram also advised me how to behave politely in a culture not my own. It explained that Belgians always shook hands in
greeting and that I should offer a quick handshake with light pressure,
not a "firm, pumping American handshake." Then the Culturegram
offered this caution:

> As in most of Europe, typical American casualness may be regarded
> in Belgium as rude and a sign of poor breeding. One should never
> talk to another with hands in pockets or with anything (e.g., chew-
> ing gum) in the mouth. It is understood that everyone should ob-
> serve good posture and never put feet on chairs or tables. Moreover,
> pointing with the finger, scratching, yawning, or using a toothpick in

Rachel and Suzanne Bunkers,
February 1988, Brussels.

public is considered rude. Using a handkerchief for any purpose
should be done discreetly.

The Culturegram explained that Belgium, Europe's second most
densely populated country (9.9 million people), had two official languages, French and Flemish, but that only 11 percent of Belgians were
bilingual. A nation since 1830, Belgium had a long history as a culturally and politically divided country where distrust and animosity between the French-speaking Walloons and the Dutch-speaking Flemish
prevailed. Brussels was itself a microcosm of the deep divisions between the Walloon and Flemish factions in the country.

As I would soon discover, I couldn't learn everything about Belgium
from a Culturegram. I had to learn it from my own daily experiences.
On the morning of January 26, 1988, after my first night's sleep in Europe, I awoke to the rumbling of trams on the cobblestone street just
outside our rooms at the Flatotel, one block from the entrance to the
Bois de la Cambre, a large forest within the city of Brussels. Two-year-
old Rachel and I had arrived in Brussels the day before. Our host, Geert
Glas, had met us and driven us to the Flatotel, a few blocks from where
Rachel's child care center was located.

When I pushed Rachel's stroller off the plane and into the Brussels airport, I had spotted a huge sign: WELCOME TO BRUSSELS — THE HEART OF EUROPE. I said, "We did it!" All those months of imagining and hoping and worrying and being afraid—and we did, despite everything, get onto that plane in Minneapolis and off it in Brussels.

JAN. 26, 1988

5:20 p.m. At the Flatotel. Poor little Rachel got really sick & vomited all over herself in the tram on our way back from the Fulbright office. She had told me earlier at a restaurant that she'd been feeling sick and that her tummy hurt. She told me again on the bus, but before I could do anything, she upchucked all over her lavender snowsuit, stroller, mittens and shoes. Somebody handed me a bunch of Kleenex to catch the vomit as it kept coming. She cried, "It's on my mittens—on my shoes, Mommy!" I held her & asked the driver when we'd get to Boulevard de la Cambre. When we did, I got her stroller off the tram and took her into the first pharmacy I saw. The pharmacists sold me acetaminophen suppositories to give her 3 times a day. I got her back to our room and bathed her; now she's asleep but red & feverish. A woman at the pharmacy told me babies get stomach ailments for 3–4 days after traveling, and I think the tram & subway rides made Rachel's case worse. The woman called it "la grippe." I need to call Geert Glas just to ask if he can be on call in case she worsens and I need to get her to a hospital. God, I hope not. Being a lone parent with a sick child is the worst feeling. God, help me!

JAN. 29, 1988

Rachel's feeling much better. She had a medical exam yesterday, and today I registered her at the garderie (childcare center). In French it's called La Garenne [the Rabbit Hutch]. She just went for her first full day from 9 a.m. till 3 p.m.

I've found a large, furnished one-bedroom apartment, just two blocks from the garderie & adjacent to the ULB campus. I got a call from Mrs. Allington in the Fulbright office last night. She had seen a "For Rent" ad and had talked to the landlord, Monsieur Lamy, who called me. He, Rachel, and I went to see the apartment early this a.m. It's on the 2nd floor of a large security-locked building, with heat & cleaning furnished, for 23,400f (about $680 per month)—more than I have ever paid for a place to live in my *whole life*—but because the dollar's so low, it seems expensive. There are few apartments available; this one is large and has dishes, pots and pans, etc. I guess I'll consider it a necessity, not a luxury. I cashed my Fulbright check for 72,500f & gave M. Lamy 20,000f as a guarantee.

JAN. 30, 1988

Monsieur Lamy called me last night to see how Rachel's first day at the Rabbit Hutch went. He told me we can get into our new apartment on Monday. M. Lamy even offered to help us move. He seems so nice. I keep wondering: what's the catch? I need to believe there isn't one, that people can & do help each other out and don't expect something back. I'm eager to move into the apartment, get everything out of suitcases and into drawers, set up my computer, and see if it works. I should check at the computer store across the street to see what adapter I need. I'm still a bit scared but excited as well. There are things to look forward to and enjoy now.

JAN. 31, 1988

Yesterday we went along on the Fulbright scholars' trip to Erasmus' house and a brewery. Rachel had her first full-blown tantrum in the bathroom at Erasmus' house. She screamed, kicked, threw herself on the floor and told me to go away, then cried and yelled some more. Finally, I had to walk out of the bathroom and stand by the door listening. A moment later I went in and held out my arms to her. She crawled over and buried herself in my arms.

Rachel still has jet lag. She has a hard time going to sleep at night. Again last night she jumped, tossed, rolled and talked till after midnight. I was exhausted and short-tempered—just wanted her to sleep so I could sleep. Finally I lay down on the sofa, & she was still sitting up in bed when I closed my eyes. I think it's best for her to be in her own bed, and for me, too. I hope she'll bounce back from all the stresses of travel. Being on my own with her is forcing me to re-examine my approach, to use what works & find new ways to address new problems brought on by the situation.

FEB. 1, 1988

Tomorrow we'll move to our new home at 28 Avenue Huysmans. Monsieur Lamy will come at 9:30 a.m. to help load suitcases. Rachel will go to daycare, and I'll probably spend the day at the apartment unpacking. I hope all goes well. We will take it a day at a time.

I just watched an early Katharine Hepburn film, "Pamela Thistlewaite," on BBC. She played a British suffragist who'd birthed a

daughter "out of wedlock" and tried to pretend her daughter was
her niece whom she was raising for her sister who'd died. Quite a
story, all about woman as "rebel" and her terrible "secret" and the
man who loved her and waited 20 years to marry her. At the end,
the Hepburn character said something to the effect that she hoped
it'd be easier for future generations of women not to have to keep
such secrets.

I started to cry. Rachel was sitting with me, and I just wanted to
hug her and protect her and make sure everything would be okay for
her—because I fear the world hasn't changed that much. Within a
certain social milieu I can be an "unwed mother"—a professor, Fulbright scholar, writer—yet I hope Rachel and I won't be judged
solely by our "illegitimate" status. That word infuriates me, makes
me sick. While watching the movie, I realized not only that I have
always been a single parent but also that I am relieved to be one.

FEB. 2, 1988

Lunch. I'm back at the little "cafe de l'université" on Avenue de
Boendaal where Rachel and I came on Sunday. I just got everything
moved into our apartment. Monsieur Lamy did most of the work for
me. He had his car and moved the books, food, suitcases and trunks
that way. It took us about two hours. Then he drove me to his home
in Boitsford to meet his wife, who gave me a little orange cake for
Rachel. They have a divan there that we can use in the apartment as
a bed for Rachel. When I paid him the rent, he told me to pay 1/2 of
the deposit now & 1/2 next month so I won't run out of money!

FEB. 9, 1988

I'm going to write more in here about daily life. I want some record
of how we have lived. It's 7:45 a.m., still dark out, and cars are going
by on the way to work. Rachel's still asleep but will be waking up
soon. It's hard to tell what time it is when I wake up because it's almost always still dark out. If I go to the kitchen window & look
out, I can see the back windows of other apartments' kitchens
across the courtyard. The whole area is enclosed, like a long triangle
with garages, small yards, and everyone's kitchens and verandas facing one another. So I can see people in kitchens making breakfast,
and clothes hung out to dry, and lots of birds trying to get the bread
crumbs that people have thrown out onto garage roofs. Most apartment buildings are at least eight stories, like ours, many taller, with
two apartments on each story.

There's no front yard. Our building is off the street. Inside the

front door are mailboxes & buzzers to ring up tenants, then a locked
door leading to the elevator. Lights are on timers, so we usually are
in the dark as we go up and down to our apt. Rachel always wants to
push the buttons to make the elevator work.

We get rid of garbage via la poubelle (a little chute out on the
back porch where we put plastic bags with trash). There are also
clotheslines there for drying small items. I use them for airing out
clothes as well.

Now it's 8:00 a.m. and it's light—but gray and windy—probably
rainy, too. I felt cold yesterday when out walking, so I stopped &
bought a wool/angora cap for 100f & a pair of maroon woolen tights
for 100f—I plan to get a second pair of tights—they feel so good
on me. I wear 2–3 layers to keep warm. The wind and rain really
cut through my trenchcoat, even with a liner. Rachel has a long
red winter coat that's good for rainy days, also a hooded sweat-
shirt and raincoat and several mittens, also a lavender snowsuit
if need be.

10:00 a.m. Now I'm in the cafeteria at the Royal Albert Library
for coffee. Then I'll go to the salle des lectures to see if the books I
requested yesterday are there yet. Supposedly this is a very hard library to get into—Jacques Steiwer told me he'd requested a reader's
pass but was refused. So I guess it is a big deal to work here.

The cafeteria looks out over the rooftops of office buildings past
the Sablon and over to the Palais de Justice. Today all is gray and
foggy and rainy, and I can't see much from here, except people working at their desks in glassed-in offices about a block away. Way off in
the distance I see a huge "Coca Cola" sign alternately flashing in
red and gold. It's a fascinating area of the city, and I hope I can get
out & do some walking on warmer days. Now, off to work.

FEB. 11, 1988

At La Baguette d'orée for lunch. First I took Rachel to the garderie,
then I went to the Royal Albert. On the tram this morning, I saw
green grass with the sun shining on it. Signs of spring. Little things
can please, even thrill, me. Finding peanut butter and a cereal variety pack for Rachel at the grocery store made me happy. Understanding what the clerk meant when she charged me "septante
francs" [seventy francs] for two newspapers had the same effect.
And hearing the reference librarian say he could understand my
English but not speak it, and my being able to say "C'est la meme
chose avec mon français" [Same thing with my French] and seeing
him laugh, sharing the joke—that made me happy, too.

FEB. 14, 1988

Rachel and I got up about 8 a.m. She's watching TV and I'm writing here. It's Valentine's Day—I gave her a card I made and two story books. She made me a little necklace out of macaroni at the garderie last week—"Your present, Mommy," she said.

I went to my first European Al-Anon meeting in Waterloo on Friday. I took a bus there and got lost but did find the building. I tried all the locked doors, looking for the meeting. At last, in desperation, I pushed one more door and into the room I fell.

Six women were sitting around a table spread with AA & Al-Anon materials. A lifeline at last. Each of us told our story. A woman named Lois told me that my Higher Power had lifted Rachel and me up out of an abusive situation and brought us safely to Brussels. Another woman named Pamela offered to drive me back to the garderie to get Rachel after the meeting.

FEB. 23, 1988

7 a.m. This is my only time to be by myself to write. Lately I go to bed early and tired out (9 p.m.), then wake up by 6 a.m. and try to come and read some Al-Anon literature and perhaps write a letter or two before Rachel wakes up about 7:30.

One day Georges Lamy came to fix something in our apartment, and he said he wished we'd be his renters for five years, not five months. I told him I was looking into coming back here. He said, "Well, we don't always get everything we want. If we get even a fraction of what we want, we can be happy."

MARCH 2, 1988

My Identity Card came today! So at last I have a Belgian Identity! On the card I'm listed as "celibataire"—or "celibate"—unmarried, as opposed to "divorced" or "single." That term "celibataire" isn't a bad one. I like its implications of being on my own, like the very old meaning of "virgin," I suppose you could say.

MARCH 19, 1988

Today I had a good day. Remember that, Suzy! It does happen. Rachel and I took the tram over to visit Pamela & her three kids. We ate lunch, had a nice visit, and stayed till 3:00 p.m., when Pamela drove us home.

Then we went to get groceries at G.B. On the way, we met a man who was taking his daughter for a walk. He and I started conversing

in French. Then we learned we were both Americans from Minnesota. We laughed and began again in English!

It turns out that the man, Bill Leslie, and his family live very
near us at 57 Square des Latines. He and his wife, Mary Jo Spenser,
just had a baby, Clare, and their older girl, Madeleine, is about
Rachel's age. They came here from Minneapolis, and he's teaching
at the International School here. They've been here two years. I plan
to look them up and hope we can visit so the girls can play.

This was probably my best day here so far. I am so glad to know I
can enjoy the present and feel happiness again.

Remember—if I live a day at a time—every day can be an adven-
ture. Any mood or event of one day need not affect how the next
day goes. These are days I can treasure in my memory, for they are
my special time with my young daughter. Every day it's clearer that
she's no longer a baby; she's becoming a girl. I love to see her grow
and change and have thoughts and ideas of her own.

I like to look back at the diary I kept during our early weeks in Brussels because it helps me remember details of the day-to-day life that
Rachel and I established there. As the weeks passed, I watched Rachel
develop from a toddler into a little girl. She told me she didn't want to
wear a diaper to bed anymore, and she began waking up in the morning
still dry. She kept her clothes in three little dresser drawers, and each
morning she'd choose her own underwear, jogging suit, and socks. She
would eagerly dress herself before joining me in the kitchen for a
breakfast of yogurt and Rice Krispies. After watching her favorite car-
toon show, *D.J. Cat*, we'd gather her favorite blanket, coat, mittens,
and stroller. Then we would take the elevator down to the ground floor
of our apartment building.

Once out the front door, Rachel would climb into the stroller, and I
would push her the three blocks to the garderie on the university campus. Her best friends, Savitri and Chloe, would be at the window,
awaiting her arrival. The three little girls would dash off to the toy
area, chattering in a mélange of French and English, while I haltingly
conversed in French with Rachel's teachers, Linda, Marcelle, and Ghislaine. They'd ask me how Rachel slept the night before, what she had
for breakfast, whether she would need a long or short nap, and what
time I'd be back to get her later in the day. Then, after smiles, handshakes, and "à bientots" all around, I would kiss Rachel good-bye and
take the tram to the Royal Albert I National Library in the city center.

When I arrived, I would collect the books I'd requested the day before and go to my assigned seat, Number 29, in the reading room of the library. There, under a large sign proclaiming SILENCE! I would work for several hours, translating information on nineteenth-century European life from French to English and copying it onto 5" x 7" notecards. Sometimes I'd watch the other scholars working around me. There was the grizzled elderly man in Number 18, who was always already at work by the time I arrived. When he shuffled across the room to the shelves, he had to hold on to other readers' chairs along the way. Over croissants and espresso in the fifth-floor cafeteria, I would speculate with two other American Fulbrighters, Elizabeth Panzer and Liza Temnikow, whether Number 18 would be back the next day, but he always was.

Then there was the scraggly-haired fortyish scholar in Number 14. He wore the same clothes (dark green corduroy pants, navy blue shirt, gray cardigan) every day. He always sat by himself at his table, mumbling in a language I didn't understand. After a few days of walking past him en route to the rest room, I didn't need to wonder why he sat alone.

I would work in the Royal Albert reading room for several hours, take a lunch break at a cafe on the Grand Place, return to the library to order the next day's books, then take Bus 71 back to the garderie for Rachel. If the weather was good, she and her friends would be busy scooping and shoveling sand on the playground. Marcelle, Linda, or Ghislaine would fill me in on how Rachel's day had gone. Then I'd get the umbrella stroller for our walk back to Avenue Huysmans, where we'd stop at the vegetable and meat markets before winding up at our apartment building.

Our landlord, Monsieur Lamy, became a regular visitor to Rachel, his "little rabbit." He would bring her "Kinder Treats," small, hollow chocolate eggs with miniature toys inside. He would also baby-sit Rachel so I could take a leisurely walk to the G.B. supermarket for our weekly groceries. When the American-made stroller I'd brought to Brussels broke a wheel on the cobblestone streets, M. Lamy arrived with a present for Rachel: a Belgian stroller that had been used by his grandchildren years before.

Monsieur Lamy soon became my friend, too. He explained that Brussels was divided into a number of communes or districts, and he was the one who took me to the Ixelles commune office to apply for my Belgian identity card—the prerequisite for opening a checking account and getting telephone service started. Monsieur Lamy told me about his visits to the United States and his family's survival strategies during the Nazi occupation of Belgium during World War II.

He also advised me on how to get along in Brussels. First, speak English, never French, when in a Flemish-speaking part of the city; speak French, never English, when in a French-speaking part of the city. Every street had a French as well as a Flemish name, so it was important to carry a city map at all times. The first time I'd tried to find the Fulbright office on Avenue de la Toison d'Or, I couldn't find that street. But, when I checked for it again under its Flemish name, Gulden Vlieslaan, there it was. When I traveled to different sections of Brussels, I would listen carefully and scrutinize signs in stores and restaurants to find out if I was in a French or Flemish part of the city. Then, since I knew no Flemish, I would speak either French or English, as the situation called for.

Each weekday, when I took the tram to the city center, I'd get off at the stop next to the Musée des Beaux Arts, the national museum of painting and sculpture. I had heard of it many years before when I studied a W. H. Auden poem by that same name. I knew that the Brueghel painting that had inspired Auden's poem was inside the museum, and I stopped by to look at *Landscape with the Fall of Icarus*. I was surprised to find that it wasn't a huge canvas, maybe three by four feet at most. It was kept behind glass, on a wall all by itself. I liked to study its details—the blue-green seawater, the ship's billowing sails, the shepherd and his flock, the plowman and his horse, the port city nestled among the white cliffs. The tiny legs and feet of Icarus were sticking out of the water, barely visible in the lower right-hand corner of the painting. Had anyone noticed the falling boy with waxen wings?

I knew that Belgium had once been a powerful force in the Belgian Congo. But my understanding of its history had been limited to what I'd read in books and seen in *The Nun's Story*. I remembered Audrey Hepburn's character, Sister Luke, a sister of Notre Dame de Namur, sent on a mission to the Belgian Congo to "save the souls of the natives." I could recall only a few scenes—one in which Sister Luke was working with African assistants at the mission hospital and a second in which another nun was murdered there. In the movie's final scene, Sister Luke, whose Mother Superior had ordered her back to Belgium, took off her habit and walked out the door of the convent, never to return. I must have been about ten years old when I saw *The Nun's Story*. I was still planning to become Sister Veronica someday, but seeing the movie had made me reconsider my aspirations.

Now, living in Brussels twenty-five years later, I wanted to view the culture as an insider would. I bought Rachel a red tricycle to ride up and down our block. I began taking her for Sunday walks in the Bois de la Cambre near our apartment. There, we blended in with hundreds of Belgians out for their Sunday stolls. We bought lemon-flavored ice cream from the Italian vendor whose cart played French and Flemish children's songs. We took the little ferry across the lake to the Chalet Robinson, where Rachel ate cookies while I ordered espresso.

One Sunday afternoon, my American friend Pamela and her three children took Rachel and me walking in the vast park in Tervuren at the southern edge of Brussels. There, we toured the Museum of Central Africa. We viewed huge stuffed carcasses of African animals, along with everyday household items from Belgium's former "colony," the Congo, now the independent African state of Zaire. Clearly, the museum emphasized a northern European perspective; even the valise of Stanley was there, next to photographs of him with Livingstone. I stopped at the forty-foot alabaster statue of a stately woman in flowing robes, her outstretched hand atop the head of a kneeling African boy. Its title read, *Belgium Bringing Civilization to Africa.* Here it was— glorious to some, shameful to others—the past that Belgium had tried to leave behind.

Another Sunday, Rachel and I joined our Fulbrighter friends, Elizabeth and Mike Panzer, for a train ride to the Belgian town of Ypres ("Ieper" in Flemish), about seventy miles west of Brussels. We planned to take part in the Festival of Cats, held biannually.

The old city square of Ypres was magnificent, featuring an immense guild hall and cobblestone streets. Most of Ypres had been destroyed in World War I. Huge military cemeteries contain the remains of the thousands of soldiers who lost their lives in the fierce battles between British and German forces that raged in and around the city. Today, the city center has been painstakingly restored to look as it did centuries ago, when the Festival of Cats first began.

The festival had its origins in medieval times when cloth was stored in the Great Cloth Guild Hall in the city square. Legend has it that thousands of mice began feeding on the cloth, and hundreds of cats were imported to get rid of the mice. Then the problem became how to get rid of the cats. Thus the Festival of Cats, which used to culminate with live cats being tossed off the guild hall's rooftop. Today, however, only stuffed velveteen cats are tossed to the tourists waiting below. A magnificent parade through the city streets, with all of the participants dressed as cats, concludes the day's festivities.

When our train arrived in Ypres, a special feature of the Festival of Cats was just about to take place: "The Trial of the Witches." Townspeople played the roles of witches in cages, with friars walking around them reading from the Bible and guards poking at them with spears.

Rachel was awestruck. She and I went up closer to look at one witch, who stuck out her tongue at us. Rachel blew her a kiss in return, and the witch had to smile down at us from her cage twenty feet in the air. Rachel blew her a second kiss. The witch laughed and waved to Rachel.

I found it chilling. Was this what the witch-hunts and the *Malleus Maleficarum* had been about? Later, though, I had to smile. Rachel and I stopped inside the guild hall for something to drink. There sat a jovial group of witches, friars, and guards on lunch break, eating sandwiches and drinking beers around a long oaken table.

That night, back home in our apartment in Brussels, Rachel and I made up stories about the day's events. The witches continued to fascinate her, and she wanted to hear more about them. She wanted them to be her friends. So did I, and we fell asleep telling stories about the "good witch" who had smiled down from her cage.

Question VI:
Concerning Witches who copulate with Devils.
Why it is that Women are chiefly addicted to Evil Superstitions.

Therefore let us now chiefly consider women; and first, why this kind of perfidy is found more in so fragile a sex than in men. And our inquiry will first be general, as to the general conditions of women; secondly, particular, as to which sort of women are found to be given to superstition and witchcraft; and thirdly, specifically with regard to midwives, who surpass all others in wickedness. . . .

As for the first question, why a greater number of witches is found in the fragile feminine sex than among men; it is indeed a fact that it were idle to contradict, since it is accredited by actual experience, apart from the verbal testimony of credible witnesses. And without in any way detracting from a sex in which God has always taken great glory that His might should be spread abroad, let us say that various men have assigned various reasons for this fact, which nevertheless agree in principle. Wherefore it is good, for the admonition of women, to speak of this matter; and it has often been proved by experience that they are eager to hear of it, so long as it is set forth with discretion.

For some learned men propound this reason; that there are three things in nature, the Tongue, an Ecclesiastic, and a Woman, which know no moderation in goodness or vice; and when they exceed the bounds of their condition they reach the greatest heights and

the lowest depths of goodness and vice. When they are governed by
a good spirit, they are most excellent in virtue; but when they are
governed by an evil spirit, they indulge the worst possible vices.
—Heinrich Kramer and James Sprenger, *Malleus Maleficarum,*
circa 1486

A few weeks after the Festival of Cats, at the invitation of our new
Belgian friend, Abbé Jean Ducat, Rachel and I took the train from Brussels to the town of Arlon in the Province of Luxembourg, on the border
between Belgium and Luxembourg. Abbé Ducat, who had heard about
my research, had offered to help me locate records on my Linster and
Claus ancestors who had emigrated from Hondelange, Belgium, a few
kilometers away. He had arranged for Rachel and me to stay in the
home of Rogér and Colette Pierret of nearby Wolkrange, Belgium. Our
train arrived in Arlon on time, and Abbé Ducat, waving a tiny American flag, met us and took us to the Pierrets' for a five-course dinner and
a tour of their backyard, where they raised chickens and rabbits. The
Pierrets also introduced us to Moustique, their gentle black cat, who
took a shine to Rachel.

Then, while Colette and Rachel played with Moustique, Rogér
Pierret and Abbé Ducat drove me to Messancy, where Monsieur Ca-
mille Gillet, the records clerk, welcomed me with "Bonjour, ma cou-
sine!" Monsieur Gillet had all of the records on the Linsters and the
Clauses ready for me to copy. He, too, was descended from the Claus
family, and he gave me a map of Hondelange with the old Claus house
circled in red. That evening, the Pierrets drove Rachel and me to Hondelange to see our ancestral Claus house. Then we drove to the village
cemetery. Amid the dandelions and lavender wildflowers, we stood
near an old tombstone bearing the name of Catherine Claus, one of my
great-great-great-grandmothers.

Although Rachel and I were living in Belgium, Luxembourg played a
central role in our lives during those months in Europe. In late February 1988, a month after we arrived in Brussels, our cousin Jacques Steiwer took us along to Luxembourg for a weekend at his parents' home
in Feulen. En route, Jacques told me that he'd heard our cousin Erny
Linden was in the Ettelbruck hospital recovering from a mastectomy.
When Rachel and I visited Erny there, we found her weak but in good
spirits, determined to survive the cancer and ready to begin chemo-
therapy. I promised Erny that Rachel and I would return to see her in
the spring.

In late March, my mother, Verna Bunkers, and our cousins Dick and

Ann Klein arrived from the U.S. for a three-week visit. We took the train from Brussels to Luxembourg City, where we rented a car and headed north to Feulen. Together, my mother, my daughter, and I walked the streets of our native village and visited our cousins, the Lindens and the Steiwers. On Easter Sunday morning, we attended Mass in the church where Angela, Susanna, and Barbara had worshiped more than 125 years before. We wove our way through the crowded graveyard, where many generations of our ancestors had been buried. We drove over to nearby Tadler to pray at the violet-covered grave of my mother's great-grandfather Michel Klein.

Later in the week, I had lunch with Jean-Claude Muller and Jean Ensch, scholars who specialized in Luxembourg immigration history. I asked them how I could learn more about the daily lives of nineteenth-century Luxembourg women, and they suggested that I examine census and notary records at the state archives. The 1855 census listed Susanna Simmerl as unmarried and living with her mother, Angela, in Oberfeulen. By the 1858 census, Susanna was no longer listed as living in Oberfeulen, but two-year-old Barbara Simmerl was listed as a member of Angela Simmerl's household. The 1864 census for Angela Simmerl's household listed three minor children named Anna, Catherine, and Barbara. These records confirmed what I had long suspected: when Susanna went to America in spring 1857, a few months after Barbara's birth, she'd left her daughter with Angela Simmerl in Feulen.

Next, I turned to a dusty packet tied with twine—notary records for Feulen during the 1860s. Midway through the thick stack, I came across a packet of brittle legal papers written in French and dated March 29, 1866. The name "Simmerl" was scrawled across the top of the first page. Here I found legal authorization for the sale of Angela Simmerl's house, garden, and belongings. Her family members were listed in the document: they included two daughters named Susanna—Susanna the elder ("l'ainée"), who had immigrated to the United States and married Frank Youngblut—and Susanna the younger ("la cadette"), who had remained in Luxembourg and married Louis Philbert Chenet, a blacksmith. The document also listed François Dupont as guardian for the legal interests of Angela Simmerl's two minor daughters, Anna and Catherine Simmerl. Barbara Simmerl, aged ten, was listed as living with her grandmother Angela in Oberfeulen. The notary records revealed that Susanna's older brother Peter Simmerl had traveled from Iowa back to Luxembourg to bring his family members to America.

Tucked inside this document were legal papers handwritten in English, labeled "Black Hawk County, Iowa, Clerk of Court" and dated

December 18, 1865. These papers stated that Susanna Simmerl Young-blut had given her brother Peter Simmerl power of attorney to sell any property or belongings she still had in Oberfeulen. Both sets of papers bore the signatures of Susanna, Angela, Peter, and Barbara Simmerl.

Together, these legal papers completed an important piece of the puzzle: Barbara had remained with her grandmother Angela Simmerl, when her mother, Susanna Simmerl, had left Luxembourg for America in 1857. During the next years, as the unfolding American Civil War discouraged immigration, Susanna had remained in the United States and her mother and daughter in Luxembourg. Finally, in 1866, the three were reunited when Angela and Barbara came to America. But Barbara did not go to live with her mother, Susanna, on the Youngblut farm near Gilbertville. Instead, she remained with her grandmother Angela, and the two joined the household of Peter Simmerl, a teacher in Luxemburg, Iowa.

Powerful emotions took hold of me as my theory of the heroic mother collapsed, replaced by my new theory of the deserting mother. Rocking Rachel to sleep in our Brussels apartment one night, I raged at Susanna: "How could you have left your baby behind in Luxembourg? What kind of a mother were you?" These questions continued to haunt me.

By early June 1988, it was time to plan Rachel's and my return to the United States. I had not heard from Bob during the months in Brussels, but friends from Mankato wrote that Bob had moved out of my home. When they went inside, they saw that Bob had removed my furniture and taken down all my curtains, photographs, and paintings. They'd been piled up in the basement and the attic. Bob had dismantled my bed and had wedged the mattress, box springs, and antique frame tightly up the attic stairs. He had stuffed presents I had given him into my underwear drawers. My friend Lydia discovered that my car was missing from the garage. Later she told me she had located the car and returned it to the garage. Other friends put the furnishings back into place as best they could.

Although the hostility underlying Bob's actions alarmed me, it didn't surprise me. My weekly Al-Anon meetings in Waterloo had helped me gain distance from and perspective on the problems I'd left behind in Mankato. My friends Lois, Pamela, and Clara explained that my Higher Power was looking out for me, that there was a good reason for what was happening in my life. They assured me that I could let myself feel the relief and imagine Rachel's and my return to our home, a safe place, a haven for us, friends, and family. I needed to envision

Rachel and myself happy together there. I needed to believe that there was a reason, a larger purpose, for all that had happened.

The months in Brussels had been good ones. We had enjoyed our spacious apartment, and Rachel had loved the garderie. I'd learned the ins and outs of getting around the city and the country. My research had gone very well. We'd made many good friends—Lois, Pamela, Clara from Al-Anon; Mike and Elizabeth Panzer, Liza Temnikow, and other Fulbrighters; Abbé Ducat, Rogér, Colette, Martine, and Françoise Pierret; Monsieur and Madame Lamy.

One spring morning, just after I'd dropped Rachel off at the garderie, I walked down Avenue Jeanne to catch my tram. Brilliant pink cherry blossoms filled the trees lining the avenue. I nodded "Bonjour" to the frail old woman who was scrubbing the floor of Ipsomat, the laundromat that I frequented down the street from our apartment. I even managed to joke in French with the shopkeeper at the boucherie where I stopped daily for sausage or mussels. When Marcelle, Rachel's caregiver at the garderie, asked me, "Comment ça va, Suzanne?" I could honestly answer, "Ça va bien, très bien."

Not long after arriving in Brussels in January 1988, I got a letter from my friend Becky Hogan, who lived in Whitewater, Wisconsin, and who, like me, was an avid reader of women's diaries. Becky and I were planning a panel discussion on women's personal narratives for the 1988 National Women's Studies Association Conference in Minneapolis in late June, after my return to the U.S. Becky, concerned about how I was adjusting to daily life in a foreign country with a small child, suggested that she and I exchange what she called "diary/letters." I would tell her about my daily life, and she would tell me about hers. At the same time, we would discuss the process of writing. In one diary/letter, Becky wrote about the process of letter-writing, then closed with this reflection:

> Would we write differently to one another, trying to cover more detail and so forth, if we didn't know we were going to be able to talk face to face soon? Maybe not. I suppose once one sits down to write one gets wrapped up in the process and tells as much as one has energy and time for. . . . Do you think it's true that we expect someone we write a letter to to "conform" to a fictionalized mode we've created for him or her? (4/20/1988)

I mulled over Becky's observations for some time before sending her my reply:

> Yes, I do imagine someone to whom I write a letter. I imagine
> her/him receiving it, opening it, reading it, replying to it. . . . I think
> it's a fact of life and of communication that one fictionalizes one's
> audience. The same is true of conversations by phone—don't we
> envision the other person as she/he talks and listens?

Then I speculated about how my research on Susanna Simmerl was
causing me not only to imagine her life but also to consider how my
experiences influenced my perspective on hers:

> My research now is a good exercise in a form of self-reflexivity.
> I'm researching this ancestor's (Susanna's) life, wondering about her
> going to the U.S. for what seems to have been an arranged marriage,
> about her leaving her four-month-old baby, Barbara, in Luxembourg
> with her mother (Angela—Barbara's grandmother). They were all re-
> united in Iowa in 1866. So I'm wondering about all of those dynamics
> of mother and daughter separated, their relationship disrupted (I
> think). And here I am with Rachel, and worried about her and my
> relationship being disrupted, about being separated from her, when
> we return to the U.S. in June. How do my circumstances shape my
> perceptions of my "subject's" experiences? How do my own feelings
> affect how I go about my research, how I interpret my findings?
> (5/11/1988)

Two days later Becky wrote back:

> I think that although ideas, structures, form, etc., are important
> factors in a piece of writing, *who* wrote it always matters more than
> anything else. And when we read, we sometimes seek for the com-
> fort of voices that are close to our own and speak our own language,
> while sometimes we want to hear voices so far from our own as to
> almost be speaking a foreign tongue. (5/13/1988)

In my last diary/letter to Becky, I addressed her comments about the
question of "voice" in our correspondence and in my current work:

> I wonder about the "voices" we use in these letters/diaries to one
> another. I know that my mood for the day, plus where I am (liter-
> ally) when writing affect what and how I write as well as where and
> how I imagine you reading the letter—at your home or at the Insti-
> tute, etc.; where I am when I read what you write (often I've been on
> the bus enroute to the Royal Albert for the first reading).

I think about what you and I have/have not written to each other—that we have been talking about the personal and at the same time weaving it into our work, our thoughts on forms of autobiography, for instance, on audience, voice. We write with preconceptions of who the other is, of who the self is—and of how many sheets of paper will fit into an airmail envelope! Or of how many "installments" will suffice for one letter . . .

Then I reflected upon the months I had just spent in Europe:

It is sad to leave here. I have created a small life for myself and for my daughter—with some budding friendships, some links to the women's studies community, to academia, and have really liked seeing the sights of Europe. So I am facing dealing with that sadness of letting go and the uncertainty of going home to a very different "home" than I left. . . . À bientot! (6/9/1988)

It was time to go. I had stuffed everything I could into our suitcases and trunks. Pamela and Lois had given a bon voyage party for Rachel and me. All of our Fulbrighter friends had met one last time for a farewell reception. I had attended my final Al-Anon meeting in Waterloo.

Rachel's last day at the garderie arrived. That morning, she rode her red tricycle down the sidewalk. When I had explained that we wouldn't be able to take it along on the plane, she decided to leave it at the garderie with Savitri and Chloe. When I arrived at the garderie to pick Rachel up that afternoon, her caregiver Linda handed me a painting with all of Rachel's playmates' handprints and names on it. Ghislaine gladly accepted the dozen pairs of Rachel's white cotton training pants I was donating to the garderie. Then Marcelle, tears in her eyes, carried Rachel over to me and gave me a hug. We all started to cry. These women had taken such good care of Rachel. They'd kept her safe and happy at the Rabbit Hutch while I did my research. I could ask for no better gift than that.

The next day, in flight back to the United States, I wrote a final diary entry about our time in Europe:

In the air, just left Brussels about noon. Feeling excited more than anxious, to go back to the U.S. I've been sad in the past few days and cried when I've needed to. Today I don't feel much like crying. I am eager to touch down in the U.S., see friends, and rest.

I cried yesterday when Georges Lamy took us over to Pamela's and we left Avenue Huysmans for the last time. He had tears in his eyes, too, when we both said we hoped to meet again some day.

At my last Al-Anon meeting, Lois gave me her copy of Anne
Morrow Lindbergh's *Gift from the Sea* and told me it was one of her
favorite books. I'm going to read it on the plane. It was sad to say
goodbye, but I was starting to feel excitement—it's not all anxiety.

Higher Power, let me feel the excitement and let me enjoy the
coming week. Let me not only feel the fear and anxiety over Rachel
and negotiations with her father about her future. Remember—his
problems are his. I've done nothing wrong, and I need not feel guilty
or believe I have to give in to him. I need to do what's right for me
and what I feel is best for Rachel.

En route to the United States, I read *Gift from the Sea*. Anne Morrow Lindbergh's words resonated with my reflections on the past
months in Europe and the research I had done there:

> For it is only framed in space that beauty blooms. Only in space
> are events and objects and people unique and significant—and there-
> fore beautiful. A tree has significance if one sees it against the empty
> face of sky. A note in music gains significance from the silences on
> either side. A candle flowers in the space of night. Even small and ca-
> sual things take on significance if they are washed in space, like a
> few autumn grasses in one corner of an Oriental painting, the rest of
> the page bare.

The small and casual things, the notes and the silences, from my
months in Europe would remain with me in my diary, letters, and
memory. Now I could accept that I would never learn everything about
Susanna's birth, childhood, and adolescence in Luxembourg. Yet I
could piece together enough to help me appreciate the circumstances
in which she had given birth to her first child, Barbara. And I could
study Susanna's life not as typical of every woman's life but as one
woman's life.

Now I understood that, for a girl growing up in nineteenth-century
Luxembourg, educational opportunities were minimal. Most children's
education consisted of time spent in a small village school memoriz-
ing prayers, catechism questions and answers, and Bible verses. By the
age of eleven or twelve, most children were needed to work in the
fields and at home. Except for those who studied to be priests or nuns,
few Luxembourgish children had opportunities for further education.
Because her father, Theodore Simmerl, had been a teacher as well as a
day laborer in Feulen, Susanna and her siblings might have had more
learning opportunities than many children. Signatures on legal papers

indicate that Susanna could write her name and that she could read some French. But whether she learned to read and write English once she had immigrated to the United States, who could say?

I also understood that in nineteenth-century Western European countries, it was not unusual for a young woman to become pregnant, then marry her child's father before its birth. Yet giving birth to a child out of wedlock would have been a shameful thing. It seemed very likely that the impetus for Susanna's emigration had been the birth of her daughter, Barbara, her *filia naturalis*.

Who had been the biological father of Susanna's first child? In one conversation, Jean Ensch and Jean-Claude Muller had suggested that I study Feulen census records to see if any single men had been living in houses near the Simmerl house about 1855. After all, one of them might have fathered Susanna's first child. But, we agreed, that would have been a search for the proverbial "needle in the haystack." Even if such a search did turn up some names, I would have no way of knowing whether a certain man had impregnated Susanna in March 1856. I decided not to expend my energy in that direction.

Instead, I decided to focus on Susanna's life after her immigration to America. How and when, I wondered, had Susanna told her husband, Frank Youngblut, of Barbara's existence? Because Susanna's marriage to Frank had occurred within months of her arrival in the United States, I suspected that it had been an arranged marriage. U.S. census records for 1860 indicated that Frank and Susanna Youngblut were living with their infant son, Frank Jr., on a farm near Gilbertville. Later census records, however, contained no mention of this child, who apparently died as a toddler. Youngblut family records added further context: Frank Jr., was his parents' second son. Their first child, George, born in 1858 or 1859, had apparently died shortly after birth; unlike Frank Jr., George Youngblut was not listed in the 1860 census records as a member of the household.

I wondered how Susanna must have felt in the early 1860s, knowing she'd left her first child, Barbara, with her mother in Luxembourg, and that her second and third children, George and Frank Jr., had both died as babies? How might these circumstances have fed Susanna's desire to help her brother Peter Simmerl bring Angela and Barbara to America?

If only I could travel back in time and talk with Susanna for just one day, for just one hour. More than ever, I wanted to talk with my Youngblut cousins in Iowa. Might they have any letters, photographs, or family documents that could shed light on Susanna's life as wife and mother? I hoped the answer would be yes.

8. Divide the Living Child in Two

The king therefore said: Bring me a sword.
And when they had brought a sword before the king:
Divide, said he, the living child in two,
and give half to the one, and half to the other.
—3 Kings, 3:24–25, *Holy Bible*, Confraternity-Douay Version

When Rachel and I had left Mankato for Brussels in January 1988, I knew that my relationship with her father was over. I felt relieved. During the months in Europe, I'd gained a clearer perspective on the situation I'd left behind. When my daughter and I returned to the United States in late June 1988, I discovered I needed to draw on the strength I'd built up as well as on the support of others on both sides of the Atlantic. Phone calls and visits from family and friends helped me adjust to the realities of my life in Mankato. Letters from cousins in Luxembourg as well as new friends in Brussels helped me reflect upon what I'd learned during the months Rachel and I had lived in Europe.

My cousin Erny Linden sent periodic reports on life in Luxembourg and on her and Nico's travels. Every postcard and letter contained another warm invitation to visit her family again:

December 18th, 1989

Dear Suzanne,
It's winter here, but we have no snow, only a lot of rain. I'd prefer "a white Christmas." You and Rachel sound well, with the cats and your daily work at the University. I'm well and so is Nico.

So you'd like to return to Luxembourg. But why not? You are always welcome and I also have a bed for you and Rachel.

Good health to you two, your mother and all your family.
Season's Greetings for 1989,

Erny and Nico

My friends from Brussels also wrote to me often. My fellow American Pamela and I wrote weekly letters in which we kept one another
up to date on our attempts to begin new lives. She was hoping that a
Belgian court would grant her a divorce so she and her three children
could return to the United States to live. Pamela and I shared an interest in holistic healing, and, after I'd written to her about some work I'd
been doing with Faye, my spiritual guide, she replied:

> When I read about your experiences with your healer, I wasn't
> surprised about your foremothers' presence. It's good to know that
> their separation is not your separation—there are certainly other
> possibilities open to you and to Rachel that were not open to
> Susanna. [9/29/88]

My Belgian friend Clara, who had taken me to weekly Adult Children of Alcoholics meetings in Brussels, sent me letters as well. Clara
and her partner, André, had been together for many years, during
which time he fought an ongoing battle against alcoholism. Clara
wrote to me about her struggle to work her own program and distance
herself from the potential effects of André's disease:

> I cannot let go no matter how hard I try. I always fall in the trap.
> Maybe this is where my limit of the alcoholic relationship lies. Only
> by growing the love and respect for myself can I solve this what I
> feel as a dilemma right now—and of course patience. I came across
> a couple of very good tapes on growing the love for the self and
> changing the thinking patterns from our usual negative ones
> through positive affirmations to positive ones—they are by Louise
> Hay and I must say they help me enormously—I listen to them in
> my car driving to and from work. They are my lifeline at the mo-
> ment. [1/1/90]

My American friend Lois, who lived with her husband, a retired professor, just outside Brussels, and whose little Yorkshire Lutine had
been one of Rachel's favorite Belgian playmates, sent me postcards
with captions like "La ou Dieu nous plante, it faut savoir fleurir"
[Wherever God plants us, we must know how to flourish]. During the

difficult first months following our return to the United States, the most powerful letter I received was one that Lois sent me in March 1989, at a time when I sorely needed guidance. Somehow, I felt my friend had sensed that need, for she wrote:

> I have recently developed another "Lois Gimmick," which is helping me a lot. It goes like this:
>
> 1. I discover that there is a fire in my house.
> 2. I get frightened and upset—how did it start, why should *my* house burn, why should I lose *my* things, what shall I do? etc., etc.
> 3. I remember that I bought some fire extinguishers just for such a case & use them up, but the fire is too strong for my extinguishers. I have used them all & the fire is still burning.
> 4. I finally remember that the fire department is ready and waiting to take care of such things. They come & I start telling them what to do & how to do it & get singed in the process.
> 5. I move aside and do my best to help without getting in the way and in order to be safe and not burn down along with the house.
>
> That is the scenario I adopt when things go wrong, but looking at it carefully & from the viewpoint of the program (or just plain common sense), I think it can be improved upon:
>
> 1. Accept the reality.
> 2. Ask the Higher Power to step in.
> 3. Do what seems indicated under the circumstances.
> 4. Do my best to keep from being damaged.
>
> It all works like a charm if I can only keep myself from wanting things to be different from what they are in reality. The trouble is that life's problems do not *seem* to be as clear cut as a fire. But most of them can be improved upon by not wasting time on magical thinking—"If Onlys" are just a waste of time during which the house burns merrily away.

I knew Lois was right: there could be no time for "If Onlys." I would spend no time on magical thinking. For my three-year-old daughter's sake as well as my own, I would look to the future and, at the same time, learn from the past. Now, better than ever, I understood the advice given in *One Day at a Time in Al-Anon*:

> I have a right to free myself from any situation that interferes with my having a decent life and pleasant experiences. Every human

being is entitled to live without fear, uncertainty, discomfort. I should take a firm stand and hold fast to whatever decision I make, to help not only myself and my family, but the suffering alcoholic as well. Constant wavering can only hinder me from breaking out of my present thinking patterns.

JULY 30, 1988

It feels like so long since I've written in this diary. I have not had energy to write. The days seem to spin by, and I'm trying to care for Rachel, get legal papers done, clean house, do wash, get groceries, write a few letters, see friends, etc.

A lot has happened. Some of it is very painful to write down, and I'm not sure how much to say. On August 5 there will be a hearing concerning custody of Rachel. Bob initiated a suit for sole custody of her. I have been very preoccupied and worried. I try not to imagine scenarios and believe that Ramona Burns, my attorney, will present my case well and that it is a strong case. Still, I feel scared of trusting the legal process with Rachel's future. My options seem limited at this point. I have problems seeing what's likely and what's improbable, what I need to do and what I need to refrain from doing.

AUGUST 2, 1988

Uncle Ray Bunkers died July 24th, and I went to his funeral in Worthington on July 27th, the 10th anniversary of Dad's death. There was a dinner, after which everyone drove down to Granville for Ray's burial. Then we all came to Mom's for cool drinks before driving home. I saw Pat Feller for the first time in years, and enjoyed talking to her. Also Phyllis Feller, Sandy Bunkers, Charlene Bunkers, etc. All in all, it was a good experience to be there—the priest gave a nice homily. I cried a lot, and it felt good to get it all out. Hard to even know what the tears were about—all sorts of things, I guess.

AUGUST 3, 1988

Rachel's been home with me since July 28th. She'd been at her dad's for three days. She and I have been together a lot—visiting friends, going swimming, reading stories, coloring and playing. She and I had dinner with Helga on Saturday, and I spoke at an AA/Al-Anon Open Meeting afterwards. It felt weird to be up there in front of Midge, Mort, Helga, and several other of Bob's fellow alcoholics.

Copies of letters to the court in support of Bob's motion for sole custody arrived by mail today, letters written by Mort, Midge, and

Helga. All attest to what a fantastic parent Bob is and make no mention of me, as if Rachel had simply sprung, fully formed, from her father's forehead. I'm feeling betrayed by all three. There they sat through my Al-Anon talk last Saturday night at the AA Open Meeting, then wrote these letters. So much for confidentiality.

Tonight Cheryl, Lydia, and I got together to talk it out. They told me they were shocked at the letters and at the depth of denial that's there. "Dry drunk behavior," they told me. That doesn't make me feel better. I see the denial as well, but these letters make me feel as if everything I am is being called into question.

AUGUST 5, 1988

The custody hearing took place at 11:15 a.m. today. Lydia, Cheryl, and my sister, Linda, came. That sure helped. First, the attorneys met with the judge, and a custody study was ordered. Then the judge heard testimony about when Rachel ought to be with which parent for the next few months—stuff about who had how many rooms in their house, who had lived where for how long, etc. That part went on and on, it seemed. Now the judge will make out a schedule for Rachel and mail it out early next week, so I don't yet know how much time each parent will have her.

AUGUST 15, 1988

I wrote to Lois and Pamela about the powerful spiritual healing session that my spiritual guide, Faye, and I had last Friday. First, Faye laid her hands on my head and rubbed the back of my neck. She helped me envision Susanna and Barbara. Then she told me she had seen two spirit guides at my shoulders—two women—it was them. I asked them if they had a gift for me and they told me they loved me and that I needn't fear the loss of Rachel—that she'd always love me and would not be separated from me. Our love will survive.

AUGUST 16, 1988

Rachel came home yesterday. She cried and told me that she'd missed me. She had been lonely for me one night and asked her dad if she could phone me. He told her no. She sobbed as she told all this to me. How it hurt to hear! She took a good nap yesterday and went to sleep about 9:30 p.m. We read Raggedy Ann and Andy stories and she loved them. In the middle of the night she came in crying, so I took her and cuddled her and she fell asleep. Then I took her back to her bed. She told me several times that she'd wanted to come home from her dad's. It was hard to hear it and be loving and realize I couldn't help except to listen and love her.

SEPTEMBER 13, 1988

On Sunday when Bob brought Rachel back to me, he'd cut off her long blonde hair. All her curls are gone, and he did it without telling me. No more braids, ponytails, curls, at least for a while. I took such delight in fixing Rachel's hair for her. Now there's barely any to comb. Well, it will grow back.

SEPTEMBER 17, 1988

At Frank's cabin near Dresbach. He and I had a good talk last night and he blessed me with some holy oil and gave it to me to take along home. He and I hiked out to Dakota Point in the late p.m. It was breezy and cool—a very comfortable hike and an excellent time to talk. Lots of sadness about losses.

Frank and I talked a lot about that last night, about healing and the grieving process. I am learning to pray and realizing what I can't change. It is very, very painful—and very draining on a daily basis. I keep wondering why I need to learn all these things, why I need to suffer? No good answer, of course. Frank said circumstances lead to pain and I didn't cause those circumstances and I can't control them. The loss, the grief, the feelings of betrayal are so acute. Feeling betrayed by Helga and Midge, two former friends, both women. That feels worse to me than betrayal by men. To see them "side" with Bob and support him hurts a lot. The whole system is male— the judge, the psychologist, etc. It all makes me see how caught in it the lives of mothers and daughters are, how caught Rachel and I are. How can I sort through what would be good for her? How can I go on with my own life from here?

OCTOBER 5, 1988

A note arrived from Helga, telling about her sadness over being separated from me. I replied that her actions and her concealment of them from me have led me to re-assess my feelings toward her. I also told her that I need to be around people where the mutual trust level is high. I sent her an excerpt from *Days of Healing, Days of Joy* about whom to trust and whom not to trust: "What recovering adult children learn is that who you ask is what makes the difference. We learn to stop taking our requests to untrustworthy people. When we do that, we discover that we will receive when we ask only those we can count on to be there for us."

Oh, it feels so good to be here in bed, with Alice curled up next to me. She has become so sweet since Vincent's gone—very close and loving toward me. Maybe Alice will have a sea change in personality now. I'm reading Alla Bozarth Campbell's *Life is Good-bye; Life is Hello*. What she says about hope and pain makes sense: "Hope is precious, but it does not wipe out pain. Pain becomes bearable when we are able to trust that it won't last forever, not when we pretend that it doesn't exist."

OCTOBER 17, 1988

Rachel's third birthday. Her birthday party went well. I got a lot of help from Marcy, Colette, and other friends with toys and games. Mom drove up with a beautiful birthday cake in the shape of a Care Bear, Rachel's favorite animal. We had pizza and devil's food cake for dinner—games, presents, etc. The party went from 5–7 p.m., but it was about 8:30 by the time everyone went home. Then Mom, Rachel, and I called it a night. I read Rachel's new books to her, and she fell asleep about 9:15. I fell asleep soon after. I had a disturbing dream: one in which a woman gave birth to three children; two were large and robust, the third white and born dead apparently, though I saw it stir and told the midwife, who thought it might be alive, but it wasn't. I was sure it had been. I think the doctors only planned to tell the woman she'd had twins, and I didn't approve of keeping the third baby a secret.

OCTOBER 31, 1988

Halloween. Rachel took her fairy princess costume along to Children's House for the party there. Later, Lydia will bring her son Mark to our house, and we will take him and Rachel trick-or-treating at the downtown mall tonight, then home for pizza and to see some kids stop by to trick-or-treat us.

Bob's attorney asked the court to order me to give them all my diaries and journals from January 1985 to the present. Ramona says we'll refuse. It feels like rape to me—and it would violate a lot of people's privacy. I know there's a lot in there about the ugly things Bob has done. Everyone I've talked to thinks this is a crazy, desperate and absolutely despicable move on his part, another power play. Nothing he does can surprise me anymore.

NOVEMBER 2, 1988

Home, watching the CBS Evening News. Tonight I'll watch some TV and read. The quiet of being home alone feels deafening. I hope someday I'll see the advantages. Right now it feels lonely with Rachel gone.

I think a lot about wanting to do what's good for her—to set aside my own feelings and to focus on making her relationships with her mom and dad as good as possible. Already I see a guardedness in her that seems to come from going back and forth between houses and towns. I pray that the court will order less shifting—more long periods here at home, and some 3–4 day periods at her dad's. The major goal is to keep myself from being down on myself and to believe I am doing the best I can.

One key for me is to be in touch with other persons, to show I care about others' lives and concerns, to get outside of myself whenever I can, instead of brooding. Cheryl took me to lunch today, and we had a long talk. She has been through it herself. I hope to be a better person after all this passes. What is most important is to do all I can to help Rachel feel happy, safe, and not caught in the middle.

NOVEMBER 5, 1988

I've been rereading my old journals—the ones Bob's attorney asked for. There's a lot in them to support what I've said. No doubt about that. I was rereading the one from 1986 when Marian Corby died, and that was sad. I find it painful to read about that whole period. It's like reliving it. I'm glad I wrote what I did in my journal, yet it does bring back such strong emotions. I wish Marian had lived. So many things would have been different.

Lately I've felt a lot of sadness—guess also it's acceptance of how things are—of what I can and can't control, of whom I can and can't be around, of whom I can and can't trust. It's sad to realize that some people I'd considered close friends are people whom it's unhealthy for me to be around because they aren't trustworthy. It amazes me how much alcoholism and enabling affect everything. I need to stay away from those people, and I do have many friends I can trust and rely on. I am accepting the hardships and the uncertainty with which I've been living for nearly a year. I'm also accepting my feelings as well as the reality that not all things can be safe, settled, and peaceful. Life takes time to work through.

DECEMBER 1, 1988

Tomorrow I have to go to Minneapolis to receive the results of the court-ordered custody study. I'm worn out from it all and from my thinking about what the psychologist might say. I think it'll be a tense two hours. Cheryl and Lydia will go along. I have no clear idea what to expect, not at all. I guess from what Ramona has said, the

worst would be complete joint custody. Who knows what the best
would be or what lies in between?

DECEMBER 3, 1988

Yesterday's session with the psychologist was grueling. Cheryl and
Lydia stayed in the office till it was time to go in. Bob sat down next
to us, stared straight ahead, and said nothing. He looks fatter, up at
the top end of the scale again.

The psychologist said early on that he'd recommend joint legal
custody and primary physical custody to me. Then we went through
his report for two hours. At the end, I sat with my copy of the report
for another half hour and made notes, as the psychologist had asked
me to do. Then he said he'd not talk with me and Bob again except
if both attorneys were also present. I was so tired afterwards. Then
Cheryl, Lydia, and I drove back to Mankato to get Rachel at Children's House.

DECEMBER 27, 1988

Enroute to New Orleans for the Modern Language Association Convention. I'm going to present a paper on women's autobiography.
Feeling preoccupied with custody issues. And I miss Rachel. This
a.m. she cried—didn't want to get dressed or brush her teeth. She
told me she didn't want to go to her dad's—wanted to stay with
me—and it tears me up to have to tell her that she has to go.

Things seem as unchanged as ever. I'd hoped it'd all be settled by
Xmas, and nothing is. It means more legal fees, hearings, perhaps a
trial. Why can't anybody see that all the back and forth is not good
for a little girl? Why can't they see that she needs the stability of
being with the parent she's always been with—me—the one she
prefers and sees as her primary parent?

DEC. 29, 1988

My paper went well yesterday. Being here at MLA makes me feel,
who cares about all the academic stuff? It's nothing compared to
being Rachel's mom and wanting to care for, love, and protect her.
The pain of possibly not being able to do that is so great. I want
things to be resolved and settled. I also want my daughter on more
than a part-time basis, and I will not give up on that.

I phoned Rachel at her dad's house. When he answered, I asked if
I could talk with her. "No," he replied and hung up the phone. I sat
there, not believing it had happened.

So, on with today, a day at a time. Yesterday I talked with two women about my diaries research and my keeping a journal myself. The irony of my doing this and feeling constrained and watched is sometimes too much to take. I will not hand over my journals to voyeurs. I won't let that scare me into not writing.

DECEMBER 31, 1988

Enroute from Dallas to Minneapolis—temperature is 8 degrees in Minnesota. Ugh. I dread the cold. I'm feeling tired, sad, angry today. I feel as if I'm a broken record, retelling the custody story, hearing again and again, "Do you have a good lawyer?" Do I? I don't know what "good" means—someone who'd go in and push for everything? Someone who'd urge a compromise? Do I have a good "case"? What does that mean? How can I refer to my desire to keep my daughter as a "case"? How can it be judged how "good" a "case" it is? Or whether Rachel and I "deserve" to have our lives together not be disrupted?

It seems that, when I'd talk about this with people at MLA, I'd get shocked looks in return—people who don't really want to hear the details, who recoil from the tremendous pain I feel and that comes across in what I say and how I say it. Most people want to say, "It'll all work out," and they need to believe that. But the feeling I get is that they are shocked that this could be going on in my life. How unbelievable! How could *this* happen to *her*? (As if to imply, she must have done something to deserve it.)

Sometimes I wonder that myself. I go over all the events of the past year and I wonder, How could it have come to this? How could I have changed things? I don't know, and the fact is, I've never had control of many of the variables here—the beliefs of judge, psychologist, attorneys, etc. What I have had is a close bond with my daughter—a bond that's been there since her conception and one that's seen as expendable so that the father can get what he wants. I can't believe this is good for Rachel, and what would it mean if I didn't resist? It'd mean at best a 50–50 split—the same result.

So, instead I fight so she and I can keep our relationship strong, and I risk being portrayed as a bitch who wants to take her from her daddy. It is so hard for me to accept this—the fear that Rachel will be irreparably harmed in this and that I am powerless to prevent it.

JANUARY 19, 1989

Rachel's in bed, asleep for the night. She wanted me to tell her bedtime stories about our time in Brussels, and she fell asleep as I told one story.

Pleasant memories of Europe are coming back to me a lot lately, and I love to remember all the details of our time together there. Maybe the memories are a way of verifying that those five months *did* happen and that that was a very special time for Rachel and me. I hope to write about it all someday. All in all, we were treated very well and we *did* make it together!

Today a Christmas card and letter came from Ghislaine, Marcelle, and Linda at La Garenne Garderie in Brussels. Rachel was *so* proud of it—she took it to show to everyone at Children's House. She just beamed when I read it to her.

Rachel's memory amazes me. She recalled yesterday that I had given her a particular birthday gift, and she's so good with names of people whom she's met only once. What a smart and savvy kid. I hope those qualities stand her in good stead through all this upheaval. Tonight she again said she didn't want to go to her dad's tomorrow—she said she'd go for the day but wanted to come home at night. I hope the judge changes all the backs and forths. Right now she transfers from one home to the other anywhere up to fourteen times in a thirty-day period.

JANUARY 20, 1989

Last night Rachel awoke at 4 a.m. with a cough and 100 degree fever. I gave her Liquiprin and cough syrup, and she fell back asleep. I took off her pj's to help cool her down and she slept till about 7 a.m. Then she woke. I wasn't sure how she was doing—she seemed better—temperature was just about 98.6. She didn't want to get dressed to go to her dad's this morning. She told me, "I'm sad, Mommy. I just want to stay home with you." She cried and begged, and I told her that I would ask the judge.

She said, "I want to come home tonight, Mommy." She said she'd told her dad that the last time she went there and it didn't help. I urged her to talk to her dad about how she felt. She told me at breakfast, "I'm sad because I don't want to go." We talked more about how it was okay for her to have her feelings, okay to feel sad.

She asked again as we put on her coat not to have to go. I told her that our guardian angels would bring us kisses and hugs through the wind while we're apart. I could see her face get blank after she had her coat and cap on; it was hard to make eye contact with her.

We got into the car and drove to Hardee's to meet her dad. Before he took Rachel out of my car, I turned to her and told her, "I love you, honey. I'll see you Tuesday morning." Her face went blank as Bob took her.

Then she said, "Dad, I want to go back home tonight."

He replied, "We'll talk about that" and put her into his truck. I told him about her fever and cough during the night. He didn't reply a word, just walked away. Another "cooperative and communicative" exchange! I really wish I could have kept her at home today. But legally, I don't have that option.

JANUARY 27, 1989

The court hearing on January 23 was short compared to the hours beforehand when the judge had the attorneys in chambers. Bob's attorney's request for a court order to get all my journals was denied unless Ramona and I use them as preparation for the custody trial. In that event, the judge would review portions and decide whether they were relevant to the case. Bob's attorney claimed that the diaries were relevant; my attorney claimed invasion of privacy. I can't help but think that they want the diaries ruled out so I can't use them. Also, Bob's attorney claimed there was evidence to show which parent was better psychologically suited to be Rachel's parent, so I can only assume that they'll try to show that I'm emotionally unstable.

Bob's and my therapists' records are to go to the judge, who will review them and determine if anything in them is relevant. It all feels very unreal. I am wondering where it'll go from here, what will happen? I may end up having to prove I'm not hysterical and unbalanced! For now, a day at a time. I will keep gathering information I feel is relevant to the case.

FEBRUARY 2, 1989

Rachel came home this morning. She said in the car, "My dad said I always lived with him, but I didn't. I've always lived with you."

I said, "Yes, ever since you were in my tummy, you've lived with me."

She said, "I told my dad that and he said no."

I said, "Your dad wasn't telling you the truth, honey."

She replied, "No, sometimes my dad doesn't tell the truth."

FEBRUARY 19, 1989

The reality of the custody trial to come is hitting me. The idea that a judge could take Rachel away from me scares me. People keep saying that won't happen, but I'm not sure, and nobody can be until events unfold. I feel that I have to dig deeper and deeper inside myself searching for some more strength—whether it's there, who can

say? So far, it has been, but I wonder how much deeper I can go? I
fear losing Rachel. I fear the exposure of myself—like being stripped
naked. I need to believe I'll have her with me—and at the same
time, prepare for the possibility that I might not. I need to ask my
friends for as much support as they can give. I need to let go of my
old desires and feelings if I am to be strong for myself.

MARCH 2, 1989

In Granville. Rachel and I came here yesterday morning for Grandpa
Klein's funeral. He died on February 26. Lots of relatives came for
the Requiem Mass. Rachel and I went up to the front of the church
to view Grandpa in his casket. Rachel waved goodbye to him. Then
we sat with Linda, Dan, Matt, Megan, Ryan, Denny, Barb, Kim, and
Kelly. Afterwards, we had dinner at the high school gym. I felt sad
and also at peace.

Grandpa was a loving man, as I knew him—very good to me all
those years he and Grandma lived next door as I was growing up.
Now it's 11 p.m. I put Rachel to bed earlier, Mom is asleep, and I'm
up alone watching T.V. It feels good to be here tonight and for now
that's what I want to enjoy—just being here.

APRIL 1, 1989

Early Saturday a.m. Rachel's still asleep. I'm listening to NPR and
having tea. I got a letter from MSU saying I'd been recommended for
promotion to full professor. Good news. I've worked hard for it, and
it helps a lot right now to realize that there are some good things
going on in my life. I need to remember that.

My "Women's Autobiography" class started yesterday, and I'm
team-teaching it with five graduate students. There are about 27–28
students in the group, all women and several who've taken courses
with me before. Good age range, from 20s through 70s—looks like a
good group of talkers, too. It took over an hour to do our introduc-
tions around the room and each woman said a bit about herself. I
was amazed at the number of single parents there—some with three
kids—some divorced, some widowed—several women who are married but not as many as I'd expected. Two of the women talked
about their lovers and partners. I felt very glad to be there and I
know I will look forward to class every Friday.

APRIL 2, 1989

A letter from Ramona Burns came, telling me my pretrial deposi-
tion with Bob's attorney has been cancelled, and she wants to meet

with me Monday p.m. to hammer out a custody and visitation settlement proposal and prepare for trial. I need to do some serious thinking about what I can and can't live with. I don't want Rachel bouncing back and forth like a pingpong ball any longer, or to be at the judge's whims of when and how often she should be switched. I may end up having her just the way it has been all these months even without a trial.

APRIL 10, 1989

In bed at 11 p.m. Rachel's asleep, and the cats are in the basement. Tomorrow Ramona and I will go to court to work out and sign the custody settlement that's been hashed out over the past few days. I have gone over and over all the drafts of various proposals and am tired of/by it all. At 9 a.m. I'm to meet Ramona at the courthouse, and we will see how final negotiations go. The entire agreement may need to be read into the record in front of the judge.

I am still amazed that the whole process could have gone on this long. I feel that the judge and psychologist have dragged out a decision that could and should have been made last August.

APRIL 11, 1989

Early a.m. Awake, listening to news on NPR. Slept well—I was awake once to check on Rachel, and then fell back asleep. Wondering about everything. How/why did I ever get involved with Bob Corby? Why couldn't I get out sooner? Why was/is he such a mean-spirited man?

Today I am pretty numb. I am feeling some relief to have this whole thing coming to an end. The irony is that it'll never end. I will need to deal with Rachel's father for years to come, and who knows under what sorts of conditions? For today, I need to go through the legal maneuverings and motions, and I need to sit through it and not let it get to me emotionally.

When I told Rachel that it had been decided that she'd continue to live with me, she hugged me and smiled. "Oh, Mommy, I'm so happy!" Then, "I love you better than Daddy."

I said, "Honey, it's OK to love both your mom and your dad. I'm glad you are going to stay living with me."

Then I got tearful and so did Rachel. She asked, "Why are you crying?"

I said, "Because I'm happy that we will be staying together."

"Me, too," she replied.

MAY 2, 1989

Pamela wrote me from Brussels. The judge there has granted her divorce and told her that she and the three kids can leave Belgium for the U.S. By September they will be here. And last night Lois phoned from New Haven, where she's visiting her son. It was so good to hear her voice.

MAY 6, 1989

Today Rachel said, "I got what I wanted." And me? I'm still sorting out all the events of the past year or so. Sometimes, late at night like this, I get too tired to care, and those are my moments and hours of peace. It doesn't all finally "add up to" or "mean" something.

Life is not fair. I know that, if I ever doubted it. People hurt and betray one another in the name of love, loyalty, and "the best interests of the children." I guess I knew these things, but now I know them in my heart and gut and will have to live with the pain that that knowledge brings. And I will keep going and believe there is some reason and purpose to it all.

JUNE 13, 1989

Here I am in my summer autobiography workshop. We all just read Auden's "Musée des Beaux Arts" and are doing journal writing re the poem and our responses to it.

My response: the suffering of the individual is important only to that individual. The world goes on; everyone else goes about their business. The tragedy of the boy (Icarus) falling into the ocean and drowning is ignored (or perhaps worse) not even seen by those in the immediate vicinity, not to mention those at a distance.

What is at the center of my universe might not, and generally does not, matter a lot to those around me. Each person has a sort of "tunnel vision" about life—seeing, hearing, feeling only that which happens to them—perhaps dimly aware (or blissfully unaware) of the next-door neighbor, the child down the street, the student in China, the street person in San Francisco, the garderie worker in Brussels, the woman who has just had a mastectomy in Mankato.

What does this make me think about? About how my life and struggles and joys must matter to me. They must be at the center of my life, and the irony (paradox) is that they can't and shouldn't be at the center of anyone else's life. What one person desperately wants,

another does not. What I see (or don't see, or choose not to see) is
not what another person sees or fails to see.

"Life" appears to go calmly on, whatever the individual's circumstances. What would it take for "Life" *not* to go smoothly on? A nuclear holocaust? genocide? a huge earthquake, typhoon, tornado?

Why do flowers continue to grow when someone is dying? Why
do birds, animals, humans continue to go about their daily business
of hunting and pecking when others are suffering and being killed?

Why not? That is the question Auden asks. He doesn't judge. He
just says, "Look, be realistic, this is how things are":

>   . . . the sun shone
> As it had to on the white legs disappearing into the green
> Water; and the expensive delicate ship that must have seen
> Something amazing, a boy falling out of the sky,
> Had somewhere to get to and sailed calmly on.

AUGUST 10, 1989

In Mason City at Linda and Dan's for three days, then will head
home, and Mom will be there for the weekend. Yesterday Rachel
and I drove here from Iowa City. I dropped in at the State Historical
Society and talked with Carolyn Hardesty, who's editor of *Iowa
Woman* magazine. I agreed to review Judy Lensink's book on Emily
Gillespie's diary, *"A Secret to Be Burried."* On our way home,
Rachel and I stopped at the Gilbertville cemetery to see Susanna's
grave. I explained to Rachel that Susanna once had lived in Luxembourg, that she had come to Iowa, and that, when she'd died, she
was buried here in Gilbertville.

Rachel said, "Hi, Susanna. We came to see you." We looked at
the faded fabric flowers on her grave, the ones I put there two summers ago. Then I explained to Rachel that both she and I have the
name *Susanna*. Rachel and I talked some more and took some pictures. From there we headed down to the local store for new flowers
to put on Susanna's grave.

When I told Rachel we'd come back to see Susanna's grave again,
Rachel said, "We'll be back, Susanna, and we won't forget you." I
was touched. I knelt down on Susanna's grave and put both my
palms onto the ground against the dry, prickly grass. I stayed there
for a moment with my eyes closed. When I opened them, I saw
Rachel doing the same thing.

She asked, "What are you doing, Mama?"
"Praying," I said.
"Me, too," she replied.

The king answered, and said: Give the living child to this
woman, and let it not be killed, for she is the mother thereof.
—3 Kings, 3:27, *Holy Bible*, Confraternity-Douay Version

By summer 1990, our lives were more tranquil than they had been for the past several years. During the year since the custody issue had been decided, Rachel's father had argued about the visitation agreement so often that the family court judge finally appointed a guardian ad litem to decide what kind of visitation arrangement would be in Rachel's best interests. Now, when Rachel went to her father's, she stayed for five-day periods twice a month as well as on numerous holidays. She also spent six one-week periods with him in the summer. I felt better about this arrangement than the one we'd had a year earlier, when Rachel had been shuffled back and forth between homes up to fourteen times each month in the judge's attempt to give both parents equal time.

I prayed that Rachel would not feel like a child torn between her parents. While I had no need or desire to be around her father, Rachel did. It was my job, as her mother, to help make her time with her father as positive as it could be.

During this period, I wrote an essay for a collection featuring autobiographical criticism by a number of scholars. My essay, titled "What Do Women Really Mean? Thoughts on Women's Diaries and Lives," focused on what I'd learned from my study of the diaries of Midwestern women. In the essay I also talked about keeping a diary myself and about continuing to do so after my ex-partner and his attorney had asked to have my diaries court-ordered into their hands:

The custody struggle was resolved in my favor out of court, just days before the trial was to begin. . . . My daughter continues to live with me, and she visits her father regularly. It hasn't been too hard for me to write these statements down as part of this essay. It is still too painful for me to reread very many of the journal entries that I wrote during the custody struggle; and it would be unwise for me to quote any more of them here, since in Minnesota the issue of custody can be reevaluated every two years at the request of either parent. I'll simply say that my experiences over the past several years have given me a good deal to ponder vis-à-vis issues of self-reflexivity in my journal writing and in my study of other women's "private" writings.

Now, more than ever, I appreciated the value of speech and silence, just like many other women whose writings I have studied. For instance, when Virginia Woolf was writing *To the Lighthouse*, a novel based on her relationship with her parents, she puzzled over how to present the death of Mrs. Ramsay and its effects on those who survived her. Woolf's solution was to write a very short middle section, "Time Passes," for the novel. In *A Writer's Diary*, Woolf described the challenge of writing "Time Passes":

> I cannot make it out—here is the most difficult abstract piece of writing—I have to give an empty house, no people's characters, the passage of time, all eyeless and featureless with nothing to cling to: well, I rush at it, and at once scatter out two pages. Is it nonsense, is it brilliance?

Whenever I'd teach *To the Lighthouse* in my literature and creative writing classes, I'd tell my students that as far as I was concerned it was brilliance. I'd also tell them what I'd come to understand all too well: some things are better implied than stated. Other things are best left unsaid.

As year's end approached, I awaited holiday greetings from Monsieur Georges Lamy, who had been our landlord in Brussels. Since our departure in June 1988, Monsieur Lamy had written regularly on behalf of himself and his wife. As a young man, he had visited the United States. He had returned many times and enjoyed practicing letter-writing in English. I would reply to each of his letters in French; and in his next letter, M. Lamy would "grade" me on how well I had done ("You get a 9 for your French").

Georges Lamy had a soft spot in his heart for Rachel, his "little rabbit," to whom he would send stickers and pictures. On July 6, 1988, he'd written:

> *Your* apartment is now in charge of a nice gentleman, age more or less 35, teaching at the ULB, in philology! Father of a girl 10 years old, and starting a divorce procedure! Je ne puis pas comprendre du

tout et je regrette toujours "such situations." . . . More news, I think and hope, within 3 or 4 weeks. I miss my shadow. We miss both of you. . . . Que le Bonheur soit votre partage.

Though I hadn't the heart to explain the custody struggle to Monsieur Lamy, especially after reading about how sorry he always felt about "such situations," I continued to write to him, telling him about how Rachel was growing and enclosing photographs of her. Our exchange of letters continued until I received a thick airmail envelope, addressed in his familiar typescript, mailed from Brussels on January 20, 1991. Inside was this letter in an unfamiliar hand:

> Mrs. Bunkers,
> I am the grand-daughter of Mr. and Mrs. Lamy and, as you probably guess, I am writing to you because something sad happened in the family: my grand-parents both died in December. Maybe you knew that my grand-mother had cancer; we knew she would die soon and it was better for her because she suffered a lot the last months.
> The surprise was the death of my grand-father because he was so dynamic. He was so worried about the illness of his wife that he died 5 days before her from a heart attack.
> That's why I send you all the pictures of Rachel I found in their house. My grandfather had already prepared an envelope to send you a card. That's why his address still is on the back side. I often heard them speak about you and Rachel and they liked to receive your cards and pictures.
> My aunts, cousins, my sister and my grandfather's brothers and sister are very sad but maybe he wouldn't have been happy alone after having been married for about 55 years.
> I hope you are both well.
>   Yours sincerely,
>   Françoise Lamy

As I read Françoise Lamy's letter and looked at the pictures of Rachel spilling across the kitchen table, my tears began to fall. By renting me the apartment at 28 Avenue Huysmans in Brussels, Georges Lamy had given my child and me a home there. On this January day, the news of his death brought that chapter in Rachel's and my life to a close.

9. The Good Mother

Motherhood—the way we perform mothering—
is culturally derived. Each society has its own
mythology, complete with rituals, beliefs,
expectations, norms, and symbols. Our received
models of motherhood are not necessarily better or
worse than many others. The way to mother is not
writ in the stars, the primordial soup, the collective
unconscious, nor in our genes.
—Shari L. Thurer, *The Myths of Motherhood: How Culture*
Reinvents the Good Mother, 1994

As important as being a teacher and writer are to me, being a mother is more important. Stories about mothers and daughters continue to pique my interest. After I returned from Brussels in the summer of 1988, a friend suggested that I read Sue Miller's *The Good Mother.* The novel tells the story of a woman named Anna Dunlop who, after her divorce, loses custody of her daughter, Molly, to her ex-husband when Anna and her lover, Leo, are accused of engaging in inappropriate sexual behavior in the little girl's presence.

I had to set the book aside unfinished; reading it was too painful. Several years later, while rearranging books in my attic study, I came across *The Good Mother,* tucked away on a shelf. This time I read it cover to cover, appreciating, as I could not have before, the complexities of Anna's feelings for her daughter:

> There was no way to retrieve my life with Molly. Whatever it was we were to have, it would be utterly different from what we'd had before; and I didn't know if I had the strength to shape it. It seemed too full of what would not be: I would not be the name she called in the night or when she was hurt. I would not know the names of school friends, baby sitters. I would miss the odd, funny turns of phrase, the wonderful misunderstandings of the world, I would never have the rocklike comfort of daily life with her. I would be the one she yearned for, as I yearned for her. There was nothing I wanted less.

Susanna Simmerl Youngblut and   *Rachel and Suzanne Bunkers,*
grandson John Wendling, circa 1888.   *1989. Photo by Peter Raeker.*

Reading these lines, I realized how fortunate I was. My daughter would be with me. I wanted her to know her father and feel she had a second home with him, but I wanted her primary home to be with me. I wanted my name to be the name she called in the night. I wanted to know the names of her teachers, her baby-sitters, her friends. I wanted the rocklike comfort of daily life with her, and I wanted her, in turn, to have that comfort with me. As a mother, I had promised that to my daughter and myself. I intended to keep my promise.

In early June 1993 Rachel completed first grade, and I finished teaching for the year. A week later, the two of us boarded a flight to Brussels for our first visit to Europe in five years. We planned to spend two days walking around Brussels, then visit our friends Lois and Lutine in Ostende, on the Belgian seashore. From there we would take the train to Luxembourg to stay with our cousins in Feulen. I wondered what, if anything, Rachel would remember from our months of living in Brussels five years before, and I wondered how returning there would be for me.

JUNE 7, 1993

> This trip has an unreal feeling about it. I'm looking forward to being back in Brussels. I remember some things from 1988, mostly good things. Those were some of the roughest months of my life, and I

focused on making sure that Rachel and I could survive on a daily basis. A lot of credit goes to Monsieur Georges Lamy. I wish he were alive and we could visit him. He was a generous man.

JUNE 7, 1993

On our flight from Minneapolis to Brussels, Rachel chatted with an eight-year-old boy seated in front of her. Like her, he had a Game Boy, and they traded small talk. At one point, she mentioned she had two houses—her mom's and her dad's—and a Game Boy at each.

"Oh, your parents are divorced," the boy said.

"No," Rachel replied, "they were never married."

A man seated across the aisle from me took off his reading glasses and looked over my way. I had to laugh at my life story being told in front of me. I was pleased at how matter-of-factly Rachel could announce it.

JUNE 9, 1993

Last night Rachel and I got to see the Grand Place, all lit up with people dining at sidewalk cafes and walking about. In front of the Hotel de Ville, a man played a trumpet rendition of "Yesterday" as we stood and listened. I looked up at the ornate gold figures atop the guild halls, silhouetted against a pink sky from which the sun had just sunk. I stood there silently, taking it all in. I surprised myself by getting tears in my eyes as the sharp, clear trumpet blew out the melody, and I mouthed the words, "Oh, I believe in yesterday." If it's possible to feel nostalgic about a place that never was my actual home, then that's how I feel toward Brussels—at home and calm in the heart of this huge city where I know very few people.

Earlier in the evening, Rachel and I met Lois and Clara for dinner at a restaurant on the Petite Rue des Bouchers, just off the Grand Place. Then we sat and talked about what has happened in each of our lives in the past five years. A lot, as it turns out.

Clara's lover, André, whom I'd known when I was here in 1988, started drinking again so badly that she refused to live with him. At one point he got so drunk that he fell and hit his head, causing brain damage. He was paralyzed for over a year before he died last year, probably only in his early fifties. Now Clara is learning how to go on alone, and she spoke frankly about what she has learned from her experience with André.

Lois' husband, Robert, died this past February. So she's adjusting

to being on her own after fifty years of marriage and several years of
caring for Robert as he grew old and feeble. She still has a lot of zip
and desire to be out and about. I can see she needs to have things to
do and people to be with. Rachel and I plan to go to Lois' apartment
in Ostende later today and spend two days there. I long to walk on
the beach, see the ocean, and visit at length with Lois. The quiet
time in Ostende will help me get ready to go on to Luxembourg.

JUNE 10, 1993

This morning Rachel and I set out walking in central Brussels.
First we went to the church of Notre Dame de Sablon and lit some
candles in front of the altar of the Blessed Virgin Mary. Then we
walked down to the Grand Place. I bought Rachel a waffle, and we
sat on the cobblestones in the Grand Place while she ate it. Next
we walked to the European Store for souvenirs, to the post office
at Gare Centrale, and back to the Chambord Hotel to meet Lois
at 4 p.m.

Enroute to our hotel, Rachel and I stopped at the Musée des
Beaux Arts. I wanted to show her the Brueghel painting of "Landscape with Icarus." I told Rachel the story of Icarus and his wings of
wax. Tonight she told me that she didn't want to fall like Icarus. I
assured her that no one would put wax wings on her and encourage
her to fly close to the sun! Then she said she felt scared of drowning
in the ocean, and I told her I'd not let her go into it alone, that I'd
stay with her.

Tonight Lois took us out to the seashore, just feet from her apartment on the top floor of a high-rise building. Rachel and I ran in the
surf and collected seashells. Lois and her little Yorkshire, Lutine,
watched from the shore. Rachel and I stayed there an hour or so,
playing "TOWANDA!"—where we'd run out and jump over waves and
yell our loudest yells.

It felt so good to walk along through central Brussels this morning. Just to be in the Grand Place, see the familiar landmarks, and
know that after five years, they are still there—that is comforting.
To see Clara and Lois and to have dinner together reminds me of
how important they have been to my survival and how far I have
come since January 1988, when I arrived in Brussels in a pretty
upset frame of mind. Now I feel much better about life in general
and about myself in particular. I'm more settled, more sure that I
am a worthwhile person.

So this trip back to Brussels may somehow bring closure to my stay five years ago. It may help give me perspective on what I learned during that stay—about day-to-day survival, about taking care of myself and Rachel, about making my way in the world.

JUNE 11, 1993

Today Lois and I talked about her life—how she spent her childhood and adolescent years, how she and Robert met on a ship and he proposed after only a few hours, how they lived in New Haven while he taught at Yale, and how she needs to redefine her life now that he has died. I wish I could spend more time with her. I'd like to see *her* life story written; she has had quite an interesting, unusual life. I have learned so much from her.

Rachel and I took the train to Luxembourg this afternoon. Nico Linden met us at Gare Luxembourg, and we drove to Mersch to get Erny, who'd spent the day taking a cruise on the Moselle River with friends. Then we came to Feulen, and Erny made cold plates—ham, bread, jam, camembert cheese, strawberries, coffee.

Later Rachel and I went for a walk through Feulen. We went to the new playground near the church; it was built with donations from American soldiers who had liberated Feulen during World War II. Then we walked behind the church into an area of old houses with barns. The town is as beautiful as always, and I saw a dozen places I'd like to photograph this weekend, if we have any sun. The forecast is for cold and rain.

Then Rachel and I walked past "La Maison des Vacances." Erny had told me that Mme. Steichen had died a few weeks ago, apparently of Hodgkin's disease and Alzheimer's. I wonder if anyone misses her? Her husband is still there, running the "Maison des Vacances." Rachel and I met two little boys who were staying there. They watched as she and I walked through the yard outside the house. It was very quiet, no sign of anyone there—not the way it used to be when Mme. Steichen would set out her geraniums and work in the garden in her apron or play with her cats. I told Rachel the story of how Frank had accidentally run over one of her cats during our stay there in 1980. Then I told Rachel about why Frank and I had not stayed there again. Rachel asked a lot of questions: Who was Hitler? Why did he want to kill people? How did the Steichens come to be outcasts in Feulen?

Not easy questions to answer, as I have discovered. I know why

people here ostracize the Steichens. But what's hard for me to reconcile is how friendly Mme. Steichen was to me with how cruel she
was to the townspeople. But I don't dispute the word of the Lindens
or the Steiwers. Laure told me that Mme. Steichen was even worse
than her husband. So how do I reconcile that image with the one I
have of the white-haired old lady with tears in her eyes for the little
cat that Frank had run over?

JUNE 12, 1993

This morning Rachel told me that tonight I ought to sleep in her
bed for a little while to help her get to sleep, then go to my bed. For
all her independence, she is still a little child who needs comforting
and reassurances that she is safe. At times she does get pesky, especially when she wants me to notice and attend to her. She likes to
interrupt and contradict me, and those times do try my patience.
But this is what kids do and how kids are. Also, Rachel is an active,
inquiring child, not one to sit back quietly and observe, but one
to get into the action and ask questions or make observations.
Here in Europe, much more so than in the U.S., quietness in children is encouraged, perhaps enforced, and being quiet is not in
Rachel's nature.

Today I think we'll spend time here in Feulen. I want to talk with
Erny and visit the Steiwers if possible. I've had little contact with
them over the five years since I was last here. I know that Antoine
has had a stroke and is in ill health. Erny and Nico told me that
Laure asked about me, so I will make an effort to see her. Erny said
that Jacques Steiwer moved to Switzerland and is teaching there. He
was good to Rachel and me when we were first in Brussels, and for
that, I am grateful.

On Monday, I need to meet Jean-Claude Muller at the archives in
Luxembourg City to go through old census and notary records. On
Tuesday, he's arranged for me to give a presentation on my research
to some colleagues; then we'll have lunch together. That same
night, Rachel and I will go to Wolkrange for a visit with Rogér and
Colette Pierret. On Wednesday, Rachel and I will take the train from
Arlon to Ottignes, where Lois will meet us.

I am starting to look forward to completing the Susanna book,
now that I have gathered a good deal of the background information.
I admit, it will be easier to tell some parts of the story than others,
and some parts of my life I probably won't discuss at all, or just give

a "once over lightly," if that. But I think I now have enough information about Susanna and about Luxembourg to do a decent job.

JUNE 13, 1993

I'm in bed after a day that exceeded any expectations I might have
had. This morning, Rachel and I took part in a Mother's Day procession in Niederfeulen, along with about 100 townspeople. The procession began in Oberfeulen, and from there the people followed a
large statue of Mary, Our Lady of Consolation, as it was carried
down the road to Niederfeulen. Rachel and I joined in as the procession passed Erny and Nico Linden's house enroute to the church.

After lunch Erny, Rachel, and I drove to Vianden, where we spent
the afternoon touring the castle. It was as impressive as it was five
years ago, when Rachel and I were there. We rode the chairlift up to
the mountain top and looked out over the castle and the town
below. Plus, we were just in time to see the Tour de Luxembourg bicyclists ride through Vianden, and Rachel got some free candy from
cars accompanying the bicyclists. She was delighted, and I loved
watching those lean and intent bicyclists zoom down the cobblestone streets of the city.

Afterwards we drove back to Feulen, and tonight we accompanied
Erny to a Mother's Day celebration at the Hennesbau in Niederfeulen. The local chorale performed several songs, and the mothers
of Feulen got gifts—huge thermos for coffee, tea, etc. There was a
drawing for flowering plants, and I won a red begonia, which I gave
to Erny. Rachel was asked to present the choir director with a bou-
quet, and for that she received a pink begonia, which she gave to
Erny. Afterwards, we went to the cafe in the Hennesbau for beers
with a local woman and her son. Then we walked home to Erny's,
and now it's off to bed till tomorrow.

JUNE 15, 1993

Yesterday Rachel and I spent the day in Luxembourg City. We drove
there and parked in the underground garage near Place Guillaume.
We went to Jean-Claude Muller's office and then to the archives,
where I was able to photograph the 1866 notary records on Angela
and Barbara's immigration to the U.S. Today I hope to see the notary
records for 1857 and perhaps find more information there about Susanna and Peter's departure. I hope that, by going through every
record for 1857, I will come upon one for them. I'd hoped to find

records from Aspelt on Frank Youngblut, but no notary records for
that village are indexed. Perhaps they're in another notary's records,
but I may not have time to check, since I'll be there only this morning prior to my presentation.

Last night Rachel and I went to Ettelbruck to the Tasté Vin for
dinner with Laure Steiwer. I have heard very little from her since
1988. Her parents are both in ill health, and she now has a friend
who lives in the house with her. The two of them take care of Antoine and Maria. Antoine is able to sit up in a chair, but he looks
wasted and very old. Maria still looks good, but Laure tells me that
Maria's memory is poor.

Laure did give me one intriguing bit of information: Mrs. Steichen is buried in the Oberfeulen cemetery. I was not sure she'd be
allowed to be buried there, but she was. I wonder if that means she
was given a funeral in the Feulen church?

Last night, when I tucked Rachel into bed, she asked me to cuddle with her a few minutes, so I did, and she looked so lovely—her
blonde hair pulled back and her soft, clear skin so pink—no blem-
ishes or wrinkles—and she clearly loved to be cuddled by her mom.
Whenever I wonder what is worthwhile in my life, I have only to
look at Rachel, and I have my answer.

JUNE 15, 1993
11 p.m. In bed at Erny's—a long day but a good one. I left for Luxembourg City about 9 a.m. and went to the archives in the morning
and again in the afternoon. I found some notary records from 1855
detailing the sale of a garden to the Grand Duchy from Angela Hottua Simmerl.

We decided to go see Rogér and Colette Pierret and family tomorrow after we return the rental car at the airport, so they'll meet us
at Europecar, and we'll go along with them to Wolkrange and Bu-
vange for the day. We'll have dinner with them, and I will help them
translate a letter from their American cousin, Father Ken Pierre,
who plans to visit them in late July. We'll also visit with the Pierrets' daughters, Martine and Françoise; and we'll meet Françoise's
husband, Philippe, and see their new baby son, Thomas. That will
be a special treat for Rachel.

JUNE 16, 1993
Rachel told me she liked staying home with Erny yesterday. They
planted flowers and worked in Erny's garden. Then Rachel took

Rachel with Erny Linden, June 1993, Niederfeulen.

Erny up the street for lunch at the "Milwaukee Saloon," where they ate hamburgers and fries! I think it's good for Rachel to have spent a quiet day here, good for Erny and her to have had a bit of time just by themselves. And good for me to have had a day by myself to do my research and my presentation.

My presentation went well. Jean-Claude needed to translate into Lëtzebuergesch what I'd said in English. Then, there'd be times when the conversation would go forward in French and I'd try to catch as much as I could. Then everyone would go into English or Lëtzebuergesch, and a mélange of languages would fill the room.

When the conversation turned to the idea of "illegitimacy," I felt uncomfortable being the only woman in a room of seven men—and, of course, being the only one in the room who has given birth to a child, who just happens to be a "filia naturalis." Although I did not talk about myself and Rachel during the conversation, the idea was always present in my mind that, no matter how academic or theoretical the discussion became, everything said would have personal resonance for me.

So, for instance, when one man noted, "I have had one such instance in my family," or when another man referred to "an accident" and wondered how a woman could have two such "accidents" (i.e., two children, each by a different father), I found myself bristling inwardly at the idea of "an accident," as if having a child were like running off a road into a ditch and rolling the car.

The possibility was raised that perhaps it was simply a slip of the pen when the parish priest in Feulen listed Angela rather than Susanna as Barbara's parent on the baptismal record. I don't believe it was an accident. Jean Ensch noted that customarily a first child had its grandparents as its godparents. If so, Angela Simmerl would have been Barbara's godparent; but Peter Simmerl and Barbara Simmerl (a younger sister of Susanna's) were listed as Barbara's godparents in the baptismal records. Surely the parish priest, who had buried Theodore Simmerl just about two years earlier (February 1855), knew who Angela was and who Susanna was. So I don't accept the theory of a "slip of a pen," unless it was a very Freudian slip! I believe there were reasons why Susanna was not listed as the mother of Barbara. And Angela did become Barbara's *de facto* mother when Susanna left for the U.S.

Jean Ensch and I talked more about ship crossings. He told me it'd typically take 5–6 weeks for a ship to sail from Le Havre to New York. The first ships to sail to the U.S. in the spring would set off in late March or early April. So I looked through notary records for 1857 to see if Peter or Susanna had sold anything prior to leaving Luxembourg, but I could not find any records.

Jean offered to look at some other sources for me, so he took me to his office to do a quick check of all his computer records on people in Luxembourg. The name *Simmerl* is not present in Luxembourg today, but it was in 1880, perhaps used by another of Susanna's younger sisters, but not Angela, Susanna, or Peter, who had all been in the U.S. for many years by that point.

JUNE 17, 1993

5:30 p.m. Brussels time. We're flying somewhere over the Atlantic, not due into Chicago till about 5:30 p.m. Midwestern time, so a long flight lies ahead.

Lois took us to the Brussels airport, and our plane left on time. All went smoothly except for a brief confrontation at security. I did not want my film sent through the x-ray machine but was forced to send it through. I hope it's not ruined. I won't know until I get it developed later on. I must cross my fingers. I was just too angry to be polite and was glad to get out of there. Goodbye, Belgium! So much for nostalgia and romance!

Our trip has gone very well. People have been happy to see us, and I've enjoyed renewing my acquaintance with Lois, Erny, Nico, and the Pierret family. I would have liked a few more days in Luxembourg City to show Rachel the casemates, but we will save that for next time.

And I could have used more time in the archives; in fact, I am considering the possibility of going back in late August. If I could go through census records as well as notary records, and if I could also look at the church records to see who was listed as legitimate or illegitimate, that'd be useful as well.

Jean Ensch and Jean-Claude Muller raised a good point: how does a researcher assess this issue of "illegitimacy"? Apparently no one has yet done so vis-à-vis Luxembourger immigration, but I would like to see how the parish priest at Feulen listed illegitimate births—and whether the case of Susanna and Barbara was truly anomalous. I do not believe that Angela's name on the church record was a "slip of the pen" by the priest who wrote it.

In May 1993 Rachel's visitation schedule called for her to spend Mother's Day weekend with her father. The next month, when she and I arrived in Feulen, Luxembourg, we were surprised to learn from our cousin Erny that on Sunday, June 13, Luxembourgers would celebrate Mother's Day. Erny invited Rachel and me to join her in a parish procession honoring the Blessed Virgin Mary.

Led by the parish priest and acolytes, who carried a statue of Mary, Our Lady of Consolation, the patron saint of Luxembourg, the procession wound its way through the streets of Niederfeulen to St. Roche's Church at the center of the village. As the priest gave the benediction, the congregation sang "Tantum Ergo" and "O Salutaris Hostia."

The strains of these Latin hymns carried me back to St. Joseph Parish Church of my childhood—to the pungent incense, the varnished wooden pews, the unpadded kneelers. As I tried to join in the singing, my voice broke, and tears rolled down my cheeks.

Rachel looked over at me and took my hand. "It's okay, Mama," she whispered.

After the benediction, she and I lingered a while inside the church. We walked down the center aisle to the entryway, and I pointed out the baptismal font, where so many of our ancestors had been christened. We climbed the narrow steps to the choir loft, where our ancestors might once have sung during Mass. There we discovered a cache of life-size statues, their paint chipped and faded, stored behind a curtain next to the pipe organ. These statues had most likely stood on the altars of the church when Susanna and, in turn, Barbara, had been girls.

Then Rachel and I retraced our steps down from the choir loft and out the front doors of the church. As we held hands and walked back down the streets of Niederfeulen, I knew that we were home.

> *Like anger, idealization is a normal and useful early response to loss. Focusing on a mother's good traits reaffirms the importance of her presence, and processing the happy side of a relationship is a gentle way to activate mourning. But every human relationship is affected by ambivalence, every mother an amalgam of the good and the bad. To mourn a mother fully, we have to look back and acknowledge the flip sides of perfection and love. Without this, we remember our mothers as only half of what they were, and we end up trying to mourn someone who simply didn't exist.*—Hope Edelman, *Motherless Daughters: The Legacy of Loss,* 1994

Hope Edelman's observation that every mother is "an amalgam of the good and the bad" makes sense to me. I no longer need to think of Susanna Simmerl as either a "heroic" or a "deserting" mother. The more I've learned about her life, the more she has begun to emerge as a flesh-and-blood woman.

Was Susanna Simmerl Youngblut a good mother? Some might say that she was a bad mother because she left her firstborn, Barbara, behind in Luxembourg when she immigrated to the United States. Others, like me, would find it a much more complicated and difficult question—one that deserves to be set out in plain view, surveyed from numerous perspectives, mulled over, and slept on. For over fifteen years, I have done this. Even now, I think that this question can be answered in a number of ways.

Nineteenth-century census records for the Feulen area have confirmed my hunch that little Barbara Simmerl did not go to America with her mother, Susanna, in the spring of 1857. In fact, census records for the late 1850s and early 1860s show that young Barbara Simmerl was living in Oberfeulen with her widowed grandmother, Angela Simmerl. The 1858 census for Oberfeulen lists the inhabitants of House #33 as follows:

Hottua	Angela	journaliere	50	veuve
Simmerl	Barbe	sans état	17	celibataire
Simmerl	Anne	"	13	"
Simmerl	Catherine	"	9	"
Simmerl	Barbe	"	2	"

The 1864 census for Oberfeulen lists the inhabitants of House #27 as follows:

Simmerl, Angelique	journaliere	58	veuve
Simmerl, Catherine	sans état	16	celibataire
Simmerl, Barbe	"	7 yr 11 mo	"

As I mull over these records, I can finally accept the fact that Susanna and Barbara probably never lived together as mother and daughter and that Angela Simmerl lies buried next to her granddaughter, Barbara Simmerl Bunkers, in St. Joseph's cemetery in Granville because Barbara cared for Angela in her old age. Angela was both grandmother and mother to Barbara. Susanna was, and was not, Barbara's mother.

Yet, despite fissures in the mother-daughter relationship, civil as well as family records indicate that Susanna and her husband, Frank, cared enough about Susanna's mother and her daughter to help Peter Simmerl sponsor their immigration to America. Even so, I cannot help but wonder about possible long-term effects on Barbara of having been separated from her birth mother during her childhood.

Did Barbara's allegiance lie with the woman who raised her—her grandmother, Angela Simmerl? Did Barbara ever reestablish ties with Susanna, her biological mother? I could not explain why I needed to know, but I did.

172 THE GOOD MOTHER

Hope Edelman's recent work on motherless daughters explains cultural resistance to mother loss as "a symptom of a much deeper psychological denial, which originates from the place in our psyches where *mother* represents comfort and security no matter what our age, and where the mother-child bond is so primal that we equate its severing with a child's emotional death." Edelman explains that, although "grandmothers, aunts, sisters, fathers, and friends act as conduits, convening information about the lost mother to the daughter as she ages," it is the mother herself who is "understandably a daughter's most valuable resource."

Did Barbara Simmerl ever learn the details of her mother's life from Susanna herself? How, if at all, could I find out? As I pondered this question, another fortuitous turn of events occurred. On a visit to Granville, I was able to take another look at the Bunkers-Graff Family Bible. This time I noticed two looseleaf pages tucked inside its back cover. It was a letter, written in the mid-1960s, from "Aunt Sophie and Virginia" of Waterloo, Iowa, to Barbara Jacobs of Granville, Iowa. "Aunt Sophie," Sophia Youngblut O'Connor, born on July 16, 1874, was the second youngest of Susanna and Frank Youngblut's children. Sophia Youngblut married Richard O'Connor on May 29, 1895. Virginia O'Connor was one of their daughters. The letter listed the names of Susanna and Frank Youngblut's children. Barbara's name had been added to the top of the list:

Barbara   Born in Luxembourg, Europe Jan. 1, 1856
       Died in Des Moines, Ia, Feb. 4, 1943
       Buried in Granville, Ia, Feb. 8, 1943

George

Frank

John   Oct. 4, 1860   Died Sept. 28, 1924
       married Margaret Roberts

Josephine   Oct. 22, 1863   Died ?
       married Ernest Martin

Frank   June 9, 1865   Died June 2, 1906
       married Anna O'Connor

Anna   June 1868   Died July 26, 1938
       married John Wendling

Susanna Simmerl Youngblut.   *Frank Youngblut.*

Mary	March 22, 1870 Died March 4, 1958
	married Abel Lavasseur
Sophia	July 16, 1874
	married Richard O'Connor
Susan	March 4, 1876 Died Sept. 14, 1954
	married Victor O'Connor

As I read "Aunt Sophie and Virginia's" letter, I wished that my cousin Barbara Jacobs had lived long enough to know that I'd walked down row after row of white gravestones in the Immaculate Conception Parish cemetery in Gilbertville, Iowa, until I'd found Susanna and Frank Youngblut's gravestones. On my visits to the Gilbertville area, many Youngblut cousins had been eager to help me piece together details of our ancestor Susanna's life.

From these cousins, I learned that Susanna married Frank Youngblut at Gilbertville in December 1857, about six months after her arrival in the United States. Susanna and Frank Youngblut's first two children, George and Frank, died as babies. Their next seven children lived to adulthood. Frank and Susanna's youngest child, Susan, was born only a few months before Barbara Bunkers' first child, Henry, and the two families stayed in touch by letters and visits. The eastern and western branches of the Youngblut-Simmerl-Bunkers family tree went back and forth for family reunions, weddings, and funerals over the

Sophia Youngblut (l.) and Susan Youngblut, daughters of Susanna and Frank Youngblut.

Josephine Youngblut Martin, daughter of Susanna and Frank Youngblut.

years; they stayed in contact until after Sophia Youngblut O'Connor's death in the mid-1960s. In fact, my Youngblut cousins Charlotte Witry and Marie Hellman remembered their grandmother Sophie's friendship with a relative they called "Aunt Kate"—Catherine Bunkers Graff, the oldest daughter of Barbara Simmerl Bunkers. Photographs from an O'Connor family album document a 1923 visit from Sophie O'Connor and her children Paul, Florence, and Marie to Kate Graff and her family on their farm east of Granville.

Youngblut descendants have assured me that Frank and Susanna Youngblut enjoyed a long, happy marriage. For many years, Frank and Susanna farmed just outside Gilbertville. In their later years, they re-tired and moved to town. First their son Frank Jr. took over the home-place. After Frank Jr.'s untimely death in June 1906, his brother John took over the Youngblut farm. Youngblut descendants still farm the old homeplace, on the banks of the Cedar River, a quarter mile from the Gilbertville railroad depot.

Youngblut family documents list the names of Frank and Susanna's children, grandchildren, great-grandchildren, and great-great-grand-children. Clearly, family ties have been meaningful down through the generations. A large portrait commemorating the marriage of Frank and Susanna's daughter, Sophia Youngblut, to Richard O'Connor on May 29, 1895, shows nearly a hundred family members and friends on hand to wish the newlyweds good luck. When I look closely at the por-

Wedding of Sophia Youngblut and Richard F. O'Connor, May 29, 1895, Gilbertville, Iowa.

trait, I think I see Susanna, an older woman in the second row, standing just behind a young woman holding a baby.

Baptismal records, death records, and a history of Immaculate Conception Parish in Gilbertville, Iowa; wills, probate records, and bank records; a history of Black Hawk County, Iowa; Youngblut family photographs and news clippings—all of these public documents have helped me piece together the story of Susanna Simmerl's life after her arrival in the United States. All indications are that it was a much better life than she could have had in Luxembourg.

A visit from the Sophia Youngblut O'Connor family to the Catherine Bunkers Graff family, 1923, Granville, Iowa. Back row (l. to r.): Barbara Graff, Paul O'Connor, Edmunda Bunkers, Catherine Bunkers Graff, Sophia Youngblut O'Connor holding Geraldine Graff, Florence Graff. Front row (l. to r.): Milo Graff, Bernice Graff, Charlotte Graff, Marie O'Connor.

The *History of Black Hawk County, Iowa*, published in 1910, tells how Frank Youngblut came to the United States, settled near Gilbertville, married Susanna Simmerl, and farmed for many years:

> [Frank Youngblut's] birth occurred near Auspelt, Luxemburg, Germany, in 1823, while [Susanna Simmerl] was born near Phalen, Luxemburg, in 1829. He worked as a farm laborer in his native kingdom and on crossing the Atlantic to America landed at New Orleans, and thence proceeded up the Mississippi River to Dubuque, from which place he made his way across the state to Black Hawk county in 1852. Here he was employed as a farm hand for a number of years and then purchased land and began farming, meeting all of the hardships and experiences which constitute the conditions of pioneer life. He paid nine dollars per acre for his land, which is today very valuable property, owing to the improvements which he placed upon it and the natural rise in land values as the result of growth of population in this district. In the later years of his life he lived retired in Gilbertville and there passed away in 1892. His wife survived him for fourteen years, dying in 1905. Mr. Youngblut was a very active and faithful member of the Catholic church and aided in building with slabs

the first church of that denomination in Gilbertville. In politics he was a democrat and did all in his power to further the success of the party. He stood for progress and advancement in all things and his worth was widely acknowledged by many who knew him.

A family copy of the will of Frank Youngblut Sr. provided additional clues about the family's relative prosperity as well as Frank's desire to provide for his wife and children after his death:

In the name of the Father and of the Son and of the Holy Ghost, Amen: I, Frank Youngblut Sr., of Gilbertville, Ia, in the County of Black Hawk of the age of 69 years and being of sound mind and memory, do make and publish and declare this my last Will and Testament in manner following—That is to say:

First—I give and bequeath to my wife Susan Youngblut one third of all the money and also one third of all the lands and real estate belonging to Frank Youngblut, Sr., and after the death of Susan Youngblut, my wife, all property whatsoever shall be divided equally amongst John Youngblut his son and Josephine Brady his daughter and Frank H. Youngblut Jr. his son and Annie Wendling his daughter and Mary Levaseur his daughter and Sophia Youngblut and Susie Youngblut his daughters.

I also give to my wife Susan Youngblut all the rent of my farm rented to Frank H. Youngblut my son, until Sophia and Susan Youngblut my daughters shall be eighteen years of age. And I also give and bequeath to Josephine Brady my daughter the note of $400 dated Mch 7th 1891 deposited in Leavitt Johnsons Bank, Waterloo, Iowa. I also give and bequeath to Mary Levaseur my daughter the note of $500.00 dated Nov. 2, 1891 Deposited in Leavitt and Johnson's Bank, Waterloo, Iowa, and I Frank Youngblut Sr. give and bequeath to Sophia Youngblut my daughter $500 and also to Susie Youngblut my daughter $500 by a note of $1000 deposited in Leavitt & Johnson's bank to be divided equally.

It is also my will that John Youngblut and Frank H. Youngblut, my son, and Annie Wendling my daughter shall not be permitted to have a full share of all the property left after the death of my wife Susan Youngblut but as they have already received $500 each which shall be deducted from their share after my wife's death. It is also my will to let my wife, Susan Youngblut, let collect all the interest of the notes deposited in Leavitt & Johnson's Bank after my death.

In witness thereof I have hereunto set my hand and seal this 3th day of April in the year of our Lord One Thousand Eight-Hundred and Ninety-Two.

His
Frank X Youngblut Sr.
Mark.

The *Registrum Defunctorum Ecclesiae*, which contains the death records for Immaculate Conception Parish in Gilbertville, Iowa, provides further information about Frank and Susanna Youngblut's deaths. Death Record No. 123, written in Latin, states that Frank Youngblut died on May 11, 1892, and was buried in the parish cemetery on May 12, 1892. Death Record No. 289 states that Susanna Youngblut died on May 20, 1906, and was buried next to her husband on May 27, 1906. In the records, the parish priest spelled the family name "Jungblut," the original Lëtzebuergesch spelling:

In copies of Youngblut family documents given to me by Charlotte Witry, I came across a small handwritten bank note, dated "12/1/1908." It is titled "Statement of final settlement of Susan Youngblut's estate," and it provides this accounting:

Funeral Expenses	$110.00
Doctor Bill	$ 8.60
Taxes	$ 10.56
Masses	$ 21.00
Sundry Expenses, repairs	$ 36.68
Ins.	$ 2.10
Marker & Lettering	$ 12.50
	$201.44

The Catholic custom of giving out holy cards at funerals to commemorate the life of the departed was also important to Susanna's survivors. Susanna's holy card invokes the names of Jesus, Mary, and Joseph, and asks survivors to pray for Susanna's salvation:

JESUS! MARY! JOSEPH!
"It is a holy and wholesome thought to pray for the
dead, that they may be released from their sins."
—II Machabees XII. 46.

In Pious Memory of

Susan Youngblut

Born in Luxembourg, Germany, April 6, 1830
Died at Gilbertville, Iowa, May 20, 1906

LET US PRAY:

O God, the Creator and Redeemer of all the
faithful, grant to the soul of Thy servant SUSAN
the remission of all her sins, that, through pious
supplications, she may obtain that pardon which
she has desired. Who livest and reignest with God
the Father in the unity of the Holy Ghost, God,
world without end. Amen.

Holy Jesus, Mercy!

(100 days indulgence.)

Sweet Heart of Jesus, be my love!

(300 days indulgence.)

Sweet Heart of Mary, be my salvation!

(300 days indulgence.)

In *Maternal Thinking: Toward a Politics of Peace*, Sara Ruddick writes, "We have no realistic language in which to capture the ordinary/extraordinary pleasures and pains of maternal work," and she warns against sentimentalizing motherhood since, in many cultures, "the ideology of motherhood is oppressive to women." Ruddick acknowledges the continuing power of mythology in reflecting and shaping maternal roles: "The idealized Good Mother is accompanied in fear and fantasy by the Bad Mother."

In *The Myths of Motherhood: How Culture Reinvents the Good Mother*, Shari L. Thurer describes cultural mores governing motherhood throughout history. During the Reformation period, Thurer notes, "The composite message was emphatic and repetitious: woman existed to serve man. The good woman was a good mother, honorably wed and fertile, and, above all, *pious, obedient, chaste*, and *silent*. Those particular qualities, repeated *ad infinitum*, have become part of our cultural heritage." Thurer continues her analysis of the history of cultural mores of motherhood, in particular unwed motherhood, during the early modern period:

Most foundlings in this period, unlike those in the centuries before, were bastards, which testified to the desperate plight of unmarried mothers. As we have seen, the religious changes brought with them an aggressive prudery about sexual matters. There was a quantum change in attitudes about moral conduct. The definition of "good

mother" hardened, and most certainly did not embrace women who
produced babies out of wedlock. Before this time, an unmarried
mother could be absorbed into a household as a servant. Prostitutes
were tolerated in a community, and illegitimate children were not
especially ostracized. Now, an "immoral" woman was threatened
with hellfire and damnation. She was barred from employment; she
had no social role. A woman who strayed—the unmarried mother—
inspired the same virulent scorn as her older counterpart, the witch.

The recent work of Ruddick and Thurer enlarges upon issues raised
nearly twenty years ago by Adrienne Rich. In *Of Woman Born: Motherhood as Experience and Institution*, Rich distinguishes between acts
of mothering and cultural mores that dictate who should—and who
should not—be a mother. In exploring the powerful nature of the
mother-daughter bond, Rich asserts: "Even a woman who gives up her
child for adoption at birth has undergone irreversible physiological and
psychic changes in the process of carrying it to term and bearing it." In
analyzing how the mores of many cultures serve to separate women,
Rich explains: "The loss of the daughter to the mother, the mother to
the daughter, is the essential female tragedy." Finally, in speaking about
the need for mothers to nurture daughters, Adrienne Rich concludes:

> As daughters we need mothers who want their own freedom and
> ours. We need not to be the vessels of another woman's self-denial
> and frustration. The quality of a mother's life—however embattled
> and unprotected—is her primary bequest to her daughter, because a
> woman who can believe in herself, who is a fighter, and who continues to struggle to create livable space around her, is demonstrating to
> her daughter that these possibilities exist.

About the time I began my search for Susanna, I typed this quotation onto a small notecard and pinned it to the bulletin board above
my desk. I have reread these words almost daily for over fifteen years,
and I know them by heart. They are meaningful because of how important it has been to me to find evidence that Susanna was a good
mother in the face of my own bitter disappointment that she did not
take little Barbara along on the *William B. Travis* when she sailed for
America in the spring of 1857.

I suspect that, had Susanna taken her infant daughter along to
America, the two of them might have had much harder lives than they
eventually did have. As an inexperienced and unmarried mother with a
babe in arms, Susanna would have had very limited opportunities,

both in Luxembourg and in the United States. One has only to look at the character of Ántonia Shimerda in Willa Cather's *My Ántonia* (1918) to comprehend the difficulties facing an unwed immigrant woman and her baby on the Midwestern prairies and plains of the late 1800s. As the Widow Stevens observes to Ántonia's friend Jim Burden:

> Well, I expect you're not much interested in babies, but Ántonia's got on fine. She loved it from the first as dearly as if she'd had a ring on her finger, and was never ashamed of it. It's a year and eight months old now, and no baby was ever better cared-for. Ántonia is a natural-born mother. I wish she could marry and raise a family, but I don't know as there's much chance now.

Although first-time motherhood might have been quite difficult for Susanna Simmerl, her mother, Angela, was an experienced mother. Church and civil records show that Angela, born in 1808, married Theodore Simmerl on February 14, 1827, in Oberfeulen. During the next twenty-six years, Angela gave birth to twelve children:

1. Peter	b.	April 22, 1827, Oberfeulen
	d.	October 14, 1885, Luxemburg, Iowa
2. John-Baptiste	b.	April 5, 1829, Oberfeulen
	d.	April 8, 1850, Oberfeulen
3. Susanna	b.	April 2, 1831, Oberfeulen
	m.	December 9, 1857, Frank Youngblut, Gilbertville, Iowa
	d.	May 20, 1906, Gilbertville, Iowa
4. Anna Maria	b.	April 22, 1833, Oberfeulen
	d.	April 7, 1834, Oberfeulen
5. Nicholas	b.	January 1, 1835, Oberfeulen
	d.	January 17, 1837, Oberfeulen
6. Susanna	b.	January 1, 1837, Oberfeulen
	d.	?
7. Theodore	b.	July 2, 1839, Oberfeulen
	d.	July 1, 1840, Oberfeulen
8. Barbara	b.	June 3, 1841, Oberfeulen
	m.	July 1872, Michael Closener, Oberfeulen
	d.	?

9. Angela	b.	June 1, 1843, Oberfeulen
	d.	October 24, 1844, Oberfeulen
10. Joanna	b.	August 11, 1845, Oberfeulen
	d.	?
11. Mary Catherine	b.	October 5, 1848, Oberfeulen
	m.	? Paul Terns, Jesup, Iowa
	d.	?
12. Anna Maria	b.	August 28, 1853, Oberfeulen
	d.	October 10, 1854, Oberfeulen

Of the twelve Simmerl children, seven lived to adulthood; one of those, Jean-Baptiste, died at age twenty-one. The other five Simmerl children died as infants or toddlers. Angela Simmerl's last child was a girl, Anna Maria, born on August 28, 1853, when Angela was in her mid-forties. That baby lived little more than a year, dying on October 10, 1854. Less than three months later, on January 2, 1855, Angela's husband, Theodore Simmerl, also died.

Susanna Simmerl became pregnant in March 1856, just fourteen months after her father's, Theodore Simmerl's, death. When Susanna gave birth to Barbara on December 30, 1856, her mother, Angela, was a forty-eight-year-old widow. Who can know what transpired between Angela and her eldest daughter when Angela learned of Susanna's pregnancy sometime in mid-1856? Who can say how supportive Angela might have been?

And what about the father of Susanna's baby? It could not have been Frank Youngblut; he had been in the United States since 1852 and had not returned to Luxembourg. Could Barbara Simmerl's father have been a man from Feulen? If so, what happened to him? Several epidemics swept through Luxembourg during the mid-1800s, killing hundreds of men, women, and children. Perhaps the biological father of Susanna's unborn child was one of them. Perhaps he was once an active and welcome partner in Susanna's life.

Who can say why Barbara remained with her grandmother in Luxembourg while her mother and uncle sailed for America? Who can imagine why Peter Simmerl returned to Luxembourg in early 1866 to bring his mother, Angela, and her granddaughter, Barbara, to the United States? Who can guess what role Peter Simmerl played in Barbara's life? As a friend pointed out to me, perhaps Barbara's biological father was even closer than the hired man down the street. Even after all these years, I cannot answer all of my questions. I can only speculate, hypothesize, gather information, put pieces together, and imagine.

What *do* I know? I know that my great-great-great-grandmother Angela Simmerl gave birth to twelve children and raised seven to adulthood. I know that my great-great-grandmother Susanna Simmerl Youngblut gave birth to ten children and raised seven to adulthood. I know that my great-grandmother Barbara Simmerl Bunkers gave birth to twelve children and raised all of them to adulthood.

Does birthing and raising children make you a good mother? Does birthing a child and entrusting it to another woman, one who you may believe can care for your child better than you, make you a good mother? Does raising your daughter's daughter make you a good mother? I'm not sure I can answer these questions or the others that continue to haunt me.

Did Barbara Simmerl feel anger toward her mother, Susanna, for leaving her behind in Luxembourg? Did Barbara ever sit in her rocking chair, lulling her child to sleep, and rage at Susanna as I had? Or did Barbara idealize her mother in what Hope Edelman says is a "normal and useful early response to loss"?

When Peter Simmerl brought Barbara and Angela Simmerl to Iowa in 1866, did nine-year-old Barbara wonder why she was going to continue to live with her grandmother in Luxemburg rather than with her mother in Gilbertville? Perhaps Barbara did not question where her home was, for her *grandmère* was also her *mère grande*.

In *The Motherline: Every Woman's Journey to Find Her Female Roots*, Naomi R. Lowinsky explains that the grandmother stands at the intersection of "family history, generational change, and archetypal meanings." The relationship between a grandmother and her granddaughter, says Lowinsky, is often easier than that between a mother and her daughter. Why? Because the grandmother can provide "a wider circle of meanings, a larger perspective, than the tight little every-day intimacy one lives in with a mother, with its irritating ambivalence, its intensity of hope and disappointment."

Lowinsky points out the unique role of the grandmother in a family's lineage:

> The appearance of the grandmother throws the mother into relief. She is seen as one of a long line of mothers, forming a pattern that lives in the female body and is expressed in the meeting of the three. The grandmother holds these three in her body and psyche, the maiden and the mother she was, the crone she has become. The

wholeness of the feminine self is evoked, and the granddaughter's potential development is stirred. Someday, perhaps, she too will have a granddaughter to whom she will tell the stories of her female line. Grandmother consciousness opens a woman to images of the past, to the face of the future, and to the symbolic pattern of a woman's life.

I believe what Lowinsky says. Nearly every day of my childhood, I could go next door to Grandma's house to visit, play the piano, join her and Grandpa Klein for supper. When the smell of incense would make me nauseous during Sunday Mass, I'd feel safer leaving church and going straight to Grandma's house rather than going home, where my mother would sigh, "Sick in church? Not again!"

I sense that my mother and my daughter share a bond unlike either that between my mother and myself or my daughter and myself. When Mom comes to Mankato to visit, she and Rachel might go off together to shop at the mall or surprise me by cleaning the house while I'm teaching a class. What would it be like if all three of us lived together? What would it be like if my daughter and I were reunited after Rachel had spent the first nine years of her life living with my mother only? How flexible would the bonds of motherhood and daughterhood be?

What is a "good mother"? Who is qualified to judge? I no longer feel such a need to determine whether Susanna Simmerl Youngblut was, or was not, a good mother. Given my own experiences over the past ten years, I'm not even sure I know what a "good mother" is. I'd like to think I am one, yet I once was accused of being an "unfit mother" who should not be allowed to continue to raise her daughter. I don't want to pass that kind of judgment on another mother. Nor do I want to senti-mentalize or mythologize motherhood, even though I know I some-times do. I *do* want others to believe I am a good mother, and I want to believe that every mother in my family line has been, is, and will be a good mother. For me, it's prudent to remember Shari L. Thurer's caveat:

> The way to mother is not writ in the stars, the primordial soup, the collective unconscious, or in our genes. Our predecessors fol-lowed a pattern very different from our own, and our descendants may hew to one that is no less different. Our particular idea of what constitutes a good mother is only that, an idea, not an eternal verity. The good mother is reinvented as each age or society defines her anew, in its own terms, according to its own mythology.

Four generations in 1990 (l. to r.): Verna Klein Bunkers,
Frances Kokenge Klein, Suzanne Bunkers, Rachel Bunkers.
Photo by Rod Hop, Captured Moments Photography.

10. *Family Secrets*

Every family has secrets. Some are benign and
constructive, protecting the family and/or its
individual members and aiding in their growth
and individuality.

  Other secrets are toxic and destructive, destroying
trust, intimacy, freedom, personal growth, and love.
What you don't know can really hurt you!
—John Bradshaw, *Family Secrets*, 1995

During the summer of 1990, while Rachel was spending time with her father, I began editing a diary kept for more than seventy-five years by an Iowa teacher named Sarah Gillespie Huftalen. Sarah was a farm girl who became a respected country schoolteacher and a leader in the rural education movement in the Midwest. Her career as an educator spanned fifty years.

Sarah was also a good writer, who crafted poetry, essays, teacher training guides, and magazine articles. All the while, she kept a diary, which eventually came to more than three thousand handwritten pages. Sarah wrote in her diary about her many roles—as daughter, sister, teacher, wife, family historian, and public figure. Her diary reflects her growing awareness of how these roles intersected.

Sarah lived on a farm near Manchester, Iowa, with her parents, James and Emily Gillespie, and her older brother, Henry. There Sarah learned from her mother how to keep a diary, who had also been keeping a diary since she was a girl. When Emily Gillespie's health began to fail in the 1880s, Sarah quit teaching temporarily to care for her mother. During this time, Emily began dictating her diary entries to Sarah, who wrote them in her mother's diary for her. After Emily's death in 1888, Sarah held on to her mother's ten volumes of diaries. Later in life, Sarah decided to donate all of her mother's diaries, as well as her own diaries, scrapbooks, family photograph albums, genealogical charts, and teaching materials to the State Historical Society of Iowa. In 1989, my friend Judy Nolte Lensink published *"A Secret to Be Burried,"* an edition of Emily's diary. Now I took on the challenge of preparing an edition of Sarah's diary.

When people would ask me why Sarah's diary interested me, I would give three reasons: first, I was amazed that someone could keep a diary for more than seventy-five years; second, I was captivated by the particulars of Sarah's life as a teacher; and third, I was intrigued by the secrecy about dysfunction in the Gillespie family.

James Gillespie was most likely an alcoholic, and his problems with drinking, alluded to in both his wife's and his daughter's diaries, did not set well with other family members, who were active in the temperance movement. Emily and James Gillespie had an increasingly unhappy marriage. Evidence from both Emily's and Sarah's diaries indicates that James was verbally and physically abusive toward his wife and his children, Henry and Sarah. As Emily's and Sarah's diaries revealed, Emily grew more obsessive about preserving her daughter Sarah's purity, while James grew more violent toward family members.

"I question myself.—is it right for us to live with such a person. He waits every time to take Ma alone and then misuses her why he told her he'd given her $40 this summer and he couldn't see for the life of him what she had done with it—so much." Diary entries like this one, made by Sarah on November 1, 1884, convinced me that Sarah knew quite well how to use speech *and* silence to shape the messages she put into her diary—as a girl, a young woman, a teacher and wife, and as an old woman.

An uneasy feeling came over me. Had James Gillespie also been sexually abusive toward his daughter, Sarah? I could find no overt evidence in Sarah's diary, but I had an intuition. When it came time for me to speculate on this possibility in an endnote to my edition of Sarah's diary, I cited Linda Gordon's study, *Heroes of Their Own Lives: The Politics and History of Family Violence*:

> Linda Gordon cites the following statistics on incestuous relationships, 1880 to 1960: the relationships were primarily heterosexual; forty-nine out of fifty of the older perpetrators were male; the perpetrators were on the average twenty-five years older than their victims. Of the younger victims, ninety-three out of ninety-seven were girls, and the average age of victims was ten. Most incestuous relationships

continued for several years; the relationships were never voluntarily ended by the older males. The incest usually ended only when the girl moved away from the household or became pregnant.

Since I had no proof, I tried to be very tentative about the possibility of sexual abuse in the Gillespie family:

> Contemporary researchers are analyzing the many kinds of incestu-
> ous sexual abuse, such as that perpetrated by a father on a daughter
> or that perpetrated by an older brother on a younger sister. . . . While
> neither Emily's nor Sarah's diary entries state that incestuous sexual
> abuse occurred in the Gillespie family, one cannot help but wonder
> about the nature of Sarah's fear of her father—and about the nature
> of Emily's "secret to be burried."

As I was more fully drawn into the lives of Gillespie family members, I started to see small parallels between their experiences and
those of my ancestors. Daily life on the farm, studies in a one-room
country schoolhouse, caregiving to an invalid parent, family squab-
bles, a daughter's need to break free and establish her own identity, an
individual's need to come to terms with family secrets—all of these
themes in Sarah's diary were a part of my own family history. If Sarah
were alive today, I wondered whether she would appreciate an observation made by Harriet G. Lerner in *The Dance of Deception: Pretending
and Truth-telling in Women's Lives*:

> Families are not fair, and we do not choose the family we are born
> into. Our parents, being human, cannot create the perfect climate,
> like a garden greenhouse, to foster the blossoming of our true, au-
> thentic selves. Too much has happened long before we even enter the
> scene. When viewed over several generations, no family is free from
> the emotional ripples or, more accurately, the tidal waves that result
> from anxious events—immigrations, cut-offs, poverty, and untimely
> losses—that affect a family's functioning over generations.

Harriet Lerner describes many kinds of family secrets. Some secrets,
she says, are dramatic ones that conceal information of critical emotional importance for members' identities and sense of reality: "Father
is alcoholic, Mother relinquished a child before marriage, Little Susie
is adopted, Grandmother is dying, Uncle Charlie jumped rather than

fell to his death from the third-floor window, six-year-old Paula is being abused."

Other secrets (e.g., where the box of Oreo cookies is hidden, who took the spare change from atop the china cabinet) are more ordinary ones. Yet, says Lerner, the consequences of concealing even ordinary secrets "can be far-reaching, because the selective sharing and guarding of information is the stuff of which 'insiders' and 'outsiders' are made in social groups." This results in secrets in the relationship process that, according to Lerner, "may be far more important than the content of the information withheld."

Lerner's observations are valid. When *"All Will Yet Be Well": The Diary of Sarah Gillespie Huftalen* was published in 1993, many people who read it told me they felt a kinship with Sarah as a diarist, a teacher, and a member of a family with secrets. Students in my autobiography workshops continue to learn that people need to come to terms with the emotional ripples and tidal waves in the many generations of their family of origin and that a writing workshop can be a relatively safe place to explore some of those. Still, there are risks involved in revealing family secrets, and a writer must be very careful and make deliberate use of speech and silence when doing so.

About the same time that I began editing Sarah's diary, I took a three-year position supervising graduate students who taught in Mankato State University's freshman composition program. Several of the thirty teaching assistants were single mothers whose wages barely paid for their rent and food. I felt an affinity for these women, and I wanted to help them become confident teachers.

One graduate student, Rita Nicholson, was in her late twenties. At the age of seventeen, she had become an unmarried mother. Her ten-year-old son, Adam, came with her to Mankato, and they became Rachel's and my friends. That year Rita helped teach one of my women's writing courses, and she enrolled in an autobiography writing workshop that I taught. Each week, Rita would write personal essays about her childhood, adolescence, teenage pregnancy, and life as a single mother.

In one essay, Rita wrote about her father, who had died of a heart attack when she was sixteen and who, over a period of years, had sexually abused her. It was, Rita told me, the first time she had written about what her father had done to her. Perhaps by telling about his secret midnight visits to her bedroom, she could exorcise the demons from her family line:

They say that incest is so often repeated in succeeding generations that it almost seems to originate genetically. I don't believe that this is the case; incest is the nuclear weapon of the family; it is, in other words, a potentiality that we don't have to use. Incest is an emblem in our contemporary world of just how far we as humans have fallen. Incest is Milton's sin; a mother who is unable to free her own children is in turn devoured by them. Sin is the absence of love.

When I read Rita's essay on being a survivor of incest, I cried for the innocence she had lost. How many other little girls had similar stories to tell? How many of those stories would ever see the light of day? Despite everything, Rita was a survivor, and her essay ended with an affirmation: "I am whole now. That lost 'other' girl has finally, joyfully, regained her freedom of speech and with it her power."

In *Family Secrets: What You Don't Know Can Hurt You*, John Bradshaw writes about what he calls "degrees of toxicity" of family secrets. Bradshaw says that the need for disclosing less toxic "Third Degree-Damaging" and "Fourth Degree-Distressful" secrets, such as mental illness, physical disability, socioeconomic status, or ethnic shame, depends on "family process and social, cultural, ethnic, and religious context." Whether to disclose such secrets is a decision that can be made on a case-by-case basis.

But, Bradshaw explains, the need for disclosing more toxic "Second Degree-Dangerous" secrets, such as eating disorders, alcohol and gambling addictions, or paternity issues, is more pressing. Second-degree secrets, says Bradshaw, are dangerous ones that always need to be confronted and disclosed. Of course, he notes, one must be cautious about how and when to disclose such secrets: "Telling about your out-of-wedlock birth would not go over well in certain neighborhoods where the population is conservatively religious. In another neighborhood an out-of-wedlock birth is a common life transition. The shifting cultural and societal context must be kept in mind as we draw up guidelines for secret-telling."

Finally, Bradshaw discusses what he calls "First Degree—Deadly (Lethal) Secrets," such as rape, incest/molestation, child pornography, and sexual abuse. These lethal secrets, says Bradshaw, always need to be confronted and disclosed because they "violate human rights and destroy people's lives." Because violence and betrayal are often at the heart of lethal secrets, a good deal of grief is usually involved in coming to terms with them; however, explains Bradshaw, "grief is the healing feeling"; it involves a "process that goes through predictable stages

and takes time." Only when this process has been completed can forgiveness occur.

Now, when I teach autobiography writing workshops, I explain Harriet Lerner's and John Bradshaw's theories of family secrets to my students, who might find themselves writing not only about secrets in
their own lives but also in the lives of families, friends, partners, and
lovers. I ask my students to consider their motives for revealing family
secrets, and I urge them to keep Bradshaw's advice in mind:

> No one claims to *know for sure* when, where, how, and to whom
> secrets should be told. The best we can do is gain as full a grasp as
> possible of our family's polarities and do our best to be responsible
> for our own dark secrets and those that we know are hurting us as
> well as other family members.
>
> Keep in mind that the goal of confronting and disclosing dark
> secrets is to restore family members' personal dignity, privacy, qual-
> ity contact, and nurturing love, to set up an emotional climate in
> which sensitive information can be shared, and to open channels of
> communication that can be deepened long after the secret has
> been revealed.

Bradshaw's analysis of "First Degree—Deadly (Lethal) Secrets" and
their impact on family members has helped me understand the dynamics that often surround personal narratives like another one written in my autobiography workshop. The narrative, titled, "Dealing
with the Sexual Abuse of My Child," began like this:

> "Mommy, if I tell you something, will you promise not to tell
> anyone?"
>
> Two years ago, my four-year-old daughter Emily began telling me
> about the "game" her teenaged half-brother Eric had played when he
> was babysitting her during her visits to their father's house in an-
> other city. Emily described how Eric took off his clothes, then her
> clothes. She told how he'd touched and kissed her genitals and told
> her to do the same to his.
>
> "Mommy, don't tell anybody, especially Daddy," Emily warned
> me. "Eric said he and I would both be grounded if I told."
>
> I took a deep breath. "Honey, your dad needs to know. What Eric
> did wasn't a game. Remember when we talked about your private
> parts and how they were yours alone? Remember when we talked
> about how nobody has the right to touch them except you?"

"Or the doctor, if I'm having an examination," Emily added.

"That's right," I nodded.

"But Mommy," Emily said, "he's my *brother*."

The narrative continued, recounting the mother's decision to tell what her daughter had told her to a guardian ad litem, who had then talked with Emily and made a mandatory report to the county. A child protection worker, along with a police sergeant, began an investigation.

The narrative told about Eric and Emily's father's reactions to the allegations. He accused the mother of being a lesbian and of sexually abusing her daughter, Emily; he refused to allow his son, Eric, to be interviewed about the allegations; and he tried to have the court-appointed guardian ad litem fired. Despite the father's attempts to obstruct the investigation, however, both the county and the court reached the same conclusion: Emily had indeed been sexually abused by her older half brother, Eric.

Emily's mother's narrative noted that, two years after the sexual abuse had occurred, Emily was once again spending vacation periods at her father's house, where her half brother Eric continued to live. The only restriction imposed by the judge was a court order stipulating that the children's father was never to leave Emily and Eric alone together again. The mother's narrative concluded:

> The sexual abuse of a young child by a juvenile can be a complicated matter, especially when the situation involves sibling abuse. Yet it is a form of incest involving age and power differentials—and very subtle kinds of threats. It is an act of violence, not a children's game.
>
> My daughter Emily is a survivor of sexual abuse. Today she seems to feel good about herself. I give her a lot of credit for being a strong, spirited child. I also give myself some credit for helping her begin to heal. But I know that she might someday experience some of the after-effects of sexual abuse and that she might need help to work through them. Just because the county has closed its files on this case does not mean that the entire matter has been resolved.
>
> Violence toward little girls is one increasingly disturbing aspect of violence against women and children in our culture. We need to know all we can about how our legal system and child protection services do and do not respond to allegations of child sexual abuse. We need to change attitudes of attorneys, judges, legislators, and social service providers who do not give sibling abuse the serious attention it deserves. We need to understand what problems exist with current

statutes so that we can work toward changing our laws to truly protect our children.

That is why I am writing this essay. I want you to know about
Emily's experience. I hope that it will strengthen your commitment
toward making the reforms necessary to protect children from sexual
abuse. I hope that someday no little child will have to turn to a parent and say, "Mommy, if I tell you something, will you promise not
to tell anyone?"

Incest is not the only "family secret." Illegitimacy is another. In the
ten years since my daughter's birth, I've received compelling reminders
of my status as the "unwed mother" of an "illegitimate child." The
first came two days after Rachel's birth. I'd been browsing through the
listings of births in the *Mankato Free Press*, and I'd noticed the listings
for the other babies who were born in local and area hospitals on October 17, 1985. But Rachel's birth wasn't listed. When I phoned the newspaper office to ask why they'd forgotten to include it, I was told that
the hospital hadn't sent word of her birth along with those of the
other babies.

"How could that be?" I asked.

"Well, the hospital sends us all the birth notices except those of babies born to unwed mothers," the voice on the other end of the phone
line responded. "Aren't you an unwed mother?"

"Yes, I am. But I'd like my daughter's birth announcement to be in
the paper. Her name is Rachel Susanna, and she was born on Thursday,
October 17, 1985, at the hospital here in Mankato."

"Can you prove that you are the mother of this child?"

"Yes. I'm in my hospital room, and I have her right here beside me."

"I'd like to take your word for it, but I'm going to have to phone
the hospital to make sure you're actually a patient there. What's
your name?"

"Suzanne Bunkers. I'm in Room 504, and my phone number is
625-4031, extension 504. Call me back after you've talked with the
hospital office."

I hung up. A moment later my phone rang.

"Hello, is this Suzanne Bunkers?"

"It sure is. Now do you believe me?"

"Ms. Bunkers, I'm sorry. I'll make sure that your baby's birth announcement is in tomorrow's paper."

Later, when I would tell this anecdote to friends, they'd laugh up-
roariously and ask me why I hadn't invited the newspaper editor to
stop up at my room so I could prove I was my daughter's mother. I'd

laugh along, but I could see a serious side to the issue. I knew that some unmarried mothers, especially those whose babies were going to be placed for adoption, would not have wanted anything put into the local newspaper's birth announcements. Nor would their families. I felt fortunate not to be in that predicament.

A year later, on October 30, 1986, I received a letter from Father Steuben, the principal of the small high school in Iowa from which I had graduated:

> Dear Dr. Bunkers:
> In the name of the staff and the Class of 1987, I am delighted to welcome you to Spalding Catholic High School to serve as our commencement speaker on Sunday, May 24, 1987. The academic procession will form at 1:45 p.m. in the Spalding cafeteria, and the ceremony will begin at 2:00 p.m. We ask you to join us in the procession.
> You may find the enclosed copy of the "Philosophy and Objectives" helpful.
> If possible, would you please send a brief autobiography of yourself and a portrait adequate for press purposes. Kindly send these items as soon as convenient because we would like to publicize our graduation event ahead of time.

On December 1, 1986, I sent the principal my letter of acceptance, along with the photograph and autobiographical information he had requested. On January 6, 1987, while grading student papers at the kitchen table, I got a phone call. It was Father Steuben.

A few days later, I wrote about it in my journal:

> I got *uninvited* to be commencement speaker at Spalding because I have a child "out of wedlock." Fr. Steuben called me up last week one night, "concerned," as he put it, about an anonymous complaint he'd gotten. He asked if it were true that I was not married and that Rachel was born "out of wedlock." I said yes. He said he wanted to "protect" me from possible criticism from parishioners if I gave the speech in May.
> I told him I didn't feel I needed protection and didn't fear criticism. I asked him what his reason really was. He said he wouldn't judge me (of course not!) but he was "concerned how it might look" if I gave the talk. I told him it was his right to "uninvite" me, which he did. But he said that if "my circumstances ever changed" (i.e., I got married) he'd like to reconsider me!

After taking a few days to simmer down, I wrote Father Steuben a long letter:

> As the principal of Spalding High School, you have exercised your prerogative in withdrawing your invitation to me. In exercising this prerogative, however, you have gravely offended me. By focusing solely on my status as an "unwed mother," you have attempted to blot out all that I am and have accomplished in the nineteen years since I graduated from Spalding. You have, in effect, attempted to deny my existence.
>
> Furthermore, you have prevented the graduating class from hearing the words of a former Spalding student who has taken much of value with her from her four years there and who has assumed a responsible role as an educator, parent, social activist, and humanist. I refuse to accept your attempted denial of who I am and what I stand for, and I resent your inability to take a courageous stand by refusing to give in to fears of complaints if I were to give the commencement address.
>
> I celebrate my decision to have a child. It has been one of the most important decisions that I have ever made. My process of self-scrutiny in living up to the dictates of my conscience gives me great pleasure. I am the product of Spalding High School's successful attempts to aid the individual in "the formulation of spiritual, moral, and material goals and in the acquisition and skillful use of the intellectual and practical means of attaining such goals," as quoted from Spalding's "Philosophy and Objectives."
>
> This letter will, I hope, offer you some insight into my perspective on this situation, and it will further the dialogue in which we have been engaged. I welcome any continuance of this dialogue on your part.

Then I sent copies of my letter to my mother, my cousin Father Frank Klein, and the bishop of the diocese of Sioux City, Iowa.

A week later, I received the bishop's reply. He commended me for having expressed myself well and offered prayers that a "reconciliation" could take place. Shortly thereafter, I received Father Steuben's reply to what he termed my thoughtful and eloquent letter. He explained that he was not making any moral judgments and that, in fact, he was not unsympathetic to my situation; nonetheless, he stressed that, as a newcomer to Granville, he felt he must accept people as they were. He asked me to understand the dilemma in which he had found himself.

Though I did not agree with his decision, I could understand, perhaps better than he might have imagined. Like my great-great-grandmother Susanna Simmerl before me, I was the mother of a *filia naturalis*. But I knew that I as an unmarried mother could count on receiving far more emotional support than Susanna would have received more than 130 years earlier, when her daughter, Barbara Simmerl, had been born. I had an education, economic independence, and a good job doing what I loved to do. Unlike Susanna's daughter, Barbara, my daughter, Rachel, would know her biological father; and, unlike her great-great-grandmother Barbara, Rachel would be listed on her baptismal certificate as the daughter of her mother.

I didn't think much about the issue of illegitimacy again until fall 1987, when I went to the Blue Earth County Government Center in Mankato to renew my passport and apply for a child's passport for Rachel. To do that, I needed Rachel's photograph and a certified copy of her birth certificate. The clerk and I made small talk as I filled out the necessary paperwork. Then she went into the back room to make a certified copy of Rachel's birth certificate. Five minutes later, the clerk returned, shaking her head.

"I'm sorry, but did you say your child was born here in Mankato?" she asked.

"Yes, she was born on October 17, 1985, at Immanuel–St. Joseph Hospital," I replied. "At 2:46 p.m."

"Gee, let me try again." The clerk disappeared into the back room. A second time, she returned empty-handed.

"I don't understand," she said. "Are you *sure* you had a baby here in Mankato in 1985?"

I hoisted Rachel up and set her on the countertop. "Yes, I'm sure, and here she is!"

The clerk blushed. She leaned toward me and whispered, "Are you an *unwed* mother, by any chance?"

"Yes, I'm not married."

"Oh, that explains it. Your baby's birth is registered in our Illegitimate Births Book, not the regular one. Excuse me just one moment."

The clerk returned to the back room, then came out, flourishing a certified copy of Rachel's birth certificate, which she handed to me.

"Do you mean to tell me," I fumed, "that Blue Earth County has *two different sets* of birth records?"

"Yes, that's how it's done: one book for babies born to parents who are married, another book for babies born to parents who are not."

"I want to see the Illegitimate Births Book," I insisted.

"I'm sorry. We can't let you. No one can see the entries in that book, and no one can get a copy of one of the Illegitimate Birth certificates except the parent."

"Listen, I want Rachel's birth certificate put into the regular book," I said. "There's no reason for it not to be. No one is hiding her birth."

The clerk eyed me sympathetically. "I sure wish I could do that for you, but I can't. Your child's birth certificate has to stay where it is, unless, of course, your circumstances change."

"What do you mean?"

"If ever you marry your child's father, the child can be declared legitimate retroactively. Then her birth certificate can be put into the regular Births Book."

She handed me the certified copy. I paid for it, picked Rachel up, and left the building quickly, before I had the chance to say something I might later regret. I vowed to write a letter to someone, complaining about the policy of not allowing births like Rachel's to be recorded in the regular county records if the parent(s) wanted it to be. But to whom could I address my complaint?

That evening I sat down and opened my *Encyclopedic Dictionary of the English Language*:

> **Legitimate:** According to law; lawful; in accordance with established rules or principles; conforming to accepted standards; born of parents legally married; of the normal or regular type or kind.
> **Illegitimate:** a. not legitimate, illegal; unauthorized or unwarranted; illegal; irregular or improper; not in accordance with good usage. Born out of wedlock. *Logic*, not in accordance with the laws of reasoning; as, an *illegitimate* inference.

I sat there with the heavy dictionary on my lap, turning pages and reading definitions. Maybe things had not changed so much since 1856, when, in Feulen, Luxembourg, a baby girl named Barbara had been born to an unmarried twenty-five-year-old mother named Susanna.

During my many years of reading and teaching works of American literature, few have drawn and sustained my interest more than those dealing with mother-daughter relationships. And works of literature that feature such relationships where some disruption is threatened have held my interest above all others.

So, for instance, when I came across Hannah Foster's *The Coquette*, first published in America in 1797, I found the title character, Eliza

Wharton, fascinating not only because her story was told in the form
of letters from one character to another but also because she embraced
such sentiments as "Marriage is the tomb of friendship. It appears to
me a very selfish state." I liked Eliza Wharton because she was not the
traditional heroine of romantic novels: the pure little poor girl who,
through a series of lucky coincidences, finds her life culminating in a
fortuitous marriage to a handsome and virtuous young man.

In fact, the story of Eliza Wharton, as told in *The Coquette*, is the
story of a "good girl gone bad." A didactic novel, it is a classic tale of
seduction and betrayal, in which Eliza is seduced, impregnated, and ultimately abandoned by her married suitor, Peter Sanford. As in most
such stories of that time, Eliza, although not by nature a "bad girl,"
nonetheless has to be punished for her "sin"—the bringing forth of a
child without benefit of marriage. Eliza's words of repentance are repeated for readers in a letter written by Eliza to her friend Julia Granby:

> Should it please God to spare and restore me to health, I shall return,
> and endeavor, by a life of penitence and rectitude, to expiate my past
> offences. But should I be called from this scene of action; and leave
> behind me a helpless babe, the innocent sufferer of its mother's
> shame, Oh, Julia, let your friendship for me extend to the little
> stranger! Intercede with my mother to take it under her protection;
> and transfer to it all her affection for me; to train it up in the ways of
> piety and virtue, that it may compensate her for the afflictions which
> I have occasioned!

Literary and cultural mores of the time did not permit the author to
allow either Eliza Wharton or her baby daughter to survive. Both had
to die in expiation for the sins of the mother. In her letter to Julia, Lucy
Sumner, another of Eliza's friends, sums up the lesson to be learned
from Eliza's fate:

> I wish it engraved upon every heart, that virtue alone, independent of
> the trappings of wealth, the parade of equipage, and the adulation
> of gallantry, can secure lasting felicity. From the melancholy story of
> Eliza Wharton, let the American fair learn to reject with disdain
> every insinuation derogatory to their true dignity and honor. Let
> them despise, and forever banish the man, who can glory in the se-
> duction of innocence and the ruin of reputation. To associate, is to
> approve; to approve, is to be betrayed!

The final image in the novel is the inscription on Eliza's tombstone:

> *"THIS HUMBLE STONE,*
> IN MEMORY OF
> **ELIZA WHARTON,**
> IS INSCRIBED BY HER WEEPING FRIENDS,
> TO WHOM
> SHE ENDEARED HERSELF BY UNCOMMON
> TENDERNESS AND AFFECTION.
>
> ENDOWED WITH SUPERIOR ACQUIRE-
> MENTS, SHE WAS STILL
> MORE DISTINGUISHED BY HUMILITY
> AND BENEVOLENCE.
>
> LET CANDOR THROW A VEIL OVER HER
> FRAILTIES, FOR GREAT WAS HER
> CHARITY TO OTHERS.
>
> SHE SUSTAINED THE LAST PAINFUL
> SCENE, FAR FROM EVERY FRIEND;
> AND EXHIBITED AN EXAMPLE OF CALM
> RESIGNATION.
>
> HER DEPARTURE WAS ON THE 25TH DAY
> OF JULY, A. D. ——,
> IN THE 37TH YEAR OF HER AGE,
> AND THE TEARS OF STRANGERS WATER-
> ED HER *GRAVE."*

A little more than fifty years after the publication of *The Coquette*, another American tale about an unmarried mother and her child was published: Nathaniel Hawthorne's *The Scarlet Letter*. Hester Prynne, initially imprisoned for the crime of giving birth to a child while un-married, is released from her prison cell and sent to live in a tiny cot-tage at the edge of the forest. Part of her punishment is her sentence to wear, for the rest of her life, the scarlet letter A (for adulteress) on the bodice of her dress.

The first time I read this story, while still in high school during the late 1960s, I found it captivating and moving because of the artistry of its author. *The Scarlet Letter* was one of the most carefully crafted and well-told tales that I had ever read. What amazed me about *The Scarlet*

Letter (and, in fact, continues to amaze me, given that the story is set in seventeenth-century Puritan New England) is that Hester Prynne gets to keep her little daughter, Pearl:

> Her Pearl!—For so had Hester called her; not as a name expressive of her aspect, which had nothing of the calm, white, unimpassioned lustre that would be indicated by the comparison. But she named the infant "Pearl," as being of great price—purchased with all she had— her mother's only treasure!

True, Hester is first imprisoned, then shunned by the townspeople. But she does not have to relinquish her baby. Nor does she have to die, although the man who had impregnated her, the Rev. Arthur Dimmesdale, is struck down dead in the novel's climactic scene.

Even more astounding to me is the story's denouement. Young Pearl, now grown to womanhood, has left the village, married, and become "the richest heiress of her day, in the New World." Her mother, Hester, who initially left with her daughter after Dimmesdale's death, has returned to the village many years later. Hester has once again taken up residence in her weathered cottage at the edge of the woods. There, she is revered as a wise and respected old woman who helps other unwed mothers:

> Women, more especially—in the continually recurring trials of wounded, wasted, wronged, misplaced, or erring and sinful passion— or with the dreary burden of a heart unyielded, because unvalued and unsought—came to Hester's cottage, demanding why they were so wretched, and what the remedy! Hester comforted and counselled them, as best she might. She assured them, too, of her firm belief, that, at some brighter period, when the world should have grown ripe for it, in Heaven's own time, a new truth would be revealed, in order to establish the whole relation between man and woman on a surer ground of mutual happiness.

As many critics of American literature have pointed out, Nathaniel Hawthorne has created, in Hester Prynne, a woman ahead of her time. While Hawthorne does not wholeheartedly applaud the way in which Hester lives her life, neither does he condemn her to obscurity or death. Early in the novel, just as Hester is being taken from her prison cell to the scaffold to face the ridicule of her accusers, Hawthorne even draws a deft tongue-in-cheek comparison between Hester and another well-known unmarried mother:

Had there been a Papist among the crowd of Puritans, he might have seen in this beautiful woman, so picturesque in her attire and mien, and with the infant at her bosom, an object to remind him of the image of Divine Maternity, which so many illustrious painters have vied with one another to represent; something which should remind him, indeed, but only by contrast, of that sacred image of sinless motherhood, whose infant was to redeem the world. Here, there was the taint of deepest sin in the most sacred quality of human life, working such effect that the world was only the darker for this woman's beauty, and the more lost for the infant she had borne.

The Scarlet Letter held my interest for another reason. Nearly every year without fail, at least one girl attending my Catholic high school would "get herself in trouble," as the popular expression put it, and she would either "have to get married" (in which case she would keep her baby) or "disappear" (at least until her baby was born and put up for adoption). Then, when she'd return, none of her friends would ask any questions. Her secret would be safe.

When I began college at Iowa State University in September 1968, an unwed mother's options remained much the same. The following year I became friends with Shelley, who lived in my dormitory. In June 1969, just before final exams week, she disappeared, and the rumor circulated that she was pregnant. I heard that her parents had made hurried arrangements to send her away to northern Minnesota to live with an aunt and uncle for a time. The following March, Shelley returned to college and moved back into our dormitory. No one asked her where she had been.

One morning, as I was brushing my teeth in our dormitory's bathroom, I heard someone sobbing. As I walked toward the bathroom door, I saw Shelley, wrapped in her bath towel, leaning against the wall of a shower stall. I asked her what was wrong, and within minutes she told me the entire story of her pregnancy and her baby's birth just weeks before. None of her brothers, sisters, or hometown friends had even known she was pregnant. Her parents hadn't contacted her during the entire time she was living with her aunt and uncle.

Shelley told me she had never seen her baby after giving birth. She only knew it had been a little girl. She had signed the adoption papers, checked out of the hospital, and taken a bus directly back to her parents' home in southern Iowa. A week later, she moved back into the dorm and began spring quarter at Iowa State University.

Over the years, I've thought about Shelley, and I've wondered what happened to her baby daughter. Their story is not an isolated one. Whenever I tell it to a friend, I can be sure I'll hear another story in return—one about a sister, a mother, or even a friend herself—who became pregnant outside marriage and faced some very difficult and painful decisions. I could empathize, for I had faced those decisions myself.

A few years ago, I decided to do some background reading on how out-of-wedlock births were perceived by twentieth-century American scholars. When I came across Leontine Young's analysis, I was surprised to find that it had been published over forty years ago. It sounded quite contemporary:

> The existence of unmarried mothers is not new in the world's history; nor is the problem of illegitimacy unique to the twentieth century. For ages past the girl who bore a child outside the limits of wedlock has been the target and frequently the victim of public attitudes and emotions. While these public attitudes have varied from one historical period to another and from one culture to another, there is, taken as a whole, an amazing and rather appalling consistency in the way she and her child have been condemned by society. In certain periods and in certain cultures she has been punished by death and her child doomed to disgrace and ostracism. Even today this practice may be found in some countries. In others she has been branded as a moral outcast, and both she and her child have been compelled to live lives of social and economic degradation in hopeless and endless expiation.—Leontine Young, *Out of Wedlock: A Study of the Problems of the Unmarried Mother and Her Child*, 1954

Leontine Young's words took me back to 1964, when I'd bought a copy of a slim paperback, *On Becoming a Woman*, at a school book fair. In Chapter 11, "All about Love," I read about how no teenage boy could be counted on to control his sexual urges and about how it was up to the teenage girl to set the sexual limits in a relationship. Chapter 11 ended with a stern warning to adolescent readers like me:

> We could make quite a case for chastity right here by pointing out that despite the wonders of modern science, despite your own faith in your self-control and ability to stop at a given point, you are by no means "protected" from pregnancy by such methods of "controlling" intercourse. Many a girl who considered herself "smart" in her indulgence in sex finds, too late, that she has made a permanent mistake.

Pregnancy outside marriage is a mistake because it hurts you and the child, your family, and the man who is the father of the child. Only a very irresponsible or immature person can ignore these responsibilities; only a selfish teen could pretend that such a pregnancy "didn't matter." So perhaps one of the most practical arguments for chastity is simply this: any one act of intercourse (even if it's your first mistake) can lead to the permanent mistake of an unplanned and unwanted pregnancy outside of marriage.

I interpret these words quite differently now, almost thirty years after first reading them in *On Becoming a Woman*. Back then, as an eighth grader fairly new to the world of roller skating parties and sock hops, my biggest worry was that French-kissing was a mortal sin. The possibility of doing anything "below the neck" (as my friends put it) was unimaginable. I would remain chaste. I would never have to worry about making a "permanent mistake" that could ruin my life.

In May 1992, I listened as Vice President Dan Quayle issued his condemnation of unwed mothers the day after that famous episode of *Murphy Brown* in which Murphy gave birth to her son, Avery, aired on TV. I sat down at my computer and dashed off a letter to the editor of the *Minneapolis Star-Tribune*:

Dear Editor:
What do Thomas Jefferson, Pablo Picasso, Lyndon Johnson, and Irish Bishop Eamon Casey have in common? They're all white men who have fathered "illegitimate" children.

Perhaps Dan Quayle can re-direct his campaign against "illegitimacy" toward assessing why such men sire children out of wedlock and assign responsibility for those children to women.

Murphy Brown—and other single mothers—can use a rest.
Suzanne Bunkers,
Mankato, MN

In the November 1992 elections, I voted for Bill Clinton, and I remained a staunch supporter of his presidency until I tuned in the *CBS Evening News* and heard him addressing the Southern Baptist Convention. When President Clinton began railing against mothers who had had children out of wedlock, I reached for my remote control and changed the channel. I could not support him any longer.

Recent news headlines proclaim, WOMEN CHOOSE MOTHERHOOD WITHOUT HUSBANDS and UNWED MOMS' BIRTH RATE UP, ESPECIALLY

AMONG WHITES. I know that many people view the situation with alarm, but I'm not convinced that having a baby without benefit of marriage is necessarily a bad thing, especially when marriage would place mother and child in an unsafe or unhealthy situation with little hope of escape.

My point of view is simple: I don't wish to pass judgment on others; all I ask is that others not pass judgment on me. I like the way Charlotte Brontë put it in her preface to the second edition of *Jane Eyre*, published in 1848: "Conventionality is not morality. Self-righteousness is not religion."

Over the years, I've read *The Scarlet Letter* many times. My most recent rereading occurred in August 1994 while I was in Luxembourg City for a conference titled "Batardise & Identité" [Illegitimacy & Identity], sponsored by the Society of Europeanists. There, along with scholars from Greece, Bulgaria, France, and Luxembourg, I took part in discussions on subjects such as definitions of illegitimacy, the integration and marginalization of illegitimate children, the naming of abandoned children, and the illegitimate individual's search for identity. My presentation centered on my research on the life of my ancestor, Susanna Simmerl Youngblut.

When my turn to speak arrived, I talked about how my search for Susanna had begun many years before. I described my solitary walks through cemeteries as well as my silent poring over church and civil records. I discussed my initial hypothesis that Susanna had taken her infant daughter, Barbara, and sailed for America in 1857; then I explained how I had learned that little Barbara had stayed behind in Luxembourg with her grandmother Angela Simmerl for ten years. I explained that I wasn't really certain how and when Barbara Simmerl came to be recognized, within the family and outside it, as Susanna's daughter.

Finally, I told the other scholars that even now, fifteen years after my search had begun, I still did not have all the answers but my objective has shifted away from an emphasis on finding out who Barbara Simmerl's biological father had been to an understanding of the context of Susanna's and Barbara's lives, both in Luxembourg and in the United States. I had decided that my study, unlike a scientific study that had to be based strictly on ascertainable facts, would be based on family stories, personal possessions, photographs, and news clippings as well as on formal documents and scholarly studies. I told the other scholars I had determined that the advice given by Marian Martinello, in *The Search for Emma's Story*, was sound advice for me to follow:

> Knowing when to quit the search for any part of the story was important. . . . The principle I learned to apply was this: if I had obtained sufficient information to formulate and answer a general question that clarified my initial wonderings and if I could answer that question sufficiently well to reconstruct a sharply focused moving scenario in my imagination, then I had found what I needed.

Then I deviated from my formal presentation to talk briefly about *The Scarlet Letter*, published only six years before Susanna Simmerl had given birth to her first child, Barbara. I turned to a pivotal scene in Hawthorne's novel and began reading some of Hester Prynne's words aloud, aware for the first time of their many layers of resonance:

> "God gave me the child!" cried she. "He gave her in requital of all things else, which ye had taken from me. She is my happiness!—she is my torture, none the less! Pearl keeps me here in life! Pearl punishes me too! See ye not, she is the scarlet letter, only capable of being loved, and so endowed with a millionfold the power of retribution for my sin? Ye shall not take her! I will die first!"

11. In the Name of the Mother

Glory be to our Mother, and Daughter,
and to the Holy of Holies,
as it was in the beginning,
is now and ever shall be,
World, without end. Amen.
—Bobby McFerrin, "The 23rd Psalm"

Susanna, Barbara, Suzanne, Rachel. Names. What do they mean? How are they given? What *is* in a name?

In my family, names are important. We have had a long tradition of selecting names that have special meaning; part of this tradition is making a favorite ancestor's (often a godparent's) name part of a child's name. So, for example, my father, Jerome Anton Bunkers, was named after a favorite uncle, his father's brother, Anton (Tony) Bunkers; and, even though my dad's actual name was Jerome, he was always called Tony. His father, Frank Henry Bunkers, was named after his father, Henry, and, I'd like to think, after another special man: Frank Young-blut, the stepfather of Frank's mother, Barbara Simmerl Bunkers. I was named Suzanne Lillian Bunkers, after my father's mother, Lillian Welter Bunkers. And my daughter is named Rachel Susanna. Her name is special, too.

When visiting Quebec City a few years ago, I came across a little import shop that specialized in postcards from France that listed French etymologies of first names. I bought two postcards. One explains the meaning of the name "Rachel" as "not very optimistic, tending to melancholy, passionate, extreme in likes and dislikes." The second postcard explains the etymology of the name "Suzanne" as "quite feminine, likable, spontaneous, charming without effort."

Our Lady of Consolation, St. Roche Catholic Church, Niederfeulen.

I've found these French etymologies engaging, but I prefer to go back to biblical and religious sources for the names that have had special meaning in our family over the generations. As I've explored the sources of such names, I've contemplated the possible repercussions of their origins and meanings for the lives of those who have given them and those who have borne them.

The name "Barbara," for instance, was a popular name given to baby girls in nineteenth-century Luxembourg. Saint Barbara, whose feast day is December 4, was a young Roman woman who, as legend has it, was imprisoned in a tower by her father, Dioscorus, for refusing to marry. According to Delaney's *Dictionary of Saints*, it is doubtful that an actual virgin martyr named Barbara ever existed; nonetheless, Christian legend reveres her as "one of the Fourteen Holy Helpers" and as the "patroness of architects and builders." Church records indicate that Susanna Simmerl's daughter Barbara was named after her godmother and aunt, Barbara Simmerl, who was Susanna's younger sister.

In Luxembourg, according to *The Practice of Popular Protection and the Cult of Saints-Protectors*, Saint Barbara became known as the patron saint of miners because she could find refuge in the crux of a rock, which, miraculously, gave her asylum after her escape from imprisonment. Norbert Thill's photographic essay "Schutzpatronin Sankt Barbara" [Protector-Patron Saint Barbara], which appeared in the *Luxemburger Marienkalender* (1982), provides evidence of just how extensively the popular legend of Saint Barbara has found expression in the statuary and stained-glass windows of churches in many Luxembourg villages, such as Steinsel, Osweiler, Bourscheid, Rosport, Differdange, Wormeldange, Heinerscheid, Esch-Alzette, and Vianden. Even today, Luxembourg churches continue to pay homage to the memory of this respected virgin-martyr.

The name "Rachel" is of Hebrew origin, and it means "innocent, gentle; blessed one." Its biblical source is the story of Rachel and Jacob, as recounted in Genesis 29. Jacob had fallen in love with Rachel, the younger daughter of Laban, who agreed that she could marry her suitor after Jacob had completed seven years of work for Laban. But Laban tricked Jacob by substituting his older daughter, Leah, for Rachel in the marriage bed. Then Laban required Jacob to work another seven years so that Rachel could become his second wife. Rachel eventually became the mother of Joseph, the favorite of Jacob's twelve sons and the founder of one of the twelve tribes of Israel.

The name "Susanna," also of Hebrew origin, means "brilliant and pure." It comes from the story of Susanna, as told in Daniel 13 in the Catholic Bible. Susanna, a virtuous wife and mother, had been accused of adultery by two male elders who lusted after her.

> "I am completely trapped," Susanna groaned. "If I yield, it will be my death; if I refuse, I cannot escape your power. Yet it is better for me to fall into your power without guilt than to sin before the Lord." Then Susanna shrieked, and the old men also shouted at her, as one of them ran to open the garden doors. When the people in the house heard the cries from the garden, they rushed in by the side gate to see

what had happened to her. At the accusations by the old men, the servants felt very much ashamed, for never had any such thing been said about Susanna.

When Susanna's case came before the judge, the elders accused her of having lured them into the garden, and she was sentenced to be executed. As Susanna was about to be led away, a young boy named Daniel stepped forward. He had overheard the elders threatening Susanna, and he questioned them, catching them in their lies and defending Susanna's purity and honor. Biblical scholar Louis F. Hartman explains the meaning of the story of Susanna: "The primary purpose of the story is to show that virtue (here in the form of conjugal chastity) triumphs, with God's help, over vice (here in the form of lust and deceit)."

The story of Susanna, considered canonical by some biblical scholars, is considered apocryphal by others. Thus, it is found in the Greek and Latin (Vulgate) versions of the Book of Daniel (the "deuterocanonical" Catholic versions), not in most canonical Protestant or Jewish versions. According to *A New Catholic Commentary on Holy Scripture*, which refers to the story of Susanna as one of the "deuterocanonical appendices," this story may have been added to the Book of Daniel "to narrate an example of how a pious woman was unjustly condemned by wicked judges and saved by God" or to serve as "an attack on lax judicial procedure" that "advocates a more rigid examination of witnesses when there was suspicion of collusion."

Recent feminist scholarship adds depth and vision to earlier, more traditional interpretations of the story of Susanna. In *The Women's Bible Commentary*, Toni Craven notes that the law did not entitle Susanna to speak in her own defense, yet she raised her voice to God to protest the unfairness of her sentence of execution. Craven concludes:

> To allow the story to increase only Daniel's reputation is to miss the importance of Susanna's actions and the association of this story with other books titled by the names of women, notably Ruth, Esther, and Judith. Even though appended to the book of Daniel, "Susanna" is still remembered as the title of this story. . . . Susanna's story tells how a woman *within* the covenant community faced death and triumphed over adversity when threatened—not by powerful foreign officials but by supposedly trustworthy Jewish leaders. Susanna, like Daniel, Shadrach, Meshach, and Abednego, honors God's sovereignty by valuing faithfulness more than life itself. She champions

prayer and the finding of one's own voice in refusing evil and choosing good. Good triumphs because of God's attention to her cry.

Catholic stories of the saints also include a brief mention of another Susanna, whose feast day is August 11. According to the Saint Joseph Daily Missal, "St. Susanna, a holy virgin, was beheaded after grievous torments in 295, for refusing to marry the [Roman] emperor's son." Delanay's *Dictionary of Saints* provides this brief biography:

> Susanna (d. 295). The beautiful daughter of Gabinus, a priest, and niece of Pope Caius, she refused Emperor Diocletian's request that she marry his son-in-law Maximian and converted two of her uncles, Claudius and Maximus, who were court officers sent by Diocletian to persuade her to marry, to Christianity. Diocletian was so enraged by what she had done that he sent one of his father's favorites, Julian, to deal with the matter. Julian had Maximus, Claudius and his wife Praepedigna, and their two sons burned to death at Cumae, and then had Susanna and her father beheaded.

Die Luxemburger und ihre Vornamen lists "Susanna" as one of the ten most common names given to a baby girl in Luxembourg during the latter nineteenth century. According to Catholic tradition, a female infant would typically be given the name of her godmother. Thus, Susanna Simmerl was named for her godmother and aunt, Susanna Hottua, the sister of Angela Hottua Simmerl.

Over the centuries, "Susanna" has also proved a popular choice for writers who wish to speak about the virtues of female purity and piety. For instance, in *The Book of the City of Ladies*, written sometime around the turn of the twelfth century, Christine de Pizan draws upon the biblical story of Susanna. As part of her attempt to address the issue of woman's role in society, de Pizan employs the narrative strategy of an ongoing exchange with the allegorical figures of Reason, Rectitude, and Justice—all of whom are personified as female.

In response to de Pizan's question, "Where does the opinion that there are so few chaste women come from?" Rectitude uses the biblical figure of Susanna as an illustration of valiance and chastity in women:

> From what I have already actually told you and from what you know about this, the contrary is quite obvious to you, and I could tell you more about this and then some. How many valiant and

chaste ladies does Holy Scripture mention who chose death rather than transgress against the chastity and purity of their bodies and thoughts, just like the beautiful and good Susanna, wife of Joachim, a rich man of great authority among the Jews?

Christine de Pizan's treatment of the story of Susanna places great emphasis on her beauty and purity, and it stands in stark contrast to images of women in the *Malleus Maleficarum*, published less than a hundred years later. As the story of Susanna has been adapted over the centuries by painters and writers, however, another shade of meaning has often entered into their interpretations. As Susan Haskins describes it,

> The original biblical account of Jewish married virtue under siege from male predatoriness became through various medieval commentators that of a temptress, whose bathing lured the Elders from the paths of righteousness. This was illustrated in numerous images of her in fifteenth- and early sixteenth-century psalters, displaying her entirely naked body to the old men, and it was as the temptress of *vanitas*, rather than victim, that later artists like Tintoretto and Rubens chose to depict her.

Such interpretations are apparent not only in the work of painters like Tintoretto and Rubens but also in the work of twentieth-century artists. Consider, for example, American painter Thomas Hart Benton's *Susanna and the Elders* (1938) and American poet Wallace Stevens' "Peter Quince at the Clavier" (1915). Here Stevens writes of the "witching chords" invoked in the "red-eyed elders" by the sight of Susanna:

> In the green water, clear and warm,
> Susanna lay.
> She searched
> The touch of springs,
> And found
> Concealed imaginings.
> She sighed,
> For so much melody.

The poem goes on to recount the discovery of the elders (the "simpering Byzantines") and the revelation of "Susanna and her shame."

Stevens' poem concludes with the poet's observation on the nature of beauty and memory.

I had recently taught "Peter Quince at the Clavier" in my American literature course. It, along with Daniel 13 and etymologies of family names, was swirling around in my head as I packed for a trip to Europe in August 1994. I planned to take part in a short conference, "Illegitimacy and Identity," as well as participate in the XXIII International Congress of Genealogy and Heraldry, both of which would be held in Luxembourg City. En route, I would spend a few days in Amsterdam, then take the train to visit my friend Lois at Louvain-la-Neuve, meet my friend Clara for dinner at the Grand Place in Brussels, and return to my old neighborhood on Avenue Huysmans once more.

AUGUST 22, 1994

> Monday 2:30 p.m. I am at the Tavern at Chausée de Boondael 475, 1050 Bruxelles, just two blocks from where Rachel and I lived in 1988. I took Bus 71 to Avenue Huysmans this morning. I walked up the street and entered the foyer of our old apartment building. I almost expected to see our name, *Bunkers,* still on the Apartment 2 mailbox.
>
> This tavern is the first place I brought Rachel for a Sunday meal when we arrived in Bruxelles in January 1988. If I recall, it was cold and I took her out in her stroller just for some relief from the Flatotel. We ended up here because it was the only place open on a Sunday. I don't recall what I had. I think I bought Rachel a little pizza, which she devoured, and we shared a "Dame Blanche"—ice cream sundae. I remember feeling so grateful for good, hot food. I would have eaten anything—I was so desperate for a hot meal and to be somewhere with people, music, and talking! After that, I'd stop by here once a week or so for coffee or a beer. It's close to the ULB [Université Libre de Bruxelles] and draws a crowd of students and area residents.
>
> The neighborhood looks just about as it did in 1988. I had a sense of déjà vu when I got off Bus 71 and saw "our" apartment building. It's sad that kind Georges Lamy has died; he was so good to Rachel and me. When I return, I have a feeling of being at home, a little nostalgia, maybe like what I feel whenever I visit Madison. It's like, "Hey, don't I still *live* here?" The years since I've been gone drop away, and I get a warm, loving feeling toward the place as one where I felt safe, protected, and comfortable.
>
> It amazes me that I sometimes feel more "at home" in a place

like this than I do in Mankato, after nearly fourteen years there. I
hope I feel this way again when I get to Luxembourg.

AUGUST 23, 1994

I'm waiting on the steps of the Musée des Beaux Arts for the 10 a.m.
opening. Then I plan to browse for a couple of hours. I don't need
to take the train to Ottignes until 3:25, and it will arrive there by
4 p.m. Lois will pick me up. We'll stay at her house in Louvain-la-
Neuve until Thursday, at which time I will take the train to Luxembourg City. It'll be a short visit to Lois, but I hope we can tape-
record some stories of her life tomorrow.

2:30 p.m. The Museum was good—interesting to see so much religious art by so many Dutch and Flemish painters—Brueghel,
Rubens, etc. One painting by de Jordaens called "Susanna and the
Elders" caught my eye. It's based on the Biblical story of Susanna,
which appears only in the canonical Catholic version of the Bible. I
want to learn more about the painter and this particular work. Also,
I wonder how the Reformation connects to the disappearance of Susanna's story from the Protestant canonical version of the Bible?
Why did that story get marginalized in some versions, deleted
in others?

AUGUST 25, 1994

I'm here! The train arrived in Luxembourg City on time, and I took
a taxi to the Centre Carrefour-Convict, where I'll be staying a few
nights. Jean-Claude Muller and the other scholars at the "Illegitimacy and Identity" conference were waiting for me, and we all went
to lunch at a restaurant in the Grund—an old brewery where, as
Jean-Claude put it, "more illegitimate births existed than anywhere
else in Luxembourg." We laughed—he drove me to the old restaurant, and the other 4 people came in another car. He asked, "Where
is Rachel?"

I replied, "With her dad for two weeks." I was amazed how easily
I said it and how comfortable I felt—really, how fortunate Rachel is
to have a dad in her life and how she needs both her mom and her
dad. No matter what he has done (or tried to do) to me, Rachel
needs & deserves a good relationship with him, and I am very happy
to be out of his life, away from his grasp.

I went out walking all over Luxembourg City. It feels like home,
and I believe it is a feeling I've had ever since the first time I came
here in 1980—with Frank—and, if not for him, I probably would

not have made that trip. For him, it was the death of his mother
that gave him a desire to find his roots. For me, it was the death of
my father that gave me that impetus. These events brought Frank
and me together, and from there everything else has come: my con-
tacts with family and friends in Luxembourg, my desire to learn
about Susanna and the history of my family.

When I come here, the tears start to flow. When I see the Luxembourg Cathedral of Notre Dame, I am overcome by a feeling that I
can't explain. When I sit in the central square and realize that so
many of my ancestors had to leave Luxembourg and could never
come back, I feel so incredibly lucky to be here. I have the ability
to be in a place that they no doubt longed for but could never
see again.

And Susanna? Who can say how she felt about her homeland, especially if she was more or less forced to leave? I can come and go.
My life is so different from what her life could ever have been.

AUGUST 28, 1994

Sunday in Niederfeulen at Erny and Nico Linden's. They were
happy to see me when I arrived for dinner last night, and we visited
a while. This morning I went with them to Mass in Oberfeulen.
The old church has been restored and looks very beautiful inside.
Now I think that is where Susanna would have gone, since the Simmerls are officially listed as part of Oberfeulen, not Niederfeulen,
but the parish records seem to cover both—and people seem to consider it all one town—Feulen.

The Oberfeulen church, built in 1730, would have been in use
when Susanna was a girl. One stained glass window depicts "The
Visitation"—Mary's visit to her cousin Elizabeth, when each told
the other she was pregnant, Mary with Jesus, Elizabeth with John
the Baptist. Would Susanna have seen this window at Mass? What
would she have thought about the Blessed Virgin Mary, who also
gave birth to a child out of wedlock?

I wonder whether Barbara was presented as Susanna's younger
sister rather than as her daughter? Census records show that Angela
Simmerl's last child died shortly after birth in 1854. Then her husband died. Would Angela have taken Barbara as a substitute for the
child who died? Barbara was born on December 30, 1856, according
to the Feulen parish baptismal records, but many records in the U.S.
list her as born on January 1, 1856, making her appear to be a year
older than she actually was. Might her actual birth date have been

concealed to make her appear old enough to pass as Angela Simmerl's youngest child?

What does account for the erasure of Susanna's name in church
records but not in civil records? Is there any chance it was acciden-
tal on the part of the parish priest? No, I just can't believe it could
have been a slip of the pen because "filia naturalis," written by the
priest, was no accident.

Does it matter who Barbara's biological father was? I could probably spend the rest of my life trying to find out, but to what end? My
goal is not to fill in that line on a genealogical chart. I want to move
away from the name of the father. My goal is to restore, claim, and
celebrate the name of the mother.

I'm going to check to see whether Peter Simmerl was born just
two months after Angela Hottua and Theodore Simmerl were
married in 1827. If so, this would lend support to my hypothesis
that it wasn't unusual for pregnancy to precede marriage, but
it was unusual for pregnancy to conclude with no marriage
taking place.

After Mass, Erny and I stopped to say a prayer at Nick Linden's
grave. It's been ten years since he had a stroke and died, the day
after Frank, the Lindens, and I went to see an American band at the
Hennesbau in Feulen. I'd left for Paris and didn't learn of Nick's
death until I got home to Mankato in early July. So Erny has been
widowed for 10 years.

Today, after a very good noon meal (pepper steak, potatoes, salad,
fruit), I went for a drive alone to take some pictures in the area. The
scenery is breathtaking as always. I drove first to Tadler and stopped
by the cemetery where my great-great-grandfather Michel Klein is
buried. His grave is still being cared for by the townspeople. I drove
on to Bourscheid to see the restored castle, and I climbed to the top.

I took a lot of photographs of the countryside as I drove along in
the hopes that some can be used in the Susanna book. I stopped a
few times at places where plaques commemorated the American
soldiers who gave their lives in the Battle of the Bulge in 1944–45.
A poster at the Bourscheid castle advertised the commemoration of
the 50th anniversary of the liberation of Luxembourg by U.S. troops
on September 11, 1994, the first liberation of Luxembourg. The
Germans pushed back in during the winter of 1944–45. Although
Americans aren't always welcome in some European countries, they
do seem to be welcome in Luxembourg, where the people have long
and vivid memories.

Tomorrow I'll drive to Luxembourg City for the opening session
of the Congress—at Kirschberg Plateau—the EEC headquarters.
I'll likely be in and out of the Congress, and I'll go to the Archives
when I can. On Tuesday I'll go to see the Pierrets in Wolkrange,
then stay at the Hotel Schintgen in Luxembourg City while the
Congress is underway.

Yesterday, as I was driving from Ettelbruck to the outskirts of
Niederfeulen, the Beatles' "Long and Winding Road" came on my
car radio. I pulled over next to the "Niederfeulen, 50 km" sign and
looked out over the valley where the fog covered the town and let
the tears fall—not sad tears, but the tears that mark some deep feeling, perhaps one that no words can explain—to myself, or to anyone
else. There is really no reason to try to explain—it is just the way it
is for me when I get here. In some way I can't explain and perhaps
will never fully understand, this is Home.

AUGUST 31, 1994

At Rogér and Colette Pierret's home in Wolkrange, Belgium. Yesterday afternoon we went to see the Abbey d'Orval about thirty miles
east of here, just on the border between Belgium and France. I
thought the countryside was lovely and the ruins of the old 12th
century abbey impressive in the late afternoon sunlight. I took quite
a few photos and am about to be done with my documentation of
this visit to Luxembourg and Belgium. I am developing a feeling of
nostalgia for some things Belgian, like stores and certain places—in
Brussels—the Grand Place, the Sablon, rue Huysmans, etc.

But this part of Belgium near Arlon is really more Luxembourg
than Belgium, despite the "partition" which took the province of
Luxembourg and made it an official part of the country of Belgium.
The people here live like Luxembourgers and speak Lëtzebuergesch
daily—at least the older generations do. Rogér told me that he and
Colette speak it but that their daughters Martine and Françoise use
French as their daily language.

The trip to Orval was also enjoyable because, after our tour of
the ruins of the old abbey, we went to a little cafe across the road
from the abbey, where the three of us had big glasses of Orval beer,
brewed by the monks. The name "Orval" came from a woman
named Matilde, who proclaimed the area a "Val d'Or." Then it was
transposed to "D'Orval." Very good beer at that. Colette bought
some D'Orval cheese and honey, while Rogér bought a case of
D'Orval beer. No doubt they will send some along with me back

to the U.S. They are good people, and despite our limited ability to communicate at times, I feel pretty comfortable around them.

The village church bells are ringing for morning Mass. It's 7:00 a.m., so soon I will get dressed for the day. I want to be in Luxembourg Ville by 9 a.m. for the roundtable discussion that Jean-Claude Muller and Jean Ensch are doing. Then I hope to spend the p.m. at the National Library and/or Archives d'état.

Everyone is preparing for the 50th anniversary of the liberation of Luxembourg by American forces. The primary celebration will take place on 11 September. There will be Masses of remembrance and state ceremonies and memorials—in Bastogne, at the castle of Bourscheid, in Luxembourg City, and elsewhere in the Grand Duchy. It is still a source of some pride to Luxembourgers to have an alliance with Americans.

During WWII, the Grand Duchess and her family left the country and sought asylum in the U.S. and Canada until shortly before the Liberation. Then they returned—the Grand Duke Heretier Jean, the Grand Duchess Charlotte, and the rest of the family. It would have been considered treacherous had they remained in Luxembourg during the war, and the Nazi occupiers may well have killed them. But the triumphant return of Grand Duchess Charlotte and her family was an important element in the liberation of Luxembourg.

Two days ago, when Erny Linden and I were talking, she showed me photographs of her husband, Nick, as a young man drafted into the Nazi youth work force. He would eventually have been put into the Nazi army, but he deserted and joined the Resistance in Luxembourg. The Steichens informed on him, and his parents were sent to a deportation camp near Poland. After the liberation, Nick Linden and his comrades came out of hiding from the forest, and his parents were returned to Feulen.

When I asked Erny how she felt about the Steichens now, she said, "I speak with them. But I do not forget."

SEPTEMBER 3, 1994   3 P.M.

I'm enroute from Amsterdam to Minneapolis.

Milly Thill came to the Luxembourg City airport to see me off. She wanted to talk about her book, *Milly's Story*, a collection of stories about her experiences as a young woman in Luxembourg during World War II. The book was published in 1990 in Lëtzebuergesch; she says that the English version will come out in November, and she'll send it to me.

Milly also invited Rachel and me to stay with her on our next trip in 1995, Luxembourg's year as the Cultural Center of Europe. It'd be fun to be here for that and to bring Rachel along. For now, however, I need to concentrate on completing work on *In Search of Susanna*.

On September 3, 1994, my last morning in Luxembourg City, I walked down to the central square, eager for one more espresso before heading to the airport to catch a late-morning commuter flight to Amsterdam. In the Place d'Armes, I came upon a flea market offering antique furniture, china, and clothing, along with "Luxembourgensia"—knickknacks, old currency, and boxes of postcards.

There, while browsing through one such box, I came across a postcard of a drowsy little girl. She stared out at me from the lap of the woman who was reading to her. The postcard was captioned, "Wenn Du noch eine Mutter hast." "If you still have a Mother." My German wasn't good enough to make a fluent translation of the verse that accompanied the caption, yet I thought I could figure it out:

> Wenn Du noch eine Mutter hast,
> So danke Gott und sei zufrieden;
> Nicht allen auf dem Erdenrund,
> Ist dieses hohe Glück beschieden.

> [If you still have a mother,
> Thank God and be satisfied;
> Not everyone the whole world 'round
> Is granted such good fortune.]

Though I knew that both the scene and verse were romanticized (indeed, oversentimentalized), still the postcard brought tears to my eyes. Was I just so tired out and jet-lagged that I'd become overly emotional? Did I need another espresso? What was it about images of mothers and daughters that stirred me so deeply, especially whenever I was in Luxembourg?

I leafed through the box of postcards until I came upon another depiction of a mother and daughter. This postcard was captioned "Almosen"—"Beggars." Here, again romanticized and sentimentalized, was a young woman in "gypsy" attire—bandanna on her head, tambourine upside down and outstretched toward me. The young woman's left arm was wrapped around the shoulders of a little girl, dressed in similar fashion, who huddled against her. The eyes of the young woman stared out at me: "Almosen."

I held the two postcards up next to each other. An absorbing counterpoint: one mother, wedding ring on her hand, cradling her beloved daughter and reading tenderly to her; the other mother, no wedding ring in sight, cradling her beloved daughter and begging for alms.

> *Alleluia, alleluia. This is a wise virgin, and one of the number of the prudent. Alleluia. Oh, how beautiful is the chaste generation with glory! Alleluia.*—From the Mass of a Virgin-Martyr, in the St. Joseph Daily Missal, 1959

Virginity. *The Encyclopedia of Catholicism* defines it as "the condition of never having had sexual relations" and explains that in early Israel "female virginity was prized." In the Old Testament, Deuteronomy stated that, if a husband found his new bride to be "otherwise," she could be stoned to death. If, on the other hand, the husband complained falsely, he would only be whipped.

Recent scholarship has revealed that the origins of the word "virgin" go back to pre-Christian times, when the word meant a woman who was sexually free and her sexuality was not under the control of a man. Most people I know, however, still use the biblical definition. And, for Catholics, the exemplar of virginity is Mary, the Blessed Virgin, the only human being born without original sin on her soul so that she could become the mother of God the Son, our Lord Jesus Christ. In 1854, Pope Pius IX issued a papal bull, *Ineffabilis Deus*, which officially recognized Mary's unique status and proclaimed December 8 as the Feast of the Immaculate Conception.

Catholic tradition holds that Mary remained a virgin her entire life—before, during, and after the birth of Jesus. Biblical references to Jesus' brothers and sisters are interpreted by Catholic theologians as actually being references to Jesus' step-siblings or cousins. As Sister Margaret explained to me in fifth-grade religion class, Mary's lifelong virginity was a Mystery of Faith. It could not and should not be explained; a good Catholic would accept it as true because it had been proclaimed by the Holy Father.

I wasn't about to question the Holy Father. In fact, I found the Blessed Virgin Mary the most appealing of any Catholic saint. An entire altar in our church was devoted to her, and I would often stop there after Mass to put a dime into the collection box, then light a match over a little votive candle in the tray of a hundred candles at the foot of the altar.

Every May, my sister, Linda, and I would set up a May altar in our bedroom. Its focal point would be the large statue of the Blessed Virgin

Mary that our mother usually kept on top of her dresser. But for one month each year, Linda and I could carry the statue into our bedroom. We'd set it up on the vanity in front of the mirror and surround the BVM with fresh lilacs from Grandma Klein's garden. Every morning before walking to school, we'd kneel in front of our May altar and say the rosary.

In religion class I'd learned that even though I could pray to our Blessed Mother, I ought not to ask her to answer my prayers. After all, she was not God, only the Mother of God. Her role was to take my requests to her son, Jesus, who, as I imagined, relayed them to God the Father and God the Holy Spirit during their daily consultations up in Heaven. Then, if the Holy Trinity determined that my prayer should be answered, Jesus would convey word back to Mary.

Even though I understood this "chain of command," I almost always prayed to Mary, especially when I needed some very special prayer answered. I'd say the Hail Mary, then the Hail Holy Queen. But my favorite prayer was "The Memorare." I thought it was just sincere and desperate enough that, if I said it, the Blessed Virgin Mary would not be able to refuse my request:

> Remember, O most gracious Virgin Mary, that never was it known that anyone who fled to thy protection, implored thy help, or sought thy intercession, was left unaided. Inspired by this confidence, I fly to thee, O Virgin of Virgins, my Mother. To thee I come, before thee I stand, sinful and sorrowful. O Mother of the Word Incarnate, despise not my petition, but in thy mercy, hear and answer me. Amen.

I still say "The Memorare" when I am in need of a good prayer. I believe it's a powerful one, and I believe that the Blessed Virgin Mary can and does answer prayers.

In recent years, Mary's name has been in the news frequently. As in earlier reports from Lourdes, France, and Fatima, Portugal, many people have claimed to have had visions of Mary—at San Damiano, Italy; San Sebastian de Garabandal, Spain; Medjugorje, Yugoslavia; and Mellarey, Republic of Ireland, to name only a few apparition sites.

In *Encountering Mary*, Sandra Zimdars-Swartz defines an apparition as "a specific kind of vision in which a person or being not normally within the visionary's perceptual range appears to that person, not in a world apart as in a dream, and not as a modification of a concrete object as in the case of a weeping icon or moving statue, but as a part of the environment, without apparent connection to verifiable visual stimuli." Those who say that Mary has appeared to them regard it as a great privilege and responsibility, for the Blessed Virgin typically leaves messages with them to convey to the rest of the world.

Take, for example, the case of Annie Kirkwood, a retired nurse living with her husband and family in a Dallas, Texas, suburb. In her recent book, *Mary's Message to the World*, Kirkwood recounts the many occasions on which the Blessed Virgin Mary has appeared to her since 1987. On each occasion, Mary has made prophecies and predictions, which Annie Kirkwood has reported to the world. Among these are Mary's predictions that the frequency of earthquakes and volcanos will increase, weather patterns will change all over the world, the polar ice caps will melt, UFO activity will increase, a third world war will not occur, and, after a shift in the earth's magnetic fields, there will be two suns and a binary solar system.

In addition to making these predictions, Kirkwood explains that the Blessed Virgin used her appearances to reveal details about her life with Saint Joseph, Jesus, and the rest of their family. According to Kirkwood's apparitions (and contrary to Catholic teaching), Mary did not remain a virgin after Jesus' birth. She and Joseph had several more children by conventional means, including James, David, Daniel, Elizabeth, Jacob, Ruth, and Mary Martha. The Blessed Virgin also provided genealogical information about her and Joseph's families and revealed that she believed in reincarnation. In fact, she had been reincarnated several times, as a nun in the Middle Ages, as a follower of Saint Francis of Assisi, and as a healer in India. *Mary's Message to the World* concludes:

> My aim is that you see the hope and the love in which this prophesy was given. Take hope into full account in your life, your inner-life, now. It gives you the impetus to seek God with all your heart, all your mind, and with all your might. In so doing, by prayer and meditation, you will be prepared to survive unto the end, to survive and to endure these last times with courage, hope, and love. This is my prayer and this is my hope: that all progress in spirit, that no one be turned off for the next 100 years because it will be a glorious time. These will be wonderful, peaceful lives you will lead on Earth.

Whether or not a person believes that the Blessed Virgin Mary actually appeared to Annie Kirkwood, this book of predictions and revelations no doubt has many readers, especially those interested in finding ways to "redeem" a modern world that seems out of control. Mary's

"Gospel according to Annie Kirkwood," if you will, is based on the precept of brotherly and sisterly love as the avenue to surviving the millennium. And the tenor of the Blessed Virgin's messages to Annie Kirkwood strikes me as far more positive than the tenor of the messages that Mary supposedly gave to Mary Ann Van Hoof, who lived on a farm near Necedah, Wisconsin. For her, the apparitions had lasted from 1950 until her death in 1984.

I'd found out about Mary Ann Van Hoof by accident during the summer of 1989, when Rachel and I were en route to Appleton, Wisconsin, to visit our Fulbright friends, Elizabeth and Michael Panzer. We spent the night at my cousin Frank Klein's cabin across the river from La Crosse, Wisconsin. The next morning, as we drove past Tomah, Wisconsin, and onto country roads, Rachel announced that she had to go to the bathroom. When she added, "It's *urgent*, Mama," I knew we had only moments to spare.

That was when I noticed the roadside sign: SHRINE OF THE QUEEN OF THE HOLY ROSARY, MEDIATRIX OF PEACE, MEDIATRIX BETWEEN GOD AND MAN. I headed in that direction. Surely, a religious shrine would have public rest rooms. When we turned the corner, I discovered we'd wandered into some sort of religious theme park. I got out of the car and, with Rachel in tow, walked toward the gift shop. We passed a rack of women's wraparound skirts. A rummage sale? No, a sign next to the rack spelled it out:

> All persons are reminded to please dress Marylike to enter the Shrine grounds as they have been venerated by Mother of God and various Saints. Knees to be covered, skirt over slacks, no shorts, no see-through materials, no low-cut dresses or blouses. Wrap around skirts available at information booth. Your cooperation is appreciated.

Standing next to the sign in long pants, Rachel giggled as, under the watchful eye of a gift shop clerk, I pulled a wraparound skirt from the rack and tied it on over my shorts. Then Rachel and I entered the park, which featured life-size tableaux of the Annunciation, the Visitation of Mary to Elizabeth, the Birth of Jesus Christ, and the Last Supper. At the center of the park was an exceptionally gory tableau depicting the Crucifixion. Rachel pointed up at the tableau and exclaimed, "Look, Mama! Somebody squirted ketchup all over Jesus!"

What had we wandered into? I was too curious to leave just yet, so we went into the gift shop, where we bought new rosaries. I picked up a copy of the *Shrine Beacon*, published bimonthly by Mrs. Van Hoof's followers. It wasn't until that night, when I was reading in bed, that I had a chance to look at the current issue. It contained a good deal of history about the shrine as well as information about an organization called For My God and My Country, whose motto was "To Pray Together—to Play Together—to Work Together—We Shall Win Together."

Articles in that issue of the newsletter condemned the loss of traditional Catholic values and argued in favor of the restoration of the Latin Mass. A lengthy article titled "In Imitation of Mary" expanded on the theme of female purity and modesty. All women should imitate the Blessed Virgin Mary, not only through prayer but also through dress and behavior. That, said the *Shrine News*, was part of "God's Plan for Man Versus Satan's Conspiracy for World Dominion."

I had had enough of the Shrine of the Queen of the Holy Rosary. Later, when I told my cousin Frank Klein what Rachel and I had seen there, he confirmed that the Catholic Church had investigated the Necedah apparitions and comdemned them as false in 1955. And when I read Sandra Zimdars-Swartz's *Encountering Mary*, I found her assessment of Mary Ann Van Hoof's revelations enlightening:

> In her own descriptions of her childhood in her published writings, Mary Ann said only that she came from a poor family and had to work hard. The ecclesiastical commission which investigated her experiences, however, found evidence of more specific problems. . . . Mary Ann's view of America as a threatened and vulnerable nation, whose every lapse could invite the intrusion of powerful evil forces, corresponded, it seems, to memories of a childhood in a dysfunctional family in which her own lapses, and probably those of other members of her family as well, brought upon her the violent anger of an abusive father. Mary Ann's mother was probably able to offer her no more protection at these crucial times than, in the worldview of her later revelations and messages, the "Madonna Maria" was able to offer a faltering America.

In April 1994, my cousin Frank Klein sent me a birthday present— *No Fig Leaves*, a collection of poems about women in the Bible. The poems were written by Sister Viola Kane, a member of the School Sisters of Notre Dame, which has its motherhouse here in Mankato. In a letter introducing the collection, Sister Viola wrote:

Whether you picked up this book accidentally to peruse it, or de-liberately to ponder it, I hope it will fascinate you. Material for the poems dates back centuries before Christ, but please don't let that scare you because these women of scripture are real. Their stories are alive in us. . . . I hope you will take the time to scan, to read, to ex-change with these women. This book is just an attempt to begin the process. I dream you will complete the dialogue with your own life experiences.

I was intrigued by Sister Viola's poetry, particularly by a poem titled "Unborns Meet," in which the scene of the Visitation is recalled. Mary, having just learned from the Archangel Gabriel that she will bear Jesus, goes to visit her older cousin, Elizabeth, who is pregnant with John the Baptist:

> Mary, unwed pregnant teenager,
> welcomes Elizabeth's hug
> Awesome days follow as each becomes
> her sister's keeper of joys, tears
> and fears.
>
> Strengthened by God and each other
> the two in fullness grow
> In a faith larger than wisdom
> preparing the way for God
> in us to know.

The image of Mary as an "unwed pregnant teenager" stayed with me after I closed the covers of *No Fig Leaves*. When I was a child, my teachers had always fudged about the issue of whether Mary had actu-ally been married to Joseph—or only betrothed—when she miracu-lously became pregnant with Jesus.

"*Betrothed* really means just about the same as *married*," I recall Sister Margaret telling my religion class. But I wasn't so sure.

On the playground at recess, I asked several girls in my class what they thought of Sister Margaret's statement. No one was buying it. None of us believed that Mary and Joseph had been "as good as mar-ried" when Mary had become pregnant with Jesus. After all, hadn't Joseph hesitated about the possibility of marrying Mary once he'd found out she was already pregnant? If I remembered, it had taken a visit from the Archangel Gabriel to persuade Joseph that Mary was, indeed, a virgin who "had not known man."

For centuries the Church has taught that chastity is paramount, for women if not for men. The newest version of the *Catechism of the Catholic Church*, just issued in 1994, explains that chastity "is a gift from God, a *grace*, a fruit of spiritual effort." The *Catechism* lists lust, masturbation, fornication, pornography, prostitution, and rape as offenses against chastity. The *Catechism* urges Catholics to accept "the virginal conception of Jesus as a divine work that surpasses all human understanding and possibility" and to celebrate Mary as "*Aeiparthenos*, the Ever-virgin."

The *Catechism* also explains that Mary's virginity manifests God's power and that Jesus, conceived in Mary's womb by the Holy Spirit, is the New Adam, who ushers in the new birth of children through faith. The *Catechism* concludes that Mary's dual status is a sign of her perfect faith: "At once virgin and mother, Mary is the symbol and the most perfect realization of the Church."

Why has it been so important to the Catholic Church to declare Mary "Ever-virgin" as a matter of faith and doctrine? Surely, it has to do with the Church Fathers' perceptions of what would be an appropriate role for the Mother of God to play. But, like many other scholars and members of the laity, I believe it also has to do with the Catholic Church's inability to reconcile sexuality with motherhood, in a theological, if not an actual, sense. For, if the Virgin Birth is a doctrinal certainty, then there is little room for discussion of such issues as whether Mary and Joseph had a sexual relationship or whether they had other children besides Jesus.

John Shelby Spong, an Episcopalian bishop, examines the doctrine of the virgin birth in *Born of a Woman* (1992). After pointing out the dangers of interpreting the Bible literally, Spong explains that Mary's status as virgin or nonvirgin was not an issue in the original Hebrew version of the Gospel of Saint Matthew 7:14, where Mary was referred to as *almah* [young woman], not *betulah* [virgin]. Only when the Bible was translated from Hebrew into Greek did *almah* become *parthenos* [virgin].

In his study, Spong analyzes theological, historical, and political implications of various translations and interpretations of the Gospels of Matthew and Luke. He asserts, "Ideas do have consequences," and he explains that his goal is "to raise some of these to our consciousness, to challenge them, and finally to counter them." Spong concludes:

The only hope for the survival of the virgin Mary as a viable symbol is her redefinition by the new consciousness. . . . Only the church that manages to free itself from its sexist definition of women, anchored significantly in the virgin Mary tradition, will survive. The virgin of a literal Bible, the virgin of the annunciation, Bethlehem, and the manger, corrupted by the years of an overlaid male theology, will have to go. But the feminine side of God in some new incarnation will inevitably rise to take her place.

In books such as *Sanctuaries of the Goddess*, by Peg Streep, scholars have traced the roots of the Blessed Virgin Mary to pre-Christian goddesses like Demeter, Persephone, and Artemis—all virgins in the ancient sense of being women who have control of their own sexuality. Most recently, in *The Truth about the Virgin: Sex and Ritual in the Dead Sea Scrolls*, Ita Sheres and Anne Kohn Blau analyze a ritual performed at Qumran and described in the Dead Sea Scrolls. This ritual involved the pledging of a select group of virgins in a ceremony reminiscent of those in ancient goddess religions.

Contemporary scholars of religious studies have also been paying increasing attention to the writing of mystics and visionaries such as Hildegard of Bingen (1098–1179), Hadewijch of Belgium (thirteenth century), and Julian of Norwich (1343–1423). All three speak of the loving, nurturing qualities of God. Not coincidentally, all three are women.

Now I know I've always believed in Mary, both as the Mother of God and as God the Mother. When I listen to Bobby McFerrin's moving rendition of "The 23rd Psalm," dedicated to his mother, I'm more certain than ever that God is not an old man with flowing white hair and beard, shaking his fist down at me from the sky.

12. Our Unescapable Common Source

For an instant some filament lighter than cobweb
spun itself out between that living center in her and
in me, a filament from some center that held us all
bound to our unescapable common source, so that
her life and mine were kin, even a part of each other,
and the painfulness and strangeness of her vanished.
—Katherine Anne Porter, "Holiday"

In September 1978, shortly after my father's death, I began writing my doctoral dissertation on women in the short stories of Katherine Anne Porter, a twentieth-century writer born and raised in the American South. I was intrigued by one of Porter's stories in particular. Although written in the 1930s, "Holiday" was not published until *The Collected Stories of Katherine Anne Porter* appeared more than thirty years later. In her preface to this collection, Porter wrote:

"Holiday" represents one of my prolonged struggles, not with questions of form or style, but my own moral and emotional collision with a human situation I was too young to cope with at the time it occurred: yet the story haunted me for years and I made three separate versions, with a certain spot in all three where the thing went off track. So I put it away and it disappeared also, and I forgot it. It rose from one of my boxes of papers, after a quarter of a century, and I sat down in great excitement to read all three versions. I saw at once that the first was the right one, and as for the vexing question which had stopped me short long ago, it had in the course of living settled itself so slowly and deeply and secretly I wondered why I had ever been distressed by it. I changed one short paragraph and a line or two at the end and it was done.

I found Porter's brief explanation of how "Holiday" had "disappeared" for more than twenty-five years unsatisfying because I suspected that her remarks in "Go Little Book . . ." did not tell the entire story about the genesis and gestation of "Holiday." In her essay "'Noon Wine': The Sources," Porter explained that a writer actually lives a story four times over: first, in the series of actual events that lead to the writing of the story; second, in memory; third, in the recreation of what she calls "this chaotic stuff"; and fourth, when the writer is "challenged to trace his clues to their sources and to expose the roots of his work in his own most secret and private life."

What was it about the events narrated in "Holiday" that was linked to Porter's "moral and emotional collision with a human situation [she] was too young to cope with at the time it occurred"? Why had the story "haunted" her? And how had the passage of time settled the "vexing question" so that it no longer distressed her?

As I worked on my dissertation, I came to believe that the key to understanding "Holiday" lay in understanding the relationship between the story's narrator and a crippled servant girl, Ottilie. The narrator is a troubled young woman writer who spends a spring holiday in the rural Texas household of the Müllers, a "family of real old-fashioned German peasants," as her friend Louise describes them. While staying there, the narrator becomes fascinated with the family's servant girl, Ottilie.

Ottilie, who cannot talk and who spends her days cooking and cleaning up after members of the Müller family, seems oblivious to the narrator until one day when she shows the narrator a family photograph of a "girl child about five years old," wearing a "frilly frock and a prodigious curl of blonde hair." The narrator struggles to understand Ottilie's pantomime: "she patted the picture and her own face, and strove terribly to speak." At this moment a link between the women is formed.

As "Holiday" draws to its conclusion, the narrator comes to recognize the inevitable: try as she might, she cannot truly understand, nor rescue, Ottilie: "She was beyond my reach as well as any other human reach, and yet, had I not come nearer to her than I had to anyone else in my attempt to deny and bridge the distance between us, or rather, her distance from me?" Everyone in the Müller family accepts the reality of Ottilie's assigned place within its structure; now the narrator must do the same.

The paradox in the conclusion to Katherine Anne Porter's "Holiday" is the paradox in my search for Susanna: try as I might, I cannot fully know or truly understand the circumstances of my ancestor's life. Because I cannot live inside her skin, I cannot fully appreciate the reasons for the decisions she made or had imposed upon her. Nor can I know or understand the circumstances of all those individuals whose lives Susanna touched.

Yet I do know more now than I knew before. I know that a "filament from some center" holds both Susanna and me "bound to our unescapable common source," and I know that her life and mine are kin, "even a part of each other." The "painfulness and strangeness of her" have vanished. All of the people and events that have found their way into my consciousness during my search for Susanna are fully alive and truly present, if not in my memory, then in my imagination.

DEC. 19, 1994

I worked hard last week to go through all of my Luxembourg journals (1980, 1984, 1988, 1993, 1994) and type excerpts to use in the "Susanna" book. Yesterday I drove to St. Paul to the University of St. Thomas for the dedication of the Luxembourg Collection at the library there. Prince Henri, the Hereditary Grand Duke of Luxembourg, was there and, thanks to Christine Heinerscheid, I met him and got his autograph for Rachel. Frank was also there, and we sat together at lunch and had a chance to visit before he drove back to Dresbach. I stayed to view the Luxembourg Collection and talk with Jim Kellen, the archivist, about working with materials in it.

JAN. 30, 1995

This morning I worked on a start to a chapter about Dad's family for the "Susanna" book. I reread my diary entries for July–December 1978, right after his death. I think that the chapter will reconstruct his life and look at the whole issue of presence and absence of mother and father in his life. I'm not sure yet how this chapter will develop, but I do know I need it in the book. I want to quote from Dad's autograph book, Grandma Bunkers' letters, Dad's letters, etc. As I look back, I can see that Dad's death was what sent me on my search, not only for Susanna but also for other links to my past.

JAN. 31, 1995

I felt drained after typing diary entries yesterday. I don't think I can deal with my own diaries in the same way I can deal with the diary of someone like Caroline Seabury or Sarah Gillespie Huftalen. When I reread what I wrote back then in my diary, the emotions come charging to the surface, and I am sometimes awash in tears, as I was yesterday. Dad died, yet the pain must be just beneath the surface because, as soon as I start to "scratch" a bit, it is right there, engulfing me. It almost makes me too scared to keep reading those old diaries—who knows what I will find there?

And the "me" writing then is and is not the "me" rereading it all now. Then, I mostly just wrote and I didn't agonize a lot or censor myself as I wrote. Now I know I'm more cautious not only about what I say but also about how I say it and how much (if any) of it I put into writing. I wonder how I'll feel in 20 years when I reread the journal entries here? I know that, when I reread old journals now, I sometimes cringe at what I wrote, or I feel sorry for the self I was then because I know so much more now about how or why certain things transpired then. But I don't regret having kept a journal all these years, and I think I can "mine" it for information to be used in other things I write.

FEB. 13, 1995

The more I actually think of Susanna as a flesh-and-blood person, the scarier it gets. As long as she remains an abstraction, she can be a symbol. But once she becomes more concrete, she has to be seen as someone specific, non-generalizable. I felt more that way as I talked by phone with my Youngblut cousin Charlotte Witry. She mentioned photographs, holy cards, family papers—and each bit of information makes Susanna all the more real.

Am I feeling anything like what an adopted child feels when she wonders about her birth mother, then gets a chance to begin to find out some of that information, bit by bit? In many ways, Barbara Simmerl was the "given-up" child—the one "left behind" in Luxembourg. What did she know about her biological mother? Whose child did she think she was?

Do I feel like the "given-up child" who's trying to learn about the birth mother's family? I yearn to see a picture of Susanna, or any of her children, descendants, etc., to see if I recognize myself in any of their faces. They had her, after all. She spent her life with them, not with my family.

FEB. 23, 1995

In today's mail I got some photos from Marie Hellman of Waterloo—my first definitive pictures of Susanna Simmerl and Frank Youngblut. These photos were apparently included in a Black Hawk

County history of 1910, but the photos are older than that, because Frank died in 1892 and Susanna in 1906.

I could sit and stare at the photo of Susanna for hours—just drinking in her features and noting all the details. It is so good to see her at last after all the years of wondering what she looked like.

The photograph shows an older woman wearing a dark dress with a brooch at the neck. Her hair, mostly gray, is pulled back, most likely into a bun. She is not looking directly at the camera but just a bit to the side, close enough that she could almost be staring at the observer. She is not smiling, not frowning. She looks settled, determined, at peace. Or at least that is how I want to interpret what I see when I look at Susanna's portrait.

Frank Youngblut has a gray bristly beard; his hair is still mostly dark, not gray, and he's balding. He wears a simple dark suit and white shirt. Perhaps these portraits were taken for a special anniversary. If they were married in December 1857, thirty years would have been 1887; twenty-five years would have been 1882. By their fiftieth anniversary in 1907, both Frank and Susanna had already died. So I'd guess that these portraits had to have been taken sometime during the 1880s.

Marie wrote to her cousin, Sister Callista O'Connor, in California to get copies of these old photographs. I will have negatives and copies made for myself and perhaps for others in the Youngblut family. The Youngblut cousins have come through for me in the past few years. And to think that when I began this work, I had no idea who any of them were. I can thank Barbara Jacobs for helping me find them.

I looked at Susanna's portrait again, and for some reason, Nora Bachmann came to mind. Maybe it is the memory of Nora's long, long hair, braided and wound up and pinned into a bun. When I was a little girl, we lived just a couple of houses away from Nora. I'd go down the block to visit "Aunt Norie," as we called her, and I'd watch her comb out her long hair, braid it, and wind it up. I remember her deep brown eyes and soft skin. She was a gentle soul, as I remember her. Now I know that "Aunt Norie" was Elnora Bunkers Bachmann, Barbara Bunkers' daughter and Susanna's granddaughter.

APRIL 14, 1995

Good Friday. Today is Grandpa Klein's birthday. He would have been 98 years old. I always liked it that he and I shared the birthday month of April, but typically, one of our birthdays would fall near

Easter, and we would wind up spending it in church. What a disappointment to have my birthday fall on Good Friday and have to spend three hours on my knees! Good Friday was the one day of the year when Mass was not celebrated, but we spent several hours in church nonetheless. It's better now that I feel free to make choices about such matters. Rachel and I will go to Mass tomorrow evening to celebrate the Easter Vigil.

APRIL 20, 1995

I'm 45 years old today. I can't say I feel that old, and I hope my life is not already more than half over. One never knows.

I just turned on the TV. The news is all about a terrorist attack on a federal building in Oklahoma City. Many people were killed, including a number of children at a daycare center. It is a tragedy and a senseless one, as these terrorist attacks usually are. I wonder whether anyone will ever be caught and charged in this horrible crime? It seems that only when it happens in the U.S. do we take such things seriously.

APRIL 24, 1995

I am going to write a letter to Al Stone. I want to respond to his request that I be more "fully confessional" in the "Susanna" book. Al wrote that he likes the last several chapters the best. In two middle chapters, he wants me to be less reticent and to bring my work life as well as my personal life more into the story. I need to consider how much I can do that. I plan to write a frank letter, outlining what has happened in the past years and explaining why I feel reluctant to "spill my guts" in this book.

JUNE 7, 1995

I spent the morning refining the seventh chapter of the "Susanna" manuscript, and I started re-arranging parts of the eleventh chapter so I can examine the issue of illegitimacy and relate it to the Blessed Virgin Mary and other female saints, especially the virgin-martyrs. I am moving around bits of information from novels, my diaries, Catholic lore, lives of the saints, etc. I want to link these up to the idea of unwed motherhood and the myth of the "good mother." I am going to call this chapter "In the Name of the Mother," after the Bobby McFerrin song that my friend Zoé told me about last year.

Jeff and Michelle (Youngblut) Lindquist sent me the diskettes with all of the Youngblut genealogical records on them. Now I can put them on my hard drive and call them up. I am impressed with how much work Jeff has done to get this information into the computer.

Rachel's Brownie Troop took part in a Girl Scout Bridging Ceremony tonight. Now they are Juniors, and they get to wear green sashes. I'm going to continue as troop leader next year, and Christy Steele will be my assistant again. She and I agreed that working with nine-year-olds is more challenging than teaching college writing classes!

JUNE 10, 1995

My final American literature class with my students from Taiwan was last Monday, and what a good class it was! Rachel went along with me, and we brought cookies and juice for everyone. I asked each student to write a letter to a friend in Taiwan, speaking about what he or she could give as advice for someone coming to MSU next fall to study English.

Then the students told me they had a surprise for me. Jeffrey wrote a whole blackboard full of Chinese characters. Then Tim sat down at the piano. He told Rachel and me to sit up front. Tim began playing, and the whole class sang "Oh, Susannah" to me—in Chinese! I was delighted. I knew the melody and could hum along, but I could make out only three words: *Susannah*, *Alabama*, and *Louisiana*. Rachel was tickled, too, and we sang along in English.

We all went outside for "class pictures," and we had handshakes and hugs all around. Then we said our "so longs," with hopes to see one another this summer. This was one of my best teaching experiences ever.

JUNE 19, 1995

This morning's local newspaper had this front-page story: last evening, a newborn baby girl was found abandoned in the lobby of the hospital in Mankato. The baby, who weighs four pounds, is about six weeks premature and is being called "Baby Jane Doe." The police are asking the baby's mother to step forward, saying she might not be charged with child endangerment since she left the baby at a hospital. No one is asking the father to come forward at this time.

JUNE 20, 1995

No word yet on the mother of "Baby Jane Doe." The police are still searching for her. Apparently, it was an unattended home birth, and the baby's umbilical cord was tied with a twistie used for a garbage bag. The police again stated that, if the mother comes forward, charges might not be filed because the mother's leaving the baby at a hospital shows a desire to protect it, to leave it where the mother knew it would be safe. Again, there's been little mention of the baby's father stepping forward and taking a share of the responsibility.

Last week, I read another story in the newspaper. It was about a young woman who had tracked down the birth mother and father who had given her up for adoption in 1963. She had brought the birth parents together, they fell in love, and they will be married in July. The headline read, "Daughter Given Up for Adoption Finds Parents, Leads Them to the Altar." A happily-ever-after story? I have to wonder.

JUNE 22, 1995

Still no word about the parents of "Baby Jane Doe." Yesterday's newspaper headline read, "Abandoned Baby Getting Lots of Care— But Not From Her Mother." There are tiny references to the possibility of a father, but clearly, the emphasis is, "Where is the baby's mother?" No one would be asking that if the mother had given the baby up for adoption in the usual manner.

I have to wonder what made the birth mother need to "give up" her baby in such a desperate way? And, at the same time, what made the mother take such care with her little daughter? The baby was dressed in a colorful sleeper and wrapped in a new blue terry-cloth towel. The labels had been cut off both, so someone was thinking ahead and did not want the sleeper or the towel traced to a certain store and city.

The newspaper stories say that many people have come forward and offered to adopt the baby, who will go to a foster family when she is old enough to be dismissed from the local hospital. It's so sad to think of that baby girl and her mother, who didn't feel she could keep her child.

And what of the father? Was he there at the birth? Did the mother deliver the baby alone, or with the help of a friend? Could the mother have been a young girl whose family didn't even know she was pregnant? Could the mother have been raped, perhaps by a relative?

Everybody says it's better that the mother took the baby to the hospital lobby than that she left the baby in a dumpster. It makes me think of Maxine Hong Kingston's story, "No Name Woman." There, the woman gives birth to her baby in a pigsty:

Full of milk, the little ghost slept. When it awoke, she hardened her breasts against the milk that crying loosens. Toward morning she picked up the baby and walked to the well.

Carrying the baby to the well shows loving. Otherwise abandon it. Turn its face into the mud. Mothers who love their children take them along. It was probably a girl; there is some hope of forgiveness for boys.

Kingston says that the mother's actions show her love for her child; she takes the baby with her down the well rather than leaving it behind. The "Baby Jane Doe" story makes me wonder, can anyone truly judge which actions most accurately reflect the love of a mother for her child?

JUNE 28, 1995

Rachel and I are in Canada at the Prince Arthur Hotel in Thunder Bay, Ontario. Yesterday we spent the day at Old Fort William, a recreation of a fur-trading post just outside Thunder Bay. It was cool and drizzly, and not many tourists were there; so wherever we went at the Fort, Rachel got a lot of attention, and the actors who played the roles of the Fort's inhabitants took time to sit and tell us about their lives and work with the Northwest Fur Trading Company in the early 1800s. We saw a demonstration of nineteenth-century medicine (bloodletting, cupping, etc.). We also saw how a carpenter worked, and we observed how the owners of the Northwest Company dealt with differences of opinion.

We also learned that all the women at the Fort were "métis" or "mixed blood" women descended from the Indian women whom the first French, English, and Scottish explorers had married "à la façon du pays" (after the custom of the country, that is, in common-law fashion, without benefit of legal or religious ceremonies). It was interesting to me because these unions were viewed as marriages, at least until the European men would decide to go back to live in Montreal. Then they'd leave their Indian wives at the Fort and find white wives in the city.

There was a certain "gentleman's agreement" about all this, but the bottom line was that the racial intermarriages lasted only as long as the white men wanted them to. These unions, also called "country marriages," were not recognized as sacred by the Catholic Church, but, according to *Many Tender Ties: Women in Fur-Trade Society, 1670–1870*, priests did acknowledge the existence of a marital bond in a state of "natural marriage." As the book says,

"The only children stigmatized were those whose father could not be identified."

JULY 4, 1995

Home again. Rachel and I got back from our marathon trip Saturday night and took most of Sunday to recuperate. We traveled over 1,400 miles.

Last night Rachel left to spend two weeks with her dad. She complained of feeling sick beforehand, so I held her and comforted her. By the time her dad drove up and sat in his car, honking the horn, Rachel was feeling better and was ready to go. I sent her softball glove and team shirt along, and off she went. Sometimes I think that the hardest part for her is that walk from our front steps to her dad's car. I have to pray (and believe) that, once she gets into the car with him, she will be all right.

By early evening I was exhausted from the emotional tension of getting Rachel ready to go. At times it hurts when she leaves, and I don't want to cry in front of her, but once she's out the door, I have to get the sadness out. At times I feel guilty that Rachel's life has to be one constant shuttle between her mom's and her dad's homes. What a luxury to be able to grow up in one home with both parents there—if they are happy together. I could not have survived, had Rachel's father and I stayed together. Sometimes, for Rachel's sake, I wish I could have given her the "one home" I had when I was growing up, despite its difficulties. But I know I can't.

JULY 20, 1995

Rachel and I came to Granville for a few days so she can be at Grandma's with her cousins, Kelly and Megan. When we arrived last evening, Kelly and Megan came dashing out to the car to greet us. They'd been up in Mom's attic and had hauled down all sorts of school books, notebooks, old letters, etc. Everything was in boxes spread across the livingroom floor.

I helped the three girls sort through the mounds of papers and books. My task was to identify the handwriting on the school papers so they could all be sorted into piles: Suzy's, Linda's, Denny's, Dale's, Dan's. All three girls were eager to get to find their own parent's old schoolwork. There was plenty to go around. Mom has been keeping all of our schoolwork since 1955, when I started kindergarten! It's been in boxes up in the attic all these years. The "big find" for Rachel was a bunch of my notebooks from high school religion, music, and English classes—a lot of which were in the worn leather binder I used during my first year at Spalding High.

Along with the school books and papers were several shoeboxes of old birthday cards and letters. The "big find" for me was a bunch of Get Well cards that relatives and friends sent to Dad in spring 1969, when he was a patient at the Veterans' Hospital in Sioux Falls and then at the Mental Health Institute in Cherokee. I was a freshman at Iowa State, and every letter I'd sent Dad was there among the Get Well cards. I opened the orange envelope addressed to "Mr. Jerome Bunkers, Mental Health Institute, Cherokee, Iowa," and took out a letter dated April 9, 1969:

> Dear Dad,
> I hope by now you're all settled and feeling better. I got back to Ames about noon and unpacked for about an hour. . . .
>
> I hope you're feeling better than last weekend. Are you taking any special pills or anything? Have you been checked over by a doctor yet? Don't worry and just take advantage of the good rest you'll be getting. And don't worry about the money 'cause it's all taken care of. Just see that you stay in bed and listen to the doctors and cooperate with them. I think that if you talk out your problems, the doctors will be able to give you good advice and then you'll realize that things aren't really as bad as they seem to be. Okay? I'll be praying for you. . . .
>
> Love,
> Suzy

As I reread that carefully typed letter, I could feel my throat tightening and my eyes filling with tears. I had to go into the bathroom, sit on the edge of the tub, and take some deep breaths. All the pain and the fear I'd felt twenty-five years ago, when I worried that Dad would never get well, had taken me by surprise once again.

This morning Mom asked me if I wanted to go along to Mass. It was being said in Dad's memory, and Mom was going to be the lector. When we got to church, Mom sat up front, but I went up the side aisle to kneel in our old family pew. Glancing up, I saw the Fourth Station of the Cross. Jesus was embracing his mother, as he'd been doing since I was a little girl. But when I looked a few pews ahead, St. Anthony was missing. Poor fellow, he's probably gathering dust in the church basement.

At the Offertory, when the priest asked us to remember the souls of the faithful departed, especially that of Jerome Bunkers, I prayed along. At the Communion, when the priest said, "Let us offer one another the sign of peace," I walked across the aisle to shake hands with several of my mother's friends and say, "Peace be with you." After Mass was over, I walked up the aisle to Mary's altar, fed some dollar bills into the coin box, and lit four vigil lights. Then I sat down in the front pew to watch them flicker.

> The sparrow even finds a home,
> The swallow finds a nest wherein
> to place her young, near to your
> altars, Lord of hosts, my King, my God!
> How happy they who dwell in your house!
> For ever they are praising You.

> —Psalms 83 : 4–5

AUGUST 13, 1995

Sunday. Rachel and I spent the day in Adrian, MN, attending the celebration in honor of Frank's 50th anniversary of his ordination to the priesthood. We drove over this morning and met Mom and her siblings (Marcel, Lois, Jim, Merlyn, and Clarice) outside the church. Over 200 of Frank's Klein and Kellen relatives packed the church for his anniversary Mass. When I whispered to Rachel, "Everyone in this church is your cousin," she gave me an "Are you kidding me?" look!

Just before Communion, we all joined hands to say the "Our Father." I held my mother's hand on one side and my daughter's hand on the other. Toward the end of Mass, Frank stepped forward to thank us all for being there to help him celebrate such an important day in his life. I will always be grateful to him and happy to have been a part of his special day.

To be hopeful in bad times is not just foolishly romantic. It is based on the fact that human history is a history not only of cruelty, but also of compassion, sacrifice, courage, kindness.

What we choose to emphasize in this complex history will determine our lives. If we see only the worst, it destroys our capacity to do something. If we remember those times and places—and there are so many—where people have behaved magnificently, this gives us the energy to act, and at least the possibility of sending this spinning top of a world in a different direction.

And if we do act, in however small a way, we don't have to wait for some grand utopian future. The future is an infinite succession of presents, and to live now as we think human beings should live, in defiance of all that is bad around us, is itself a marvelous victory.—Howard Zinn, *You Can't Be Neutral on a Moving Train: A Personal History of Our Times*

Memorial Day 1995. Rachel and I had just spent Sunday night in Mason City, Iowa, visiting my sister, Linda; her husband, Dan; and their children, Matt, Megan, and Ryan. Now Rachel, Megan, and I were en route to Waterloo, an hour and a half east of Mason City, to visit our cousins Charlotte Witry and Michelle (Youngblut) and Jeff Lindquist. Charlotte had loaned me the originals of several old Youngblut family photographs, which I had copied and planned to return to her. Jeff and Michelle were going to show me their genealogical work on the Youngblut family, which Jeff had done, using a sophisticated computer program. He wanted to enter my name, and my daughter's, into his database.

Before visiting our cousins, however, I wanted to go back to the Immaculate Conception Parish cemetery in Gilbertville, Iowa, and put flowers on Susanna's grave, as I did every summer. En route, I told Rachel and Megan more about their great-great-great-grandmother Susanna's life. When we arrived, they put lavender fabric flowers and tiny American flags on Susanna and Frank Youngblut's graves.

Then I asked the girls to help me try to decipher what remains of the faded inscription on Frank and Susanna's family tombstone:

Thou no more will join our number,
Thou no more our song will know,
But again we hope to meet thee,
When the day of life is fled,
And in heaven with joy to greet thee,
Where our farewell tears are shed.

Soon Rachel and Megan ran off to the school playground next to the cemetery. I went walking, past the graves of Frank and Susanna's children John Youngblut, Frank Youngblut, and Sophia Youngblut O'Connor and their families. Then I walked back to the oldest part of the cemetery. I'd heard that Susanna's younger sister, Catherine Simmerl, had also come to America and had married someone named Terns. Could I find any trace of Catherine here?

Sure enough, there it was: the tombstone of Katharina Terns, inscribed with her date of death, 1887, and her age, thirty-nine years. Next to her was the grave of her son Nicholas, and next to him the grave of her husband, Paul Terns, inscribed "1842–1920."

So Catherine, born in Luxembourg in 1848, had joined her older sister Susanna in Gilbertville. Perhaps Susanna and Frank Youngblut had found a nice young man named Paul Terns for Catherine to marry. Sketchy Youngblut family records indicate that Catherine and Paul had four children. Even though I couldn't research that family line on Memorial Day, I knew I could verify details about the Katharina (Simmerl) and Paul Terns family the next time I had a chance to study the Gilbertville parish records.

This is how my research has progressed: by walks through cemeteries, conversations with cousins, glances at photographs in old family albums, visits to church and civil record offices. My search for Susanna is not over, not as long as there is one more bit of information to be found, one more descendant to be acknowledged, one more cousin to be embraced.

When my daughter asks me, "Mama, where did I come from?" a richer texture underlies my answers, shaped by the quilt of experience that I have sewn. My sense of "home," of "the home tie, the blood tie," continues to evolve. As I continue to study Susanna's life, I reflect on the wisdom of literary scholar bell hooks, who writes:

> I had to leave that space I called home to move beyond boundaries, yet I needed also to return there. . . . Indeed the very meaning of "home" changes with experience of decolonization, of radicalization. At times, home is nowhere. At times, one knows only extreme estrangement and alienation. Then home is no longer just one place. It is locations. Home is that place which enables and promotes varied and everchanging perspectives, a place where one discovers new ways of seeing reality, frontiers of difference.—bell hooks, *Yearning: Race, Gender, and Cultural Politics,* 1990

Rachel Bunkers, October 1995, at the Plaza of Heroines, outside the Carrie Chapman Catt Building, Iowa State University, Ames. Just in front of Rachel is the brick commemorating the life of Susanna Simmerl Youngblut. Next to it is the brick for Sarah Gillespie Huftalen.

Conclusion: A Vibrating Web of Connection

The life that was unused in me was the part that
could wait and watch and discover that I live in a
vibrating web of connection. That web connects
dreams to the world, the living to the dead, and the
living to each other. We are forever tearing it. Now
that I know I live in a cosmos and not a chaos, I have
to try to mend the gaps I can see.
—Joan Weimer, *Back Talk: Teaching Lost Selves to Speak*, 1994

"For whom are you searching?"

Had someone asked me this question fifteen years ago, I would have answered, "Susanna."

Now I know that although I have been searching for information about a woman named Susanna Simmerl Youngblut, she has not been the only object of my search. My family's ancestral origins in Luxembourg; the links to present-day cousins there; the circumstances surrounding Susanna's, Angela's, and Barbara's immigrations to the United States; Frank and Susanna Youngblut's life together with their children; Barbara and Henry Bunkers' life with theirs; the web of Susanna's descendants in this country; my own roles as a daughter and as a mother—these, it turns out, have been the objects of my search all along, whether I realized it or not.

And, finally, I have been the object of my own search. In *Back Talk: Teaching Lost Selves to Speak*, Joan Weimer writes about her journey back into the life of Constance Fenimore Woolson, a nineteenth-century author. Weimer's research leads her to explore what she calls "the ghosts of my buried selves."

I have been doing something similar: discovering that web of connection, examining the tears, trying to mend the gaps. I have been doing these things through the interaction of memory and imagination,

242

through stories that I have heard and told over the years, through the reinvention of what could not be learned or remembered, through the pages of the book that you are holding in your hands.

Writing about the intersections of history, memory, and narrative, Mark Freeman observes, "The process of self-understanding is itself fundamentally recollective, taken here in the sense of gathering together again those dimensions of selfhood that had heretofore gone unarticulated or had been scattered, dispersed, or lost." Like many others before me, I have been gathering the scattered, the dispersed, and the lost; sifting through raw materials; piecing them into various patterns—this time on the computer keyboard rather than on the living room floor; exploring the nature of the home tie, the blood tie; and doing what Kem Luther recommends: finding "the tale whose telling will bind the scattered lives of a family line." I think back to 1990, when I was advising my student Martha Olson as she worked on her master's thesis, "Soul-Tending: Coming Home to Holiness." What Martha said there still rings true for me:

> My history entwines with my family, country, and culture's; where does one end and the other begin? I search for boundaries, for clarity and definition. I can't help myself. It's got to make sense to me. And I must look back sometimes in order to go ahead, caught in the now between past and future.
>
> I'm learning new places to look, where I can find, name, and express my truths. There's power in memories.

In January 1983 I asked my mother to give me a special birthday present. I handed her a blank journal, its cloth cover decorated with tiny red, gold, and blue flowers.

On its first page, I wrote my mother a letter, asking her if she would spend some time writing in this journal for me, telling me about her childhood, her marriage to my father, her memories of me as a little girl, her feelings now as she looks back on all those years.

Just before my birthday that April, a small package arrived in the mail. Inside was the journal I'd given my mother; it was filled with her reminiscences.

Mom wrote of her childhood on a northwest Iowa farm, with her parents and six brothers and sisters. She wrote of her days working as a "hired girl." She wrote of the early days of her marriage to my father during the 1950s and of the births of their five children. She recounted funny stories about my childhood. Yet, the most moving entry in her journal was the final one, for it spoke to me of a mother's memories and a mother's love:

> There was much to be done in a household of five children, but everyone helped and time and the years passed happily! Dad, myself and the kids, we all had our jobs to keep us busy. Sometimes now I wonder just how we handled it all. And sometimes now, I almost tire when I think of the busy years gone by, and how we struggled along.
>
> But I wouldn't want to trade those years; some were very good, some not so good, but all in the process of a family growing up. And sometimes now, I wish I could go back and relive some of those years, the busy years, when this house was full of kids, fun, and laughter! Sometimes I just wish . . .
>
> There are days when I wish I could make myself go up into the attic and do some cleaning, and maybe the closets, too, but everywhere are memories. In the far southwest corner of the attic is the old high chair you kids all used, far to the north end is a small red rocker, the half-intact doll house and cases of Barbie doll clothes! It's all been there for quite a few years, gathering dust and taking up space! But there it can stay, until the day someone decides it has to go.
>
> There must be many things I've forgotten to mention in this book. It's been hard to relive the past, and I find it hard to put together times and places. I've tried to recall times and occasions as they were, and hope, Suzy, you enjoy the things I've put together!
>
> It's been fun, and though I may have shed a tear or two in between the lines, I've enjoyed penning this book for you, Suzy!
>
> My best to you always. I'm proud to call you my daughter, you have accomplished so much! May the good Lord bless and keep you.
> All my love,
"Your Mom"

The concept of biography itself has changed profoundly in the last two decades, biographies of women especially so. But while biographers of men have been challenged on the "objectivity" of their interpretation, biographers of women have had not only to choose one interpretation over another but, far more difficult, actually to reinvent the lives their subjects led, discovering from what evidence they could find the processes and decisions, the choices and unique pain, that lay beyond the life stories of these women.
—Carolyn Heilbrun, *Writing a Woman's Life*, 1988

*The Bunkers family,
Christmas 1965.
Back row (l. to r.): Linda,
Suzy, Denny. Front row
(l. to r.): Tony, Dale,
Verna holding Danny.*

I appreciate Carolyn Heilbrun's assessment of writing about women's lives because I've had to choose which interpretations of events to accept, and I've had to reinvent, through the interaction of memory and imagination, aspects of the lives that my subjects might have led. I've learned that no single theory or interpretation can account for all the complexities of an actual life. I must concur with Michael Ondaatje, who, near the end of his memoir, *Running in the Family*, observes: "There is so much to know and we can only guess."

Like my theory of Susanna as the "heroic mother," my theory of Susanna as the "deserting mother" has been shattered. In fact, the more I have reconstructed (and reinvented) Susanna's life, the less qualified I feel to pass judgment on her actions. And the less willing I have become to believe that I can neatly sum up what her life meant—or what it means.

The dynamics of mother-daughter relationships are complex; feelings between mothers and daughters are powerful and often contradictory. As I have studied Susanna's relationships with Barbara and Angela through the filter of my relationships with my own mother and daughter, I have become better able to appreciate the distinctions that scholars have drawn between acts of mothering and the cultural institution of motherhood, past and present.

My search for Susanna has deepened my understanding of how my own experience of daughterhood and motherhood has inevitably

The Bunkers family at Granville's centennial celebration, June 1991.
Back row (l. to r.): Dale Bunkers, Dennis Bunkers, Ryan Kennedy, Daniel
Kennedy, Daniel Bunkers. Middle row (l. to r.): Barbara Ahrens Bunkers,
Matthew Kennedy, Suzanne Bunkers. Front row (l. to r.): Kelly Bunkers,
Kimberly Bunkers, Verna Bunkers, Megan Kennedy, Linda Bunkers
Kennedy, Rachel Bunkers. Not pictured: Julie Castillo Bunkers; Margery,
Lisa, Lori, Jennifer Castillo; Daniel Bunkers, Jr. Photo by Rod Hop,
Captured Moments Photography.

affected my interpretations of what Susanna did and why she did it. My search has helped me gain perspective on a woman whom I never knew but whose experiences and decisions are interwoven with my own. It has made me grateful for my close relationships with my mother, Verna, and my daughter, Rachel.

My search has turned out to be a search for many "missing persons"—Susanna Simmerl Youngblut, Frank Youngblut, Barbara Simmerl Bunkers, Frank Bunkers, Tony Bunkers. My search has helped me recognize how important it is for my daughter to enjoy the presence of both her mother and her father in her life so that one day she will have her own memories and her own stories to tell. I hope that Susanna's story will be one of them. Slowly pieced and carefully woven, it will become a warm and cherished coverlet for her descendants.

Appendix: Genealogies

My research into various ancestral lines has led to the following discoveries about family origins in Luxembourg, Belgium, and Germany.

Paternal Ancestry

My paternal ancestors, the *Linsters and Ahrends*, originated in Hondelange (originally a part of Luxembourg but since the early 1800s part of the Luxembourg Province of Belgium). My great-great-grandparents John Linster and Elizabeth Ahrend married on January 8, 1849. They became the parents of seven children (Jacques, Nicholas, Pierre, Henry, Jean, Anna, and Jean-Baptiste), four of whom survived to adulthood. John and Elizabeth Linster and children came to the United States about 1870 and settled first near Fredonia, Wisconsin, and later near Granville, Iowa. The dates of John and Elizabeth Linster's deaths are as yet undetermined.

My paternal ancestors, the *Welters and Grethens*, also originated in Luxembourg. My great-great-grandmother Mary Margaretha Grethen was born in Waldbredimus, Luxembourg, on August 3, 1826. She married my great-great-grandfather Mathias Welter Sr. in Luxembourg; several of their nine children (Magdalena, Nicholas, John, Mathias, Peter, Catherine, Nicholas, Isadore, and Elizabeth) were born in Luxembourg. The 1860 U.S. census lists the family as living near Fredonia, Wisconsin.

Eventually the Welters, like the Linsters, moved to western Iowa, settling near Granville and Alton in Sioux County. Mathias Welter Sr. died on September 8, 1888. Mary Margaretha Welter died on October 21, 1907.

My great-grandfather Mathias Welter Jr. married my great-grandmother Anna Linster on February 4, 1885, in Alton, Iowa. Matt and Anna Welter had four children (Mary, Lillian, Theresa, and Silverius). The Welter family lived for a time near Grafton, North Dakota, but they eventually returned to Granville, Iowa, where they ran the Welter Saloon and Pool Hall. They retired to Bird Island, Minnesota, where Matt died on October 1, 1916.

Following her husband's death, Anna Linster Welter returned to Granville to live with her daughters, Lillian Welter Bunkers (my paternal grandmother) and Theresa Welter O'Connor. Anna Linster Welter died on November 10, 1931, in Granville.

My paternal ancestors, the *Simmerls* and the *Hottuas*, had their origins near Bissen, Luxembourg. My great-great-great-grandfather Theodore Simmerl married my great-great-great-grandmother Angela Hottua in 1827. The couple lived in Oberfeulen, Luxembourg, where their twelve children (Peter, Jean-Baptiste, Susanna, Anna Marie, Nicholas, Susanna, Theodore, Barbara, Angela, Joanna, Mary Catherine, and Anna Maria) were born. My great-great-grandmother Susanna Simmerl, who was born in Oberfeulen, Luxembourg, on April 2, 1831, gave birth to her first child, a daughter named Barbara Simmerl, on December 30, 1856. Shortly thereafter, Susanna Simmerl immigrated to the United States in 1857 with her older brother Peter Simmerl. Peter settled in Luxemburg, Iowa, while Susanna went to Gilbertville, Iowa.

My step-great-great-grandfather, *Frank Youngblut* [Jungblut], was born in Aspelt, Luxembourg, on January 11, 1824, to Michel Jungblut and Marie Feipel. Frank's father, Michel Jungblut, was born on February 11, 1774, in Aspelt. Frank's mother, Marie Feipel, was born on November 16, 1778, in Obermotgen, Germany. Michel Jungblut and Marie Feipel married on December 20, 1802, in Aspelt. Michel Jungblut died on August 14, 1831, in Aspelt. Marie Feipel Jungblut died on February 3, 1835, in Aspelt. Frank, an orphan at the age of eleven, apparently lived with relatives in Aspelt. Records indicate that Frank Youngblut [Jungblut] immigrated to the United States in 1852, traveling first by ship to New Orleans, then making his way up the Mississippi and settling near Gilbertville, Iowa.

Susanna Simmerl married Frank Youngblut of Gilbertville on December 9, 1857. Susanna and Frank had nine children (George, Frank,

John, Josephine, Frank, Anna, Mary, Sophia, Susanna). Frank Young-blut died on November 5, 1892, at Gilbertville. Susanna Simmerl Youngblut died on May 20, 1906, at Gilbertville.

My paternal great-great-grandparents *Theodore and Elizabeth [surname unknown] Bunkers*, had their origins near Hanover, Germany. They married and came to the United States early in the 1840s, settling at Dyersville, Iowa, near Dubuque. They had four children (B. Herman, Henry, Theodore, and Barney). Their second son, Henry Bunkers, married Barbara Simmerl, the eldest child of Susanna Simmerl Youngblut.

Henry and Barbara Simmerl Bunkers, who married on July 20, 1875, in Luxemburg, Iowa, eventually moved westward to the Granville, Iowa, area. They became the parents of twelve children (Henry, Elizabeth, Catherine, John, Frank, Anton, Joseph, Otto, Clara, Emil, Elnora, and Edmunda). Henry Bunkers Sr. died at Granville, Iowa, on February 15, 1924. Barbara Simmerl Bunkers died at Granville, Iowa, on February 4, 1943.

Frank Bunkers, born on March 16, 1893, in New Vienna, Iowa, married Lillian Welter on June 2, 1908, in Granville, Iowa. Frank and Lillian Bunkers had eight children (Larry, Dick, Ray, Cletus, Vincent, Bernice, Jerome [Tony], and Viola). Frank and Lillian Bunkers became my paternal grandparents.

Maternal Ancestry

My maternal ancestors, the *Kleins* and the *Simons*, had their origins in Luxembourg and Germany, respectively.

My maternal great-grandfather, Theodore Klein, was born to the widowed Mary Müller on September 26, 1853, in Niederfeulen, Luxembourg. Theodore's father, Michel Klein, had died a few months before Theodore's birth. In 1871 Theodore immigrated to the United States, joining his older brothers, Nick and Jake, in northwest Iowa.

My maternal great-grandmother, Elizabeth (Lizzie) Simon, was born to Franz Simon and Katherine Melcher on September 8, 1860, in Schönholthausen, Germany. In 1880 Franz and Katherine Simon and their four children (Franz Ferdinand, Henry, Fred, and Elizabeth) had come to Chicago, where Lizzie found work as a nursemaid.

In 1882, Lizzie was invited to northwest Iowa to visit her friends the Pennings. While there, she met their cousin, Theodore Klein, and, after spending a Sunday afternoon with him, she agreed to marry him. On January 16, 1883, Theodore Klein married Elizabeth Simon, and the two farmed near Granville, Iowa. Fifteen children were born to them, nine of whom (Mary, Frank, Anton, Emma, Fred, William, Theodore Jr., Bertha, and Cecelia) survived to adulthood.

My maternal ancestors, the *Nemmerses* and the *Kokenges*, had their origins in Luxembourg and Germany, respectively.

Nicholas Nemmers, my great-great-grandfather, was born to Nicholas Nemmers and Marie Freyman in Dondelange, Luxembourg, on September 12, 1845. In 1847, Nicholas and Marie Nemmers and their children (Nicholas, Michael, and Catherine) immigrated to the United States, settling near St. Donatus, just south of Dubuque, Iowa.

Anna Kaiser, my great-great-grandmother, was born to Hubert Kaiser and Barbara Erhlinger in Luxembourg [village as yet undetermined] on December 25, 1852. Like the Nemmers family, the Kaiser family immigrated to the United States and settled near St. Donatus.

After Anna Kaiser and Nicholas Nemmers married at St. Donatus on February 24, 1873, they immigrated westward to the Alton, Iowa, area. Their daughter, Josephine Nemmers, was born on May 25, 1877, at Alton.

John Bernard Kokenge, my great-great-grandfather, was born in 1814 in Oldenburg, Germany. After the death of his first wife, Elizabeth Fordman, he married Marie Anna Mayrose, born in 1828, also in Germany [name of village unknown]. John Bernard and Marie Kokenge immigrated to the United States around 1850, settling in Cincinnati, Ohio. Their children Bernard, Mary, Elizabeth, and Josephine were born in Ohio. The family moved westward to New Vienna, Iowa, in the late 1850s, where two more children were born—Henry, on June 28, 1859, and Sophie, on April 7, 1862.

Henry Kokenge, my great-grandfather, married Catherine Goebel on February 21, 1882, in New Vienna, Iowa. They had three children (John, Anton, Ernest) there before moving westward to Alton, Iowa, in 1888. Three more children (Mary, Anna, and Bernard) were born in Alton before Catherine Kokenge died there on April 13, 1894.

On June 4, 1897, Henry Kokenge married his second wife, twenty-year-old Josephine Nemmers. Henry and Josephine Kokenge became the parents of ten children (Joseph, Dorothy, Frances, Alfred, Irene, Aloysious, Cyril, Edna, Maureen, and Emmett). On June 15, 1918, Josephine Nemmers Kokenge died at Alton, from complications of a goiter. Henry Kokenge lived until April 14, 1936, when he died at Alton.

Theodore Klein Jr. (son of Theodore and Elizabeth Simon Klein) married Frances Kokenge (daughter of Henry and Josephine Nemmers Kokenge) on January 16, 1922, at Alton, Iowa. Theodore and Frances Klein had seven children (Marcel, Verna, Lois, James, Merlyn,

Clarice, and Thomas). Theodore and Frances Klein became my maternal grandparents.

My Parentage
Jerome (Tony) Bunkers was born on November 16, 1921, at Mahnomen, Minnesota. Verna Klein was born on October 8, 1924, at Granville, Iowa. Tony Bunkers and Verna Klein married on June 14, 1949, at Granville, Iowa. They became the parents of five children (Suzanne, Linda, Dennis, Dale, and Daniel). Tony Bunkers died on July 27, 1978, at Granville. Verna Bunkers still lives in Granville, Iowa.

Singular Lives